ANARCHISM
A COLLECTION OF
REVOLUTIONARY WRITINGS

PETER KROPOTKIN

Edited by
Roger N. Baldwin

DOVER PUBLICATIONS, INC.
Mineola, New York

Copyright

Copyright © 1970, 2002 by Dover Publications, Inc.
All rights reserved under Pan American and International Copyright Conventions.

Published in Canada by General Publishing Company, Ltd., 895 Don Mills Road, 400-2 Park Centre, Toronto, Ontario M3C 1W3.
Published in the United Kingdom by David & Charles, Brunel House, Forde Close, Newton Abbot, Devon TQ12 4PU.

Bibliographical Note

This Dover edition, first published in 2002, is an unabridged, slightly corrected republication of the work originally published by Vanguard Press, New York, in 1927, under the title *Kropotkin's Revolutionary Pamphlets*. Dover Publications first published the work in 1970, under the same title. The Introduction to the Dover Edition was written by Roger N. Baldwin for the 1970 edition.

Library of Congress Cataloging-in-Publication Data

Kropotkin, Petr Alekseevich, kniaz', 1842–1921.
    [Selections. English. 2002]
    Anarchism : a collection of revolutionary writings / Peter Kropotkin.
        p. cm.
    Originally published by Vanguard Press, New York, in 1927 under the title: Kropotkin's revolutionary pamphlets.
    Includes bibliographical references.
    ISBN 0-486-41955-X (pbk.)
      1. Anarchism. I. Title.

HX833 .K7213 2002
335'.83—dc21

2001047465

Manufactured in the United States of America
Dover Publications, Inc., 31 East 2nd Street, Mineola, N.Y. 11501

CONTENTS

INTRODUCTION
TO THE DOVER EDITION

IT is forty years now since I compiled these pamphlets and forty more years since most of them first appeared. Yet their philosophy retains a fresh relevance to the enduring conflicts between authority and freedom, to human rights and to the age-old ideals of a society of equality and justice.

Kropotkin's confidence in the capacity of mankind to achieve such a society may seem naive. But evidence is not lacking, even in this violent and confused era, to sustain a belief in it. Personal freedom, voluntary association, and democratic control of power are still vital forces in political thought and practical struggles.

My belief in those principles attracted me years ago to Kropotkin's writing and led me to edit these scattered pamphlets in book form. I was then engaged in social and political reform and searching for answers to the problems of the injustices of power, coercion, poverty and inequality. I had explored the gospel of salvation according to Marx and rejected it as rigid and alien dogma. However, Kropotkin offered, not dogma or a blueprint for a revolution, but working principles, as revolutionary in themselves as the Golden Rule or the ethics of Jesus. Like Tolstoi, he called them anarchism—with a non-Christian sanction. I never accepted the whole doctrine nor put a tag on my beliefs, but I took from the philosophy only what seemed relevant to the practical direction of aims of social justice.

I have found those principles applicable to much that has marked world history since Kropotkin's time. The revolution that has ended European colonial rule over subject peoples and brought national independence to them, along with the dignity of sovereign equality, is surely in line with the growth of freedom, despite its expression in the form of coercive political states. With the revolution has come the recognition of racial equality, the decline of white superiority, and so a basis for a world order of all peoples. Kropotkin's principles, though they did not deal directly with the subjection of the colonial peoples, would fit this epochal revolutionary change in attitudes and power. So, too, only in less degree, has the emancipation of women—squared with the thought of Kropotkin, presenting today a picture of legal political participation all over the world —been accomplished in the remarkable span of less than a generation.

I like to think that Kropotkin would have endorsed the first charter of human rights ever adopted by the world community, the Universal Declaration of Human Rights, accepted as goals, not practical law, by almost all States. Although the product of governments most unlikely to observe or enforce them at present, it sets forth the rights of "every person" against the abuses of power. It presents the old dilemma of authority versus freedom, but at least the world has its first code of rights and in terms of personal freedoms.

Whatever speculation may suggest as to Kropotkin's influence on events since his time, he has still a considerable audience throughout the world in elite circles. His larger works, unlike these pamphlets, are widely translated and distributed (*Mutual Aid, The Conquest of Bread, The Great French Revolution,* etc.). Unlike his chief opponent Karl Marx, he has no organized following, but his anarchist ideas still mark a few revolutionary movements, especially in Spain and among those working-class circles that call themselves syndicalists. Anarchism, as far as it ever had any organized expression, has almost disappeared.

I was struck on a visit to the Soviet Union in 1967 by the recognition accorded Kropotkin, and that by a government whose dictatorial power represented everything Kropotkin detested. It is to be explained by the tribute the Russians pay to a great revolutionist against the Tsars, a world-renowned scientist and an author of social criticism and idealism. It must be noted that Kropotkin called his system of ideas anarchist communism, and that in common with Marx he believed in the abolition of the State as coercive. "While the State exists," said Lenin, "we cannot speak of liberty. When we can speak of liberty, there will be no State."

But more than that, as I recount in "The Story of Kropotkin's Life," he had the personal admiration of Lenin, so great that Lenin journeyed to call on him at his country home. And whom Lenin admired let no Communist reject. So in Moscow I found him honored above any Russian, except Communist leaders, by having a subway station named after him—apparently the highest honor of all—along with an avenue, a street and a village. His birthplace, a handsome house in a little park-like setting, is marked by a bronze plaque.

But it is marked also by a use that I am sure would have delighted Kropotkin. Leased by the American Embassy, it has been completely renovated as a school for English-speaking children, just opened indeed at the time of my visit in 1967. I was delighted, on my own account. I had lived in the house forty years before for a few months one summer as the guest of Mme. Kropotkin, his widow; it was so soon after his death that the faded wreaths of his funeral were still kept among souvenirs in the house.

Later I wrote a brief account for the children of what I had learned of Kropotkin's boyhood in that house and how even at the age of twelve he had given up his title of prince so that he could feel closer to the common people. I told them how he had always struggled for greater freedom for everybody, in Russia and in his long exile abroad, and how he had come home after the revolution to die, and how from the very house in which they studied the great funeral started which took him one bitter winter day to his last home.

I hope the children will understand the spirit of freedom embodied in the gentle, kindly man whose profile in bronze marks their school—perhaps quite as well as some who read these pamphlets.

ROGER N. BALDWIN

New York
January, 1970

THE SIGNIFICANCE OF KROPOTKIN'S LIFE
AND TEACHING

THE revolutionary movement against the Russian Czars during its hundred years of struggle aroused the idealism of the
youth in the cities. Thousands of young men and women
in the professional classes risked their positions, their chances
for careers and their family ties to engage in revolutionary
and educational propaganda among the peasants and workers
and later in secret conspiracies against the government. Hundreds of them were hanged or exiled. Their agitation continued unceasingly for years under a persecution unmatched
in modern history. The revolution finally triumphed in the
overthrow of the Czar and the seizure of power and property
by the workers and peasants.

Kropotkin grew up in the midst of this struggle,—in the
years of intense agitation for the abolition of serfdom and
for a constitutional government. He was born a prince of the
old nobility of Moscow, was trained as a page in the Emper-
or's court, and at twenty became an officer in the army. The
discovery that he was engaged in revolutionary activities in
St. Petersburg while he was presumably devoting his life to
scientific geography, caused a sensation. He was arrested
and held in prison without trial. He became at once one
of the most hated and most beloved representatives of the
revolutionary cause. He was one of the very few of the
nobility to go over to the revolution, and his family connec-

I

tions and training at the court made him a conspicuous figure. After making a dramatic escape in broad daylight from his fortress prison in St. Petersburg after a year's confinement, he found refuge in England. For forty-two years he lived virtually in exile, chiefly in England, engaged in scientific research and anarchist propaganda. He returned to Russia in 1917 after the Kerensky revolution,—an old man of seventy-five.

But he could feel no enthusiasm for a revolution which set up a new governing class, particularly when followed by the dictatorship of a political party. Yet he looked upon it with far-seeing eyes. He regarded the revolution as a "natural phenomenon independent of the human will, similar to a typhoon," and waited for it to spend its force in order to begin a real reconstruction through the free cooperation of peasants' and workers' associations.

He died four years later in his little cottage in the country a few miles from Moscow,—continuing to the end his writing on social problems. His family and friends refused the State funeral offered by the government as a gesture contrary to his principles. The Soviet Government turned over to his friends the house in the old nobles' quarter where he was born, to be used as a museum for his books and papers and belongings, and renamed one of the principal streets of Moscow for him,—as a tribute to his services to the revolutionary cause in Russia.

But it is neither as a scientist nor as a Russian revolutionist that Kropotkin is most significant to the world at large. It is rather as a revolutionary anarchist, who put into anarchism the methods of science. He was in fact a scientist in two wholly unrelated fields,—geography and revolutionary social ethics,—for his anarchism was essentially applied ethics. He was one of the leading authorities of his time both in geodetic mathematics and Siberian geography. He was the first man to formulate a scientific basis for the principle of anarchism, —in its opposition to authority in all forms and in its advocacy of complete social reorganization on the basis of the free cooperation of independent associations. He brought to social science a wealth of training in the natural sciences. Unlike most scientists he states his observations and conclusions so simply that his works were published in popular book and pamphlet form in almost all languages. Their wide appeal was due also to his passion for the education of the masses in revolutionary ideas, feeling that once they understood their powers and mission, they would unite to destroy the State, monopoly and private property.

Mutual aid, sympathy, solidarity, individual liberty through free cooperation as the basis of all social life—these are the positive ideas at the root of Kropotkin's teachings. Abolition of the State, of authority in all forms, of monopoly and class rule, are their negative forms. Coupled with them was a belief,—shared by many revolutionists of all schools,—in an approaching social revolution, a universal seizure of property by the workers and peasants, which would end exploitation and class rule and usher in free cooperation and individual liberty.

He shared with socialists their criticism of capitalism, and in large part their conception that the forms of the economic life of a people determine their social institutions—law, government, religion, and marriage. But he disagreed with them in the use of political methods as a means of achieving power and in their conception of a workers' State. Anarchist-communism, he described, as the "no-government system of socialism." But anarchism as a principle of freedom carried him outside the economic and political struggle into all social relations,—marriage, education, the treatment of crime, the function of law, the basis of morality.

Kropotkin's social outlook was colored by his early contacts with the Russian peasantry. When he thought of the masses, he unconsciously pictured to himself peasants oppressed by landlords and Czars, quite capable of handling their own affairs when a revolutionary upheaval once gave them freedom. His outlook on the working-class was also colored by his limited contacts. He was not close to the working-class struggle as a whole. His only intimate connections were with the Jura Federation in Switzerland, the Russian Jewish workers in London and to a lesser degree with the anarchist workers in Paris. His bitter hostility to Marxian socialism cut him off from the German workers' movement. He knew little of the practical problems of leadership, or of the psychology of action among the workers. And, like many intellectuals, he idealized their capacities.

Kropotkin, unlike many others who called themselves anarchists, notably the Tolstoians, was not opposed to the use of violence. He did not condemn deeds of violence, particularly the assassination of tyrants, but considered them useful acts in the struggle toward liberation. Civil war he regarded as inevitable in the conflict of classes, though he wished it to be limited to the "smallest number of victims and a minimum of mutual embitterment." Even international wars he regarded as sometimes significant of conflict between advanced and reactionary forces. This attitude explains how he could champion the Allied cause in the World War, for he feared the triumph of German militarism would be fatal to the progress of the revolutionary forces which he believed were far more advanced in the Allied countries. His profound love for France, and a strong sentimental attachment to Russia, probably influenced this attitude.

Of the non-resistant anarchism of Tolstoi he wrote, "I am in sympathy with most of Tolstoi's work, though there are many of his ideas with which I absolutely disagree,—his asceticism, for instance, and his doctrine of non-resistance. It seems to me, too, that he has bound himself, without reason or judgment, to the letter of the New Testament." He was also scornful of Tolstoi's idea that the propertied classes could be persuaded to give up their prerogatives without a violent struggle.

Kropotkin objected to being called a "philosophical anarchist" because he said he learned anarchism not from philosophy but from the people. And like many other anarchists he objected to the implication that it was only a philosophy, not a program of action, not a movement rooted in the struggle of the masses. "Philosophical" sounded aloof, too respectable, too pacific. It smacked of books and the study.

To concepts of anarchism other than "anarchist-communism,"—the school founded by Michael Bakunin,—he was inhospitable. The anarchist schools of thought have only one point in common,—the abolition of the State as an institution of compulsion,—and all sects emphasize their points of difference. He regarded "individualist anarchism" of the school of Benjamin Tucker in America and Max Stirner in Germany, as hopelessly conservative, committed only to winning personal liberty without a revolutionary change in the economic system. He said of individualism in general, so often conceived as the leading principle of anarchism: "Individualism, narrowly egotistic, is incapable of inspiring anybody. There is nothing great or gripping in it. Individuality can attain its supreme development only in the highest common social effort." He called the individualism of Nietzsche "spurious," remarking that it could exist "only under a condition of oppression for the masses" and in fact destroyed individuality "in the oppressor himself as well as in the oppressed masses." Ibsen he regarded as the only writer who had achieved a conception of true individualism, but "had not succeeded in expressing it in a way to make it clearly understood." The French anarchist thinker, Pierre Proudhon, inspirer of the "mutualist school" of revolutionary economic changes through the reorganization of banking and money, he considered an impractical dreamer.

Kropotkin did not carry his differences of opinion into the open, except in his relentless opposition to all forms of authoritarianism, which meant a constant state of warfare with authoritarian socialism as represented by the followers of Marx. Besides his opposition to him on principle he had a strong personal dislike for Marx,—whom he never met,—largely due to Marx's treatment of Bakunin. Marx, according to common report, had helped spread false rumor that Bakunin had been in the employ of the Russian secret service.

Yet when these two once met at the home of George Sand, Marx greeted Bakunin effusively. Kropotkin could not tolerate what he regarded as unpardonable hypocrisy. This feeling was intensified by the discovery that parts of the *Communist Manifesto* had been lifted almost word for word from a work by Considerant. Kropotkin took almost a boyish delight in scoring anything on Marx, and, furthermore, he had contempt for him as a politician.

But aside from a personal feeling which was doubtless the result of his hostility to authoritarian socialism, his differences with Marx on other fundamental points were great. Although he was a materialist, accepting in large part the socialist economic interpretation of history, he did not regard economic forces as so overwhelming a factor in the class struggle. All through his work the power of ideas is stressed,— a factor accepted by the Marxians as important but secondary, and originating in the struggle of classes. That struggle itself seemed to Kropotkin less influential in revolutionary progress than arousing the "people" to revolutionary thought and feeling. Such a concept was doubtless based on his early outlook in Russia, where the masses of the peasants stood opposed to a small ruling class. The socialist conception was a sharper, clearer picture of class lines and interests in the industrial west. Yet in his *Great French Revolution* Kropotkin embodies an interpretation that is shared by the whole socialist-communist school. Indeed, the Soviet Government offered him large returns for the right to use it as a text-book in Russian schools—an offer which Kropotkin characteristically refused because it came from a government.

In his social thinking Kropotkin tended to develop his facts from his theories. He described his method as "inductive-deductive." In his geographical scientific work he got his facts first and developed his theories. The difference in his approach to the two fields was doubtlessly due to his strong feeling on all social issues. Regarding them he was a propagandist at heart, tending to ignore or brush aside the facts that contradicted his interpretations. He maintained that he was always ready to alter his theories in the light of facts, but like all men of deep convictions he cherished them too profoundly to see opposing facts except to demolish them. While much of his work in the social sciences is really scientific,—especially *Mutual Aid* and *Fields, Factories and Workshops,*—preconceptions color large parts of it,—a fact which, however, does not detract greatly from its value.

In his personal life he held with equal tenacity to the standards he had developed. He scrupulously refused to take a penny in compensation for his work for the movement. He refused loans or gifts even when living in pressing poverty. And even at such times he would share the little he had with all who came to him in distress. His habits were marked by moderation in everything but work, in which he was tireless. He was rigid in his opposition to tactics which he thought out of harmony with the broad principles of anarchist-communism, even when the ends appeared good. He condemned comrades who jumped bail in political cases both because of the breach of faith with bondsmen and the practical effect on securing bail in other cases. He refused to countenance aid to the Russian revolutionists from the Japanese Government at the time of the Russo-Japanese war, both because of its demoralizing influence and his hostility to governments.

Kropotkin is referred to by scores of people who knew him in all walks of life as "the noblest man" they ever knew. Oscar Wilde called him one of the two really happy men he had ever met. Romain Rolland said Kropotkin lived what Tolstoi only advocated. In the anarchist movement he was held in the deepest affection by thousands,—"notre Pierre" the French workers called him. Never assuming a position of leadership, he nevertheless led by the moral force of his personality and the breadth of his intellect. He combined in extraordinary measure high qualities of character with a fine mind and passionate social feeling. His life made a deep impression on a great range of classes,—the whole scientific world, the Russian revolutionary movement, the radical

movements of all schools, and in the literary world which
cared little or nothing for science or revolution.

The significance of his revolutionary teachings in its
practical relation to the world of today remain to be examined.

The years since Kropotkin did his most important work
have been marked by the colossal events of the World War
and the Russian Revolution, with the consequent tightening
of the conflict between capitalism and the working-class,
and with sharp changes in the revolutionary movement based
on the Russian experience.   The general revolution which
Kropotkin felt was imminent broke in Russia alone, with a
complete expropriation of the owning class by the workers
and peasants, followed by a dictatorship committed to working out communism.   This revolution is the best available
test of the significance of anarchist principles in action.
Both Kropotkin's attitude to it and the activities of other
anarchists make it clear.   Let us first state the situation in
Russia.

The enormous obstacles against which Soviet Russia has
contended in the world of capitalism, in internal opposition
and in the indifference of the peasantry have prevented, with
other lesser factors, any consistent progress toward communism and even necessitated a retreat toward capitalism.   The
economic order is a state socialism, with considerable private
capitalism in the form of limited concessions, and a huge
land-owning peasantry largely unconcerned with "progress."
The political order is a dictatorship by the Communist Party,
the only legal party, which uses the state power to silence
all opposition and to insure, as far as possible, the unimpeded
execution of its program.   It is in fact and spirit the realization of the very ideas which Kropotkin so vigorously fought
in Marxian socialism.

The communist movement throughout the World, which
developed after the Rusian Revolution from the old socialist parties, carries on a militant struggle to direct the labor
and radical forces toward similar revolutions elsewhere.   The
communists are everywhere opposed equally to the parliament-

ary ideas and tactics of the socialists and to the non-political and anti-State tactics of the anarchists and syndicalists,—all of whom they regard as impotent from a revolutionary standpoint. The socialists and anarchists,—long bitter opponents in the radical camp,—now share a common hostility to the Soviet government for its forcible suppression of their activities in Russia, and for its imprisonment and exile of their comrades there. The socialists hope the dictatorship may be dissolved into a democratic, parliamentary régime; the anarchists that it may give way to free federations of the decentralized workers' and peasants' organizations as the economic system. But because of the common hostility to capitalism, socialists and anarchists are on the whole reluctant to play into the hands of the capitalist enemies of Soviet Russia. Both defend Soviet Russia against capitalist attacks (with some conspicuous exceptions) while condemning it bitterly for its forcible suppression of opposition. The communists on their side, while repressing anarchist and socialist activities in Russia, help defend them in capitalist countries when they are attacked for revolutionary or working-class activities. The differences in the communist attitude inside Russia and outside are accounted for by the practical necessities of the tactics making for revolution and the responsibilities of a government based on such a revolution. The Soviet Government will make the compromises with capitalism necessary to insure increased production of goods and trade, while refusing to tolerate radical opposition to those compromises. Even in their own Communist Party it is silenced. But outside Russia they must encourage all the forces making toward the growth of working-class power.

In this paradoxical situation the anarchist-communists in Russia play varying roles. Some cooperate with the Soviet Government in its economic work, accepting the necessity of the dictatorship while holding to their anarchist faith, pointing out that even Lenin believed in the ultimate validity of anarchist-communism while ridiculing and opposing it now as barren of tactics for achieving its own objects. Others have accepted the necessity of silence in Russia, preferring such a dictatorship to living under a capitalist dictatorship anywhere else. Others continue to express their anarchist beliefs and to criticize Soviet policy,—and scores of them are in prison or exile. Still others have left Russia,—by actual or self-imposed exile,—and are living quietly elsewhere. A few continue active anti-Bolshevik propaganda on foreign soil. Among other than Russian anarchists, similar differing attitudes to the Soviet Government and communism dictate their activities,—though practically all of them oppose the forcible suppression of revolutionary opposition in Russia.

What Kropotkin himself would have done had he been younger, or even had he lived longer, can be gathered from his comments appearing on pages 256-259. He visualized the function of anarchists as participation only in the voluntary organizations of the peasants and workers. His advice to anarchists both in Russia and outside was to work constructively in the building of a new economy, and express that constructive purpose through the syndicalist trade unions.

What practical effect both the anarchist opposition and collaboration have had on the development of the Russian Revolution is difficult to say. The movement in Russia was weak,—far weaker than the socialist,—but its policies had a direct bearing on the central economic problems confronting the Bolsheviks. The chief policy—freedom for the trade unions, cooperatives and peasants' associations,—has gained as a practical working measure in the face of the failure of rigorous centralized control by a governmental bureaucracy.

Outside Russia, in the world of working-class struggle, the movement represented by Kropotkin's theories is widely spread but comparatively small. The anarchist-communist movement was never really well organized, and it was always barren of practical technique. It flourished chiefly on uncompromising protest, and visions of a revolutionary goal to be achieved by abolishing the State. It was simple and daring. From a vigorous movement of protest from 1870 to 1900, it has diminished in numbers and influence. Today it is represented chiefly in the syndicalist trade-union movement in Latin countries,—notably in Spain, Portugal, Mexico and South America, but with strong smaller movements in Germany, France and Sweden. Scattered anarchist journals appear as the mouth-pieces of little groups all over the world, with one anarchist daily in Buenos Aires. A syndicalist international, organized in 1922 under the name of the old International Working Men's Association, to which Kropotkin belonged, represents the syndicalist trade-unions, with headquarters in Berlin.

But quite outside any organized movement, anarchist ideas are held by many people in all classes of society and are expressed in a great variety of activities, modifying and directing other movements. It has been said that all of us are naturally anarchists at heart,—which is only to say that we all desire the largest possible personal freedom and the least possible external restraint. This instinctive attitude accounts for the response to anarchist ideas in widely different groups, particularly when they do not bear that label, feared because of old associations of violence and popular caricature. Anarchism, as Kropotkin so often pointed out, is only the formulation of a universal and ancient desire of mankind. On that basis the viewpoints of scores of distinguished philosophers, writers and religious leaders may be labeled anarchist. And anarchist writers have claimed for the philosophy such diverse personalities as Emerson, Thoreau, Whitman, Jesus, Lao-tse, Ibsen, Nietszche and Anatole France.

It is commonly said of anarchism that it is a beautiful dream for a remote future when we shall all have become civilized enough to get along without government and police. Or, according to the Marxians, when the class struggle is over. But that view misses the essential point that anarchism is an ever-present working principle of growth toward larger freedoms, and in all social activity. If means create ends, no really free society is possible without the constant building up of habits of freer relationships, of increased individual liberty, and of larger independence for all social groups. It is significant that under the Bolshevik dictatorship in Russia, this very principle which is so scorned and ridiculed in political life, is the one that works best in building up education, the cooperatives, the trade unions, and the great network of economic and social organizations. It is significant, too, that all over the world social advances in any field are being made only on the solid basis of increased individual responsibility, voluntary association and free federation. The highway of progress lies only through increased liberty for groups and individuals, whether in education, with its new type of schools in which adult authority is minimized, or in dealing with crime, with the growing tendency to substitute friendly treatment for the brutality of the prison régime, or in family life, or in the trade unions and cooperative organizations of producers and consumers.

Kropotkin's teachings, embodying these principles, will long serve to inspire faith in freedom and to clarify thinking as to how to achieve it. It will help shape policies and develop movements in a world which has still many years of struggle before it between the forces of authority and liberty.

ROGER N. BALDWIN
1927

THE STORY OF KROPOTKIN'S LIFE

KROPOTKIN is remembered chiefly as he became in his later years, a kindly, beaming philosopher-scientist, whose light blue-gray eyes looked out through spectacles with serenity and penetration. Bald, with a wide forehead and bushy white beard, he at once impressed all he met as a man of great intellectual force, but without the slightest self-consciousness or sense of superiority. Though his kindliness and courtly manners marked him in all relations, they were not of the patronizing aristocrat, but of a genuine lover of his fellow-men who made no distinctions between them. Whether lecturing to a scientific association or an anarchist group, dining with the aristocrats or working people, he was simple, warm, earnest,—overflowing with feeling for the cause he had at heart, but with no concern for himself, no sense of leadership or position.

Although he was a direct descendant of the Ruriks, who were Czars before the Romanoffs, he never referred to himself as a prince, and he disliked titles. He says in his *Memoirs* that he dropped his title at the age of twelve "under the influence of republican teachings," and never used it thereafter. He even rebuked his friends, when they so referred to him.

The young Kropotkin of Russian revolutionary memory already showed all the traits which later distinguished him. The same duality of interest marked him from his teens,—on the one side a love of intellectual pursuits, dispassionate and scientific, and on the other a passionate interest in the oppressed. He came early to science and philosophy largely through the interest of his older brother, to whom he was bound by an unusual affection. His revolutionary convictions were the expression of naturally warm sympathies, aroused by the condition of his father's serfs and by the agitation around him.

His early years in a great establishment in Moscow, divided into masters and serfs, impressed him deeply. He was born in 1842 when the agitation for freedom of the serfs was well under way. Growing up in a home in the nobles' quarter, where his father, a wealthy landowner, kept fifty servants to do the work for a family of eight to twelve, he was at once faced with the iniquities of the feudal system. He saw the serfs,—his nurses, his friends,—punished, sometimes cruelly beaten. His father ordered the establishment like a factory, for all the goods were made at home or on the country estate where the family went for the summers, and from which the peasants brought in all the supplies for the long winters. That father was a little autocrat, absolute master of the lives, loves and welfare of all his peasants and serfs numbering over one thousand two hundred and fifty. He had inherited them with three great country estates and the Moscow house, and the little family lived in luxury off their labor.

The father had no occupation. The old Moscow nobility had lost their jobs at court when the capital had been moved to St. Petersburg, and held only honorary positions. But he busied himself in military style,—for he was trained as an officer in the army,—in ordering the affairs of his estates and in doing favors for all who sought his help. He enjoyed playing the man of influence, and put endless energy into the petty affairs of strangers just to get the satisfaction of being looked up to. He kept open house and entertained lavishly.

It took five cooks to prepare the food, a dozen men servants to wait on table, with a dozen more to tend the dozen horses. A private orchestra of the servants played for meals and for the gay card parties and dances that often kept the house open till the small hours.

Kropotkin's mother, a beautiful woman, daughter of a

governor-general of Siberia, died of tuberculosis when he was only between three and four years old. He with his two older brothers were reared by French tutors and German nurses. The eldest boy was separated by some years from Peter and his brother Alexander, who was a year and a half older. The two small boys were raised together. They saw little of their father. He was even to them an autocrat, a distant and fearful figure. He married again two years after their mother's death, a marriage arranged solely for social advantage. The new mother caused all connections with the boys' mother's family to be broken, but gave them no attention herself. The servants and a French tutor raised the two youngsters.

At the age of ten, Kropotkin's future training was determined quite accidentally by being favored with the attention of the Emporer at a costume ball in Moscow, in which the children of the nobility took part. As a result of being picked out for his charm and good looks, young Peter was invited to become a page of the Emperor, for which a limited number of boys each year were trained in a special school in St. Petersburg. But he did not enter the corps for three years. When he was only twelve,—still studying at home in Moscow,—he began to write novels and to read French and Russian political books. It was then he dropped his title of prince in referring to himself, coming to the decision through reading libertarian tracts. But he appears to have kept his decision quiet. His brother Alexander was even more pronounced in his interest in liberal ideas, in philosophy and in political economy. Both boys used to discuss together by the hour the great issues of the day. At thirteen, Peter went to the corps of pages at St. Petersburg and the brothers were separated.

There he attended the military school in which all the pages were entered, carrying on their studies and serving in court. He became absorbed in mathematics, physics, astronomy and history. He even started writing a text-book on physics. On the practical side he turned to surveying. And here in this school strangely enough, he got his first knowledge of the revolutionary movement, which at once gripped him. At seventeen or eighteen he read his first revolutionary paper, Alexander Hertzen's *Polar Star*, published in London and secretly circulated in Russia. It advocated nothing more radical than a constitution for Russia, but that advocacy was considered revolutionary by the Czars.

It was at this time that the agitation for the freeing of the serfs came to a head, and the Emperor's proclamation issued in 1861, just as Peter was finishing his schooling, gave him profound joy. He was now an officer in the army with his choice of service. He elected to go to Siberia as aide to the Governor-General with headquarters at Chita. There he tried to reform the conditions of the prisoners and the exiles, and to improve the local town governments. Geographical research was part of the job, and Kropotkin went into it intently, making the studies which led to his later work. After he had been there two years his brother Alexander, to his great joy, joined him, for he too was an officer in the army. Both of them resigned together three years later,—in 1867, when Peter was twenty-five,—as a result of their revulsion at the cruelty to Polish exiles.

Peter went to the University in St. Petersburg; his brother to the law. For five years he studied mathematics and the geography of Siberia. His report on Siberia was published. He discovered, after long and painstaking research, what to him was a supreme joy,—the general principle that the mountains in Siberia are formed in just the opposite direction to that assumed by all previous geographers, a discovery with far-reaching effects. He became secretary of the section of the Russian Geographical Society dealing with physical geography, and refused the secretaryship of the whole society only because he felt himself too strongly drawn to the cause of the peasants.

At this time, at the age of thirty, he took a trip to western Europe to study workers' movements. He went to Zurich, where he joined a local of the International Working

Men's Association, but quit in disgust when he saw the
workers' interests being sacrificed to the political fortunes
of a friendly lawyer.   But in the Jura Federation, composed
chiefly of watchmakers, he found what he instinctively was
drawn to,—an association without political ambitions, and
with no distinctions between the leaders and the rank-and-
file.   This federation had been greatly influenced by Bakunin's
anarchist teaching.   It was Kropotkin's first direct contact
with anarchism.   He says of it in his *Memoirs*:

"The theoretical aspects of anarchism, as they were then
beginning to be expressed in the Jura Federation, especially
by Bakunin; the criticisms of State socialism—the fear of an
economic despotism far more dangerous than the merely
political despotism—which I heard formulated there; and the
revolutionary character of the agitation, appealed strongly to
my mind.   But the equalitarian relations which I found in the
Jura Mountains, the independence of thought and expression
which I saw developing in the workers and their unlimited
devotion to the cause appealed far more strongly to my feelings; and when I came away from the mountains after a
week's stay with the watchmakers, my views upon socialism
were settled.   I was an anarchist."

He never met Bakunin, who died a few years later, but he
was greatly influenced by his personality.   He was impressed
with Bakunin's not posing as an intellectual authority, but
with his being a "moral personality,"—which could be said
also of Kropotkin himself.   He was won to revolutionary
thought in its class significance, not as political reform.   He
says of this view;

"I began to understand that revolutions—that is, periods
of accelerated rapid evolution and rapid changes—are as
much in the nature of human society as the slow evolution
which incessantly goes on now among the civilized races of
mankind.   And each time that such a period of accelerated
evolution and reconstruction on a grand scale begins, civil
war is liable to break out on a small or larger scale.   The
question is then not so much how to avoid revolutions as to

how to obtain the greatest results with the most limited amount of civil war, the smallest number of victims and a minimum of mutual embitterment. For that end there is only one means; namely, that the oppressed part of society should obtain the clearest possible conception of what they intend to achieve and how, and that they should be imbued with the enthusiasm which is necessary for that achievement; in that case they will be sure to attach to their cause the best and the freshest intellectual forces of the privileged class."

Returning to Russia after these months in Switzerland, he at once joined the "Circle of Tchaykovsky," a secret educational organization of students, who later became socialists, which was part of the movement "to the People," regarded as revolutionary. Still casting about for the most practical means of working for the revolutionary ideal, Kropotkin was divided between going to his estate, just inherited upon his father's death, to start a peasant land movement, or to agitate among the courtiers for a constitution. While he was debating this, he continued his geographical work, going to Finland to finish a study there. For two years in St. Petersburg he worked day times on geography, and at night in his revolutionary circle, going to meetings dressed as a peasant and under an assumed name.

He finally decided to go to his estate to start the land league, but waited in St. Petersburg longer than he had intended in order to present a paper to the Geographical Society. At the meeting he was proposed for president, which he declined to consider, knowing that he might be arrested at any time. Many of his friends had already been imprisoned. As he was leaving his lodgings the next day he was pursued, identified by one of the workers in his own circle who had turned spy, and taken to jail. He was lodged in the Fortress of Peter and Paul. His arrest caused a sensation, for the proof of his connection with the revolutionary cause was clear. He was then thirty-two (March, 1874.)

Then followed almost two years in prison awaiting trial.

He was allowed to read and write, indeed to continue his scientific work. His brother Alexander was arrested after a visit to him, simply for writing a letter to an exile in London. He was sent to Siberia, where he lived the rest of his life, committing suicide after twelve years. Kropotkin fell ill in the fortress and was transferred to the prison hospital. As he convalesced there, a daring plot was formed by his friends to effect his escape. Incredible as it seems, he was able to run from the inside court-yard where he exercised daily, through a door opened to let in some wagons, and out to the street before the astonished guards could collect their wits enough to shoot. Once in the street he jumped into a waiting cab and was lost in the traffic. Disguised, he made his way out of Russia to Sweden where he got a boat to England. There he intended to stay only briefly, and to return to Russia to continue his revolutionary activities. But he soon changed his mind. He says of the decision which kept him in virtual exile for forty-two years:—

"I was soon taken up by the wave of the anarchist movement which was just then rising in western Europe; and I felt that I should be more useful in helping that movement to find its proper expression than I could possibly be in Russia. In my mother country I was too well known to carry on an open propaganda, especially among the workers and peasants; and later on when the Russian movement became a conspiracy and an armed struggle against the representatives of autocracy, all thought of a popular movement was necessarily abandoned; while my own inclinations drew me more and more intensely toward casting in my lot with the laboring and toiling masses. To bring to them such conceptions as would aid them to direct their efforts to the best advantage of all the workers; to deepen and widen the ideals and principles which will underlie the coming social revolution; to develop these ideals and principles before the workers, not as an order coming from their leaders, but as a result of their own reason; and so to awaken their own initiative, now that they were called upon to appear in the historical arena as the builders of a new, equitable mode of organization of society—this seemed to me as necessary for the development of mankind as anything I could accomplish in Russia at that time. Accordingly I joined the few men who were working in that direction in western Europe, relieving those of them who had been broken down by years of hard struggle."

He made contacts in England with the scientific journals, to which he contributed articles and reviews, and so earned a meagre living. He left Russia with nothing, and his estate was of course confiscated. For the rest of his life he continued to make his living solely by his scientific writings, refusing to take anything for his labors in the anarchist movement, though he was often desperately poor.

But England depressed him. He said of it. "Life without color, atmosphere without air, the sky without a sun, had the same effect on me as a prison. I suffered for air. I couldn't work." So he moved a year later to Switzerland, where he joined the Jura Federation and settled down among the workers. Bakunin had just died (1876), but the conflict between his ideas and those of the authoritarian Marxists raged. Of that struggle Kropotkin wrote:—

"The conflict between the Marxists and the Bakunists was not a personal affair. It was the necessary conflict between the principles of federalism and those of centralization, the free commune and the state's paternal rule, the free action of the masses of the people and the betterment of existing capitalist conditions through legislation,—a conflict between the Latin spirit and the German geist, which after the defeat of France on the battlefield, claimed supremacy in science, politics, philosophy, and in socialism too, representing its own conception of socialism as 'scientific,' while all other interpretations it described as 'utopian.' "

He found a congenial group of friends in James Guillaume, an intellectual, a highly educated man who was the author of serious works, in Elisée Réclus, the distinguished French geographer, then in exile, and in Enrico Malatesta, Italian anarchist and follower of Bakunin. Most of the Russians in Switzerland he found had become Marxists, and so his friends were among the Latins. He met at this time a young Russian student, Sophie Ananieff, living also in virtual exile in Switzerland. Shortly after they were married there.

As Kropotkin studied the forces about him he came to see that anarchism needed a deeper interpretation than its significance to politics and economics. His philosophical and scientific outlook moved him to probe for a synthesis, a unity which should establish it as a principle of life. This conception colored practically all his thinking, all his work in social ethics, and led him to ceaseless activity in research and interpretation to the day of his death. Even his writing in the natural sciences, notably his *Mutual Aid,* a classic reply to the school of the "survival of the fittest," was impelled by this desire to prove on a scientific basis the case for voluntary cooperation and freedom. Of this period of growth he says:

"I gradually came to realize that anarchism represents more than a new mode of action and a mere conception of a free society; that it is part of a philosophy, natural and social, which must be developed in a quite different way from the metaphysical or dialectic methods which have been employed in sciences dealing with man. I saw that it must be treated by the same methods as the natural sciences; not, however, on the slippery ground of mere analogies such as Herbert Spencer accepts, but on the solid basis of induction applied to human institutions. And I did my best to accomplish what I could in that direction."

With the exception of a trip back to England and to Paris, Kroptkin lived in Switzerland for five years, until he was thirty-nine,—doing what he describes as his best work, with the help of his wife and Elisée Réclus. It was chiefly in the form of articles and editorials for a fortnightly paper, *Le Révolté,* which he started at Geneva in 1879, and which he continued for many years, despite persecution and suppression, under the later names of *La Révolte* and *Les Temps Nouveaux.* Most of the material in the pamphlets reprinted in this volume was first published in his paper. The pamphlets achieved large editions in a dozen languages. Elisée Réclus collected the best of his early writing in the paper into a book, *Paroles d'un Revolté*, published only in French, in 1885 by Marpon Flamarion, while Kropotkin was at the Clairvaux prison.

The little group did not find Switzerland an easy land of refuge. The Jura Federation, frankly anarchist, was broken up by the Swiss authorities following anarchist assassinations in Europe, with which of course it had no connection. After the killing of Czar Alexander II in 1881, Kropotkin was expelled from Switzerland, doubtless at the instance of the Russian Government, which always kept close watch on him through its secret agents. The Russian Holy League, organized to defend the Czar's régime, often threatened him with death.

Finding refuge again in England, Kropotkin continued his writing and his lecturing for a year, but to tiny audiences. Interest in radical ideas was at low ebb. Then, because of Mme. Kropotkin's ill health in that climate, they went to Thonon, where her brother was very ill. There Kropotkin continued his paper for anarchist propaganda while writing scientific aticles for *The Encyclopedia Britannica*—the same strange combination of disrepute and respectability which marked him all his life. His distinction as a geographer was also recognized by his election to the British Royal Geographical Society, an honor which he declined because of his hostility to any association with a "royal" organization.

When a little later a demonstration took place at Lyons, in which some bombs were thrown, Kropotkin was arrested along with some sixty anarchists in France, though he was at Thonon and had no relation to the affair. All were charged with "membership in the International Working Men's Association," although Kropotkin alone was a member. They were tried together at Lyons in 1883 and all were convicted in an atmosphere made hysterical by the press. Kropotkin was among the four to get the maximum five year sentence, and was sent to Clairvaux prison. There he stayed for three years, while friends and sympathizers all over France worked for amnesty for the whole group, finally succeeding in getting a vote of pardon in the Chamber. Among many distinguished Frenchmen who worked for his freedom was Georges Clemenceau, then a radical, who was unceasing in his efforts in the Chamber.

At Clairvaux conditions were fairly good for the political prisoners,—no compulsory labor, a chance to study and write, to buy their own food and wine, and to work outdoors in a garden—a privilege secured for politicals by Clemenceau. They organized classes for study among the prisoners. Ernest Renan sent Kropotkin part of his library for use. Sophie Kropotkin came to Clairvaux after a year and was allowed to see her husband daily. Yet Kropotkin bristled at the whole system. His *Prisons and their Moral Influence on Prisoners,* (pages 219-235) was chiefly the result of his observations and experience at Clairvaux. He also wrote up his early and later prison experiences in book form in *In Russian and French Prisons.* The whole edition was at once bought up and destroyed by the Russian secret service, and Kropotkin himself was unable to obtain an additional copy in response to advertising.

After his release he went to Paris, only to be expelled, finding refuge for the third time in England, where he settled in a cottage outside London. His only child, Alexandra, was born at this time, which gave him great joy, although his life was saddened then by the news of the suicide of his beloved brother Alexander in exile in Siberia. This was his last family tie in Russia. The eldest brother had gone other roads from early youth and Kropotkin had no contact with him.

He found a new spirit in the English workers far more vital than five years before. He was encouraged to start an anarchist paper in London, *Freedom,* a monthly still published by the group which he got together. He continued his French paper, now *La Révolte,* for *Le Révolté* had succumbed to a prosecution for anti-militarist propaganda. A series of his early articles in *Freedom* were later revised and published in book form as *The Conquest of Bread,* the most comprehensive and effective work in existence on anarchist economics.

At this time, too, he was inspired to write *Mutual Aid,* the most widely known of all his books. He says he got the statement of the main idea, that of cooperation as a factor in the survival of animal and human societies, from the Russian geologist Kessler, but the inspiration came from Huxley's *Struggle for Existence* (1888) which aroused his anarchist soul to combat. *Mutual Aid* was published as a series of articles in the *Nineteenth Century* (London), for which Kropotkin wrote extensively. His researches for this work led him into a study of the guilds and "free communes" of medieval Europe, to which he referred time and again as examples of non-political economic organizations freely cooperating. He embodied these studies in a work, *The State; Its Historic Rôle,* which he followed some years later with *The Modern State.*

For thirty years after his return from France Kropotkin lived in England, in or near London, until his return to Russia in 1917. They were years of tireless writing and studying, relieved by manual craftsmanship in book-binding and carpentry, and a devotion to music which was a lifelong passion. He took occasional trips to France and Switzerland in later years when the authorities forgot the ban on him, and he made two lecture tours in the United States in 1897 and 1901. In these years of ceaseless labor, interrupted only by ill-health, he wrote four books, *Fields, Factories, Workshops, The Great French Revolution,* his crowning achievement in research and interpretation, the *Memoirs of a Revolutionist,* first published as a series of articles in the *Atlantic Monthly* (Boston), and *Modern Science and Anarchism.* In addition he wrote a pamphlet, *Anarchist Morality,* reprinted in this volume, and numerous articles, many published later as pamphlets. He continued of course his scientific geographical studies and writing from which he earned his living.

He was offered the chair of geography at Cambridge University, but with the offer went a pretty plain intimation that the university would expect him to cease his anarchist activities while in their service. Kropotkin of course declined the offer.

It was as a speaker at the British Association for the Advancement of Science, holding its meeting in 1897 at Toronto, that Kropotkin first went to America. Interested friends in the United States secured an engagement for him to give three lectures on *Mutual Aid* at the Lowell Institute in Boston after the Toronto meeting. He also lectured in New York. On this first American trip Kropotkin was induced to undertake the writing of his *Memoirs*. Robert Erskine Ely and other American friends impressed on him the importance of the story, and secured the consent of Walter Hines Page, then editor of the *Atlantic Monthly*, to run it as a series of articles, despite objections by the *Atlantic's* editorial council. Mr. Ely wrote the introduction, which brought Kropotkin's significance before a wide public hardly familiar with anarchist philosophy or revolutionary struggle. When it appeared in book form through Houghton, Mifflin & Company in 1899, it carried an introduction by George Brandes. It ranks high among life stories, vividly and modestly told. His intimate picture of the struggle against the Czars is unique. It deals chiefly with his early years, and brings his story only to 1889, when he was forty-seven.

On this trip, Kropotkin went out of his way to visit Pittsburgh to meet his fellow-anarchist, Alexander Berkman, then serving a long sentence for an attempt on the life of H. C. Frick of the Carnegie Steel Corporation. As Berkman was at the time in solitary confinement, Kropotkin was refused permission to see him. It is said that some years later, Andrew Carnegie invited Kropotkin, among other notables, to a party at his castle in Scotland. Kropotkin wrote a dignified declination on the ground that he could not accept the hospitality of a man in any way responsible for keeping Berkman in prison.

But it was in 1901 that he made his more memorable visit to the United States, traveling as far west as Chicago, lecturing at leading universities, and again at the Lowell Institute, Boston where he gave a series on Russian literature, later published in book form as *Ideals and Realities in Russian Literature*. In New York he spoke before the League for Political Education; before an audience at Cooper Union on anarchism, with Ernest Crosby, the biographer of Tolstoi, as chairman; and twice at a Fifth Avenue hall, where he talked anarchism as well as Russian literature to a fashionable assemblage. In Boston the Rev. Edward Everett Hale invited him to speak in his church, but Kropotkin refused because of his hostility to the church as an institution, though he finally was persuaded to reconcile his scruples to speaking in the church's lecture room.

He spoke at Harvard, where he was warmly received by Prof. Charles Eliot Norton and others, and at Wellesley College. He did not neglect his anarchist friends, speaking at many meetings arranged by them. The Russian secret police kept track of him even on this tour. The press was fair, even friendly, and his audiences large and alert, plying him with questions at the close of each address. He spoke from notes and in an English strongly accented, in a professorial but very earnest style.

Robert Erskine Ely, who assisted in arranging some of his lectures, relates an incident of his stay in New York in which Kropotkin was the unwitting means of bringing together two persons as little likely to meet as any two in the country. Ely had taken Kropotkin to call on Mrs. Jefferson Davis, widow of the president of the Confederacy, at her request. During the interview, Booker Washington, who was in search of Mr. Ely, was announced as in the hotel lobby, and Mrs. Davis expressed a desire to meet the Negro educator. So these three extraordinary people sat and politely conversed as if it were a most ordinary occasion.

These American trips were the only real breaks in the years of study and writing in England. Kropotkin's health became uncertain and in later years did not permit his undertaking the strain of public lectures. But his health did not seriously affect his studies and his writing, nor his activity as a propagandist and as adviser to the scores of comrades who came to him as the guiding intellectual force of the anarchist movement.

When the 1905 Russian Revolution broke out, Kropotkin aided by publishing a paper in London, and by such activities as exiles could undertake. He later wrote a pamphlet on it, *White Terror in Russia,* in English. His home was a center for Russian revolutionary refugees, whether anarchists or not.

He foresaw the World War, urging his French comrades long before it broke out not to oppose an extension of the period of military service, for he feared German militarism. He broke with many of his anarchist friends on his espousal of the Allied cause in what to them was a purely nationalist-capitalist war. His attitude during the war split the anarchist camp even further than the traditional sectarianism of the radical movement had already done.

When the Russian Revolution began in March 1917, and the Czar was overthrown, Kropotkin at once prepared to return, overjoyed that he had lived to see the success of the great struggle to which he had given his early vigorous years and to which he had always contributed as best he could in exile. He went back in June, settling first in Petrograd, and later in Moscow.

Despite his seventy-five years, he took an immediate and active interest both in the working out of the Revolution and particularly in the conduct of the war. Kerensky consulted him constantly. He appeared in the "democratic convention" of all factions held in Moscow where he urged a renewed military offensive. On the side of the Revolution

he accepted membership on a commission of intellectuals
which undertook the task of promoting further revolutionary
changes without bloodshed,—but it never really got under
way.

The Bolshevik seizure of power in October, 1917, ended
these activities, and Kropotkin soon moved out of Moscow
into Dmitrov, a small town nearby.   There he and his wife
and daughter had a four or five room wooden house, a garden
and a cow.   He got only the regulation food allowance for
an old man, despite the fact that he was in ill-health and his
family complained bitterly of his inability to work because
of the lack of the essentials of life.   But he did not complain
himself, except to friends, and he refused to ask the Government for anything.   His friends, however, did,—but without success until they finally got to Lenin, a great admirer
of Kropotkin, who at once ordered the local Soviet to let
Kropotkin keep his cow and to give him an extra allowance
of food.   His daughter has Lenin's order written in hand on
the back of some printed form.

Kropotkin refused to have any relations with the local
Soviet.   However, in 1920 when Margaret Bondfield of the
British Labour Mission was visiting him he accompanied her
to a meeting of the local Soviet in the school house at which
she had been asked to speak.   According to Henry Alsberg,
who was in the party, all the members arose as he came in and
cheered him.   He appeared very uneasy.   When Miss Bondfield had finished, the chairman turned to Kropotkin and
invited him to speak, saying that all Russians were proud of
him as a very great man.   He arose, half pleased and half
angry, grew very red, and sat down without speaking a
word.

Although Kropotkin could take no active part in the
development of the revolution under the Bolsheviks, he was
very deeply concerned over the terrorism both as a detriment
to the Revolution itself and on humanitarian grounds.   A
friend, who was also a friend of Lenin, came with a message
saying that Lenin was anxious to see Kropotkin and willing to

come to Dmitrov in order to discuss it.   The interview was
at once arranged.   Although Lenin was cordial and ap-
preciative of Kropotkin's view, nothing came of the meeting.
Irreconcilable as he was to the Bolsheviks, Kropotkin even
more vigorously opposed foreign intervention in Russia or
counter-revolutionary movements.   He even stopped his
friends when they made bitter tirades against the government.   His advice to anarchists was to aid in "reconstruction" through the unions and associations outside the
government.   To young anarchists abroad he advised join-
ing the syndicalist movement as the best way to the realization of the anarchist goal.

Of the revolution under the Bolsheviks, he wrote once in
1919 for the British Labour Mission, and once, after much
urging, in November, 1920, just before his death.   These
statements are so revealing of his big outlook, so wise in
their tolerant understanding, that we are reprinting them in
this collection under the head, *The Russian Revolution and
the Soviet Government.*

But Kropotkin took no part in any movement.   He was
old and feeble and engrossed in his studies, chiefly the writing
of a book on *Ethics,* published after his death.   He continued
to grow feebler and was actually taken ill with pneumonia.
He died in the little house in Dmitrov on February 8, 1921,
seventy-eight years of age.

The Soviet Government offered his family a State funeral,
which they, of course, declined.   Instead, the anarchist group
in Moscow arranged the funeral in the Trade Union house.

Twenty thousand people marched in the two-hour proces-
sion to the grave in such bitter cold that the musical instruments froze.   Black banners were carried demanding "the
release from prison of the friends and comrades of Kropotkin."
At the grave, speeches were made by Emma Goldman, by
representatives of the released prisoners, of the Tolstoians,
of scientific and labor organizations, of the students, of the
Social Revolutionists, and of the Communist Party.

The little Dmitrov house was given by the Government

to the widow for her personal use. Kropotkin's birthplace in Moscow—the big wooden house in the old nobles' quarter with its six massive square columns—was turned over to his wife and friends by the government for use as a museum for his books, papers, letters and belongings, and is now maintained by the contributions of old friends and admirers throughout the world.

ROGER N. BALDWIN
1927

NOTE ON THE EDITING OF THE PAMPHLETS

Kropotkin's work in the field of anarchist teaching was popularized through cheap pamphlets, sold up into the hundreds of thousands in practically every European language,—and Chinese and Japanese as well. He wrote only a few pamphlets as such. The score or more different pamphlets were chiefly reprints of articles and speeches which he adapted to the needs of anarchist propaganda.

Written in a simple style and resounding with calls to action, they appealed also by close reasoning and vivid illustrations. They met the need of workers for a systematic and scientific treatment of the problems confronting those who believed in the revolutionary mission of the working-class, and who rejected the appeal to political methods or to the concept of a State dictatorship by a party of the working-class. They aroused both the spirit of freedom and of revolution. And they voiced the drama of combat against the whole range of authoritarian forces, in the camps of capitalism and of socialism alike.

These pamphlets first appeared in French or English, oftener in French, for most of the articles or speeches from which they were taken were in French. A few were written in Russian. Kropotkin wrote in all three languages. Most of his scientific articles and his larger books were written in English. The pamphlets were translated into a dozen languages,—their greatest circulation being in Latin and English-speaking countries. Their circulation in Japanese has been surprisingly large.

The profound changes in the radical and working-class movement throughout the world following the World War and the Russian Revolution, decreased interest in pamphlets dealing with conditions before the war. Their circulation fell off everywhere. The anarchist movement itself lost in numbers and vigor from the dissension among its own followers, from the emergence of communism as a stronger fighting force, and from the general depression of working-class militancy in the face of capitalist consolidation and persecution. Anarchist publications of all sorts have accordingly decreased. But it is noteworthy that much of Kropotkin's work has been published in Sweden and Germany since the war, and a complete bibliography covering over five hundred titles in all languages appeared in 1926.

These pamphlets represent far more than the phases of revolutionary struggle of Kropotkin's time. They make a lasting contribution to thought in the confused conflicts which mark the long transition to a socialist economy and to the freedoms which lie in and beyond it. It is to present the essence of that thought that these pamphlets have been edited in book-form, omitting only the references and illustrations no longer pertinent, and controversial material of no current interest. They appear as they were written except for these omissions, for improvements in phrasing and punctuation, and for better translations.

All the pamphlets ever published in English are reprinted here except four,—*The Commune of Paris,* which deals with one event to which Kropotkin refers clearly enough in other work; *War,* a little treatise quite out of date now; *The Place of Anarchism in Socialist Evolution,* which duplicates other material here printed; and *The State, Its Historic Role,* which is available in book form (see page 302). Pamphlets which were reprints of chapters from *The Conquest of Bread,* now available in book form, are also omitted. In addition to including all these pamphlets previously published in English, two translated from French have been added,—*The Spirit of Revolt* and *Prisons and their Moral Effect on Prisoners.* No others in other languages contain material which would add to a presentation of Kropotkin's revolutionary thought.

These pamphlets are arranged to give a clear and comprehensive picture of Kropotkin's social teaching. No one of his books covers so wide and varied a field,—in economics, politics, law, the State, the treatment of crime, revolution and science. There is also included as an appendix a large part of the article on anarchism from *The Encyclopedia Britannica*, written by Kropotkin. Its objective treatment is of interest to those who may want a ready reference to the best brief statement of the history and aspects of the whole movement.

I should like to acknowledge here my appreciation of the aid and counsel of Arnold Roller, who translated the section of *The Spirit of Revolt* that appears in this volume, and who has been patient and never failing in suggestion and editorial advice.

ROGER N. BALDWIN
1927

NOTE FOR "THE SPIRIT OF REVOLT"

This brief and vivid statement of the role of revolutionary periods in human progress is as fresh as when it first appeared as an article in *Le Révolté* in Geneva in 1880,—later revised slightly and printed as a pamphlet in French. The part referring specifically to the French Revolution has been omitted.

Kropotkin points out the function of a new class rising to power, transforming its propaganda of words into deeds, overthrowing governing institutions that appear so strong but are decayed within. In the complete pamphlet he cites the French Revolution as the classic process, and points out the means of propaganda by which the rising class achieved its power. But he argues the case for a revolution of the workers that will not be merely a change of government, not merely the exercise of old powers by a new class, but a wholly new cooperative régime based on socialized property.

34

THE SPIRIT OF REVOLT

THERE are periods in the life of human society when revolution becomes an imperative necessity, when it proclaims itself as inevitable. New ideas germinate everywhere, seeking to force their way into the light, to find an application in life; everywhere they are opposed by the inertia of those whose interest it is to maintain the old order; they suffocate in the stifling atmosphere of prejudice and traditions. The accepted ideas of the constitution of the State, of the laws of social equilibrium, of the political and economic interrelations of citizens, can hold out no longer against the implacable criticism which is daily undermining them whenever occasion arises,—in drawing room as in cabaret, in the writings of philosophers as in daily conversation. Political, economic, and social institutions are crumbling; the social structure, having become uninhabitable, is hindering, even preventing the development of the seeds which are being propagated within its damaged walls and being brought forth around them.

The need for a new life becomes apparent. The code of established morality, that which governs the greater number of people in their daily life, no longer seems sufficient. What formerly seemed just is now felt to be a crying injustice. The morality of yesterday is today recognized as revolting immorality. The conflict between new ideas and old traditions flames up in every class of society, in every possible environment, in the very bosom of the family. The son struggles against his father, he finds revolting what his father has all his life found natural; the daughter rebels against the principles which her mother has handed down to her as the result of long experience. Daily, the popular con-

science rises up against the scandals which breed amidst
the privileged and the leisured, against the crimes committed
in the name of *the law of the stronger,* or in order to maintain these privileges. Those who long for the triumph of
justice, those who would put new ideas into practice, are
soon forced to recognize that the realization of their generous, humanitarian and regenerating ideas cannot take place
in a society thus constituted; they perceive the necessity of
a revolutionary whirlwind which will sweep away all this
rottenness, revive sluggish hearts with its breath, and bring
to mankind that spirit of devotion, self-denial, and heroism,
without which society sinks through degradation and vileness
into complete disintegration.

In periods of frenzied haste toward wealth, of feverish
speculation and of crisis, of the sudden downfall of great
industries and the ephemeral expansion of other branches
of production, of scandalous fortunes amassed in a few years
and dissipated as quickly, it becomes evident that the economic institutions which control production and exchange
are far from giving to society the prosperity which they are
supposed to guarantee; they produce precisely the opposite
result. Instead of order they bring forth chaos; instead of
prosperity, poverty and insecurity; instead of reconciled interests, war; a perpetual war of the exploiter against the
worker, of exploiters and of workers among themselves.
Human society is seen to be splitting more and more into
two hostile camps, and at the same time to be subdividing
into thousands of small groups waging merciless war against
each other. Weary of these wars, weary of the miseries which
they cause, society rushes to seek a new organization; it
clamors loudly for a complete remodelling of the system
of property ownership, of production, of exchange and all
economic relations which spring from it.

The machinery of government, entrusted with the maintenance of the existing order, continues to function, but at
every turn of its deteriorated gears it slips and stops. Its
working becomes more and more difficult, and the dissatisfac-

tion caused by its defects grows continuously. Every day
gives rise to a new demand. "Reform this," "Reform that,"
is heard from all sides. "War, finance, taxes, courts, police,
everything must be remodelled, reorganized, established on a
new basis," say the reformers. And yet all know that it is
impossible to make things over, to remodel anything at all
because everything is interrelated; everything would have
to be remade at once; and how can society be remodelled
when it is divided into two openly hostile camps? To satisfy
the discontented would be only to create new malcontents.

Incapable of undertaking reforms, since this would mean
paving the way for revolution, and at the same time too impotent to be frankly reactionary, the governing bodies
apply themselves to half-measures which can satisfy nobody,
and only cause new dissatisfaction. The mediocrities who,
in such transition periods, undertake to steer the ship of
State, think of but one thing: to enrich themselves against
the coming *débâcle*. Attacked from all sides they defend
themselves awkwardly, they evade, they commit blunder upon
blunder, and they soon succeed in cutting the last rope of
salvation; they drown the prestige of the government in ridicule, caused by their own incapacity.

Such periods demand revolution. It becomes a social necessity; the situation itself is revolutionary.

When we study in the works of our greatest historians
the genesis and development of vast revolutionary convul-
sions we generally find under the heading, "The Cause of the
Revolution," a gripping picture of the situation on the eve
of events. The misery of the people, the general insecurity,
the vexatious measures of the government, the odious scandals laying bare the immense vices of society, the new ideas
struggling to come to the surface and repulsed by the incapacity of the supporters of the former régime,—nothing is
omitted. Examining this picture, one arrives at the convic-
tion that the revolution was indeed inevitable, and that
there was no other way out than by the road of insurrection.

Take, for example, the situation before 1789 as the historians picture it. You can almost hear the peasant complaining of the salt tax, of the tithe, of the feudal payments, and vowing in his heart an implacable hatred towards the feudal baron, the monk, the monopolist, the bailiff. You can almost see the citizen bewailing the loss of his municipal liberties, and showering maledictions upon the king. The people censure the queen; they are revolted by the reports of ministerial action, and they cry out continually that the taxes are intolerable and revenue payments exorbitant, that crops are bad and winters hard, that provisions are too dear and the monopolists too grasping, that the village lawyer devours the peasant's crops and the village constable tries to play the role of a petty king, that even the mail service is badly organized and the employees too lazy. In short, nothing works well, everybody complains. "It can last no longer, it will come to a bad end," they cry everywhere.

But, between this pacific arguing and insurrection or revolt, there is a wide abyss,—that abyss which, for the greatest part of humanity, lies between reasoning and action, thought and will,—the urge to act. How has this abyss been bridged? How is it that men who only yesterday were complaining quietly of their lot as they smoked their pipes, and the next moment were humbly saluting the local guard and *gendarme* whom they had just been abusing,—how is it that these same men a few days later were capable of seizing their scythes and their iron-shod pikes and attacking in his castle the lord who only yesterday was so formidable? By what miracle were these men, whose wives justly called them cowards, transformed in a day into heroes, marching through bullets and cannon balls to the conquest of their rights? How was it that *words*, so often spoken and lost in the air like the empty chiming of bells, were changed into *actions?*

The answer is easy.

Action, the continuous action, ceaselessly renewed, of minorities brings about this transformation. Courage, devotion, the spirit of sacrifice, are as contagious as cowardice, submission, and panic.

What forms will this action take? All forms,—indeed, the most varied forms, dictated by circumstances, temperament, and the means at disposal. Sometimes tragic, sometimes humorous, but always daring; sometimes collective, sometimes purely individual, this policy of action will neglect none of the means at hand, no event of public life, in order to keep the spirit alive, to propagate and find expression for dissatisfaction, to excite hatred against exploiters, to ridicule the government and expose its weakness, and above all and always, by actual example, to awaken courage and fan the spirit of revolt.

When a revolutionary situation arises in a country, before the spirit of revolt is sufficiently awakened in the masses to express itself in violent demonstrations in the streets or by rebellions and uprisings, it is through *action* that minorities succeed in awakening that feeling of independence and that spirit of audacity without which no revolution can come to a head.

Men of courage, not satisfied with words, but ever searching for the means to transform them into action,—men of integrity for whom the act is one with the idea, for whom prison, exile, and death are preferable to a life contrary to their principles,—intrepid souls who know that it is necessary to *dare* in order to succeed,—these are the lonely sentinels who enter the battle long before the masses are sufficiently roused to raise openly the banner of insurrection and to march, arms in hand, to the conquest of their rights.

In the midst of discontent, talk, theoretical discussions, an individual or collective act of revolt supervenes, symbolizing the dominant aspirations. It is possible that at the beginning the masses will remain indifferent. It is possible that while admiring the courage of the individual or the group which takes the initiative, the masses will at first follow those who are prudent and cautious, who will immediately describe this act as "insanity" and say that "those madmen, those fanatics will endanger everything."

They have calculated so well, those prudent and cautious

men, that their party, slowly pursuing its work would, in a hundred years, two hundred years, three hundred years perhaps, succeed in conquering the whole world,—and now the unexpected intrudes! The unexpected, of course, is whatever has not been expected by them,—those prudent and cautious ones! Whoever has a slight knowledge of history and a fairly clear head knows perfectly well from the beginning that theoretical propaganda for revolution will necessarily express itself in action long before the theoreticians have decided that the moment to act has come. Nevertheless the cautious theoreticians are angry at these madmen, they excommunicate them, they anathematize them. But the madmen win sympathy, the mass of the people secretly applaud their courage, and they find imitators. In proportion as the pioneers go to fill the jails and the penal colonies, others continue their work; acts of illegal protest, of revolt, of vengeance, multiply.

Indifference from this point on is impossible. Those who at the beginning never so much as asked what the "madmen" wanted, are compelled to think about them, to discuss their ideas, to take sides for or against. By actions which compel general attention, the new idea seeps into people's minds and wins converts. One such act may, in a few days, make more propaganda than thousands of pamphlets.

Above all, it awakens the spirit of revolt: it breeds daring. The old order, supported by the police, the magistrates, the *gendarmes* and the soldiers, appeared unshakable, like the old fortress of the Bastille, which also appeared impregnable to the eyes of the unarmed people gathered beneath its high walls equipped with loaded cannon. But soon it became apparent that the established order has not the force one had supposed. One courageous act has sufficed to upset in a few days the entire governmental machinery, to make the colossus tremble; another revolt has stirred a whole province into turmoil, and the army, till now always so imposing, has retreated before a handful of peasants armed with sticks and stones. The people observe that the monster is not so terrible as they thought; they begin dimly to perceive that a few energetic efforts will be sufficient to throw it down. Hope is born in their hearts, and let us remember that if exasperation often drives men to revolt, it is always hope, the hope of victory, which makes revolutions.

The government resists; it is savage in its repressions. But, though formerly persecution killed the energy of the oppressed, now, in periods of excitement, it produces the opposite result. It provokes new acts of revolt, individual and collective; it drives the rebels to heroism; and in rapid succession these acts spread, become general, develop. The revolutionary party is strengthened by elements which up to this time were hostile or indifferent to it. The general disintegration penetrates into the government, the ruling classes, the privileged; some of them advocate resistance to the limit; others are in favor of concessions; others, again, go so far as to declare themselves ready to renounce their privileges for the moment, in order to appease the spirit of revolt, hoping to dominate again later on. The unity of the government and the privileged class is broken.

The ruling classes may also try to find safety in savage reaction. But it is now too late; the battle only becomes more bitter, more terrible, and the revolution which is looming will only be more bloody. On the other hand, the smallest concession of the governing classes, since it comes too late, since it has been snatched in struggle, only awakes the revolutionary spirit still more. The common people, who formerly would have been satisfied with the smallest concession, observe now that the enemy is wavering; they foresee victory, they feel their courage growing, and the same men who were formerly crushed by misery and were content to sigh in secret, now lift their heads and march proudly to the conquest of a better future.

Finally the revolution breaks out, the more terrible as the preceding struggles were bitter.

The direction which the revolution will take depends, no doubt, upon the sum total of the various circumstances that determine the coming of the cataclysm. But it can be predicted in advance, according to the vigor of revolutionary action displayed in the preparatory period by the different progressive parties.

One party may have developed more clearly the theories which it defines and the program which it desires to realize; it may have made propaganda actively, by speech and in print. But it may not have sufficiently expressed its aspirations in the open, on the street, by actions which *embody the thought it represents*; it has done little, or it has done nothing against those who are its principal enemies; it has not attacked the institutions which it wants to demolish; its strength has been in theory, not in action; it has contributed little to awaken the spirit of revolt, or it has neglected to direct that spirit against conditions which it particularly desires to attack at the time of the revolution. As a result, this party is less known; its aspirations have not been daily and continuously affirmed by actions, the glamor of which could reach even the remotest hut; they have not sufficiently penetrated into the consciousness of the people; they have not identified themselves with the crowd and the street; they have never found simple expression in a popular slogan.

The most active writers of such a party are known by their readers as thinkers of great merit, but they have neither the reputation nor the capacities of men of action; and on the day when the mobs pour through the streets they will prefer to follow the advice of those who have less precise theoretical ideas and not such great aspirations, but whom they know better because they have seen them act.

The party which has made most revolutionary propaganda and which has shown most spirit and daring will be listened to on the day when it is necessary to act, to march in front in order to realize the revolution. But that party which has not had the daring to affirm itself by revolutionary acts in the preparatory periods nor had a driving force strong enough to inspire men and groups to the sentiment of abnegation, to the irresistible desire to put their ideas into practice,—(if this desire had existed it would have expressed itself in action long before the mass of the people had joined the revolt)—and which did not know how to make its flag popular and its aspirations tangible and comprehensive,—that party will have only a small chance of realizing even the least part of its program. It will be pushed aside by the parties of action.

These things we learn from the history of the periods which precede great revolutions. The revolutionary bourgeoisie understood this perfectly,—it neglected no means of agitation to awaken the spirit of revolt when it tried to demolish the monarchical order. The French peasant of the eighteenth century understood it instinctively when it was a question of abolishing feudal rights; and the International acted in accordance with the same principles when it tried to awaken the spirit of revolt among the workers of the cities and to direct it against the natural enemy of the wage earner —the monopolizer of the means of production and of raw materials.

NOTE FOR "ANARCHIST COMMUNISM: ITS BASIS AND PRINCIPLES"

This summary of the leading principles of anarchist communism was written for the conservative readers of the *Nineteenth Century*, London, where it was published in two articles in 1887. Kropotkin revised it for pamphlet form. It is the simplest, clearest statement of the case for free communism in all his writing.

The first section sets forth the relation of anarchism to the socialist movement, traces the evidence to support the free as against the State-controlled form of it, and cites the agreement of evolutionists with this conception of ultimate freedom from governmental control. He takes up the organization of production to show how cooperative control and equality in sharing wealth would increase the world's goods to meet everybody's needs. The appropriation of wealth by the privileged few is shown as the evil which has always blocked cooperative production, and which must be abolished to guarantee further progress to equality and freedom. This economic discussion reflects the common view of the socialist-communist-anarchist movements, without any peculiar contribution from the anarchist viewpoint.

It is in the second section that Kropotkin arrays the evidence for free communism from a standpoint that is not shared by the other revolutionary schools. He answers the objections to his contentions,—covering such familiar practical questions as "What will you do with those who do not keep their agreements?" "How about the people who won't work unless compelled?" and "You've got to have a government to protect society against criminals." Most significant are his practical illustrations of the non-governmental activities by which the chief work of the world is done.

44

For those who want a practical application of the anarchist principles to political and economic life, the evidence here is put in the simplest and most convincing form.

After the Russian Revolution of 1917, however, he changed his opinions concerning the distribution of the products. See note at the end of this pamphlet.

ANARCHIST COMMUNISM:

ITS BASIS AND PRINCIPLES

I

ANARCHISM, the no-government system of socialism, has a double origin. It is an outgrowth of the two great movements of thought in the economic and the political fields which characterize the nineteenth century, and especially its second part. In common with all socialists, the anarchists hold that the private ownership of land, capital, and machinery has had its time; that it is condemned to disappear; and that all requisites for production must, and will, become the common property of society, and be managed in common by the producers of wealth. And in common with the most advanced representatives of political radicalism, they maintain that the ideal of the political organization of society is a condition of things where the functions of government are reduced to a minimum, and the individual recovers his full liberty of initiative and action for satisfying, by means of free groups and federations—freely constituted—all the infinitely varied needs of the human being.

As regards socialism, most of the anarchists arrive at its ultimate conclusion, that is, at a complete negation of the wage-system and at communism. And with reference to political organization, by giving a further development to the above-mentioned part of the radical program, they arrive at the conclusion that the ultimate aim of society is the reduction of the functions of government to *nil*—that is, to a society without government, to an-archy. The anarchists maintain, moreover, that such being the ideal of social and political organization, they must not remit it to future centuries, but that only those changes in our social organization which are in accordance with the above double ideal, and constitute an approach to it, will have a chance of life and be beneficial for the commonwealth.

As to the method followed by the anarchist thinker, it entirely differs from that followed by the utopists. The anarchist thinker does not resort to metaphysical conceptions (like "natural rights," the "duties of the State," and so on) to establish what are, in his opinion, the best conditions for realizing the greatest happiness of humanity. He follows, on the contrary, the course traced by the modern philosophy of evolution. He studies human society as it is now and was in the past; and without either endowing humanity as a whole, or separate individuals, with superior qualities which they do not possess, he merely considers society as an aggregation of organisms trying to find out the best ways of combining the wants of the individual with those of cooperation for the welfare of the species. He studies society and tries to discover its *tendencies*, past and present, its growing needs, intellectual and economic, and in his ideal he merely points out in which direction evolution goes. He distinguishes between the real wants and tendencies of human aggregations and the accidents (want of knowledge, migrations, wars, conquests) which have prevented these tendencies from being satisfied. And he concludes that the two most prominent, although often unconscious, tendencies throughout our history have been: first, a tendency towards integrating labor for the production of all riches in common, so as finally to render it impossible to discriminate the part of the common production due to the separate individual; and second, a tendency towards the fullest freedom of the individual in the prosecution of all aims, beneficial both for himself and for society at large. The ideal of the anarchist is thus a mere summing-up of what he considers to be the next phase of evolution. It is no longer a matter of faith; it is a matter for scientific discussion.

In fact, one of the leading features of this century is the

growth of socialism and the rapid spreading of socialist views among the working-classes. How could it be otherwise? We have witnessed an unparalleled sudden increase of our powers of production, resulting in an accumulation of wealth which has outstripped the most sanguine expectations. But owing to our wage system, this increase of wealth—due to the combined efforts of men of science, of managers, and workmen as well—has resulted only in an unprecedented accumulation of wealth in the hands of the owners of capital; while an increase of misery for great numbers, and an insecurity of life for all, have been the lot of the workmen. The unskilled laborers, in continuous search for labor, are falling into an unheard-of destitution. And even the best paid artisans and skilled workmen labor under the permanent menace of being thrown, in their turn, into the same conditions as the unskilled paupers, in consequence of some of the continous and unavoidable fluctuations of industry and caprices of capital.

The chasm between the modern millionaire who squanders the produce of human labor in a gorgeous and vain luxury, and the pauper reduced to a miserable and insecure existence, is thus growing wider and wider, so as to break the very unity of society—the harmony of its life—and to endanger the progress of its further development.

At the same time, workingmen are less and less inclined to patiently endure this division of society into two classes, as they themselves become more and more conscious of the wealth-producing power of modern industry, of the part played by labor in the production of wealth, and of their own capacities of organization. In proportion as all classes of the community take a more lively part in public affairs, and knowledge spreads among the masses, their longing for equality becomes stronger, and their demands for social reorganization become louder and louder. They can be ignored no more. The worker claims his share in the riches he produces; he claims his share in the management of production; and he claims not only some additional well-being, but also his full rights in the higher enjoyments of science and art. These claims, which formerly were uttered only by the social reformer, begin now to be made by a daily growing minority of those who work in the factory or till the acre. And they so conform to our feelings of justice that they find support in a daily growing minority among the privileged classes themselves. Socialism becomes thus *the* idea of the nineteenth century; and neither coercion nor pseudo-reforms can stop its further growth.

Much hope of improvement was placed, of course, in the extension of political rights to the working classes. But these concessions, unsupported as they were by corresponding changes in economic relations, proved delusions. They did not materially improve the conditions of the great bulk of the workmen. Therefore, the watchword of socialism is: "Economic freedom as the only secure basis for political freedom." And as long as the present wage system, with all its bad consequences, remains unaltered, the socialist watchword will continue to inspire the workmen. Socialism will continue to grow until it has realized its program.

Side by side with this great movement of thought in economic matters, a like movement has been going on with regard to political rights, political organization, and the functions of government. Government has been submitted to the same criticism as capital. While most of the radicals saw in universal suffrage and republican institutions the last word of political wisdom, a further step was made by the few. The very functions of government and the State, as also their relations to the individual, were submitted to a sharper and deeper criticism. Representative government having been tried by experiment on a wide field, its defects became more and more prominent. It became obvious that these defects are not merely accidental but inherent in the system itself. Parliament and its executive proved to be unable to attend to all the numberless affairs of the community and to conciliate the varied and often opposite interests of the separate parts of a State. Election proved unable to find out the men who might represent a nation, and manage, otherwise than in a party spirit, the affairs they are compelled to legislate upon. These defects become so striking that the very principles of the representative system were criticized and their justness doubted.

Again, the dangers of a centralized government became still more conspicuous when the socialists came to the front and asked for a further increase of the powers of government by entrusting it with the management of the immense field covered now by the economic relations between individuals. The question was asked whether a government entrusted with the management of industry and trade would not become a permanent danger for liberty and peace, and whether it even would be able to be a good manager?

The socialists of the earlier part of this century did not fully realize the immense difficulties of the problem. Convinced as they were of the necessity of economic reforms, most of them took no notice of the need of freedom for the individual. And we have had social reformers ready to submit society to any kind of theocracy, or dictatorship in order to obtain reforms in a socialist sense. Therefore we have seen in England and also on the Continent the division of men of advanced opinions into political radicals and socialists—the former looking with distrust on the latter, as they saw in them a danger for the political liberties which have been won by the civilized nations after a long series of struggles. And even now, when the socialists all over Europe have become political parties, and profess the democratic faith, there remains among most impartial men a well-founded fear of the *Volksstaat* or "popular State" being as great a danger to liberty as any form of autocracy if its government be entrusted with the management of all the social organization including the production and distribution of wealth.

Recent evolution, however, has prepared the way for showing the necessity and possibility of a higher form of social organization which may guarantee economic freedom without reducing the individual to the role of a slave to the

State. The origins of government have been carefully studied, and all metaphysical conceptions as to its divine or "social contract" derivation having been laid aside, it appears that it is among us of a relatively modern origin, and that its powers have grown precisely in proportion as the division of society into the privileged and unprivileged classes was growing in the course of ages. Representative government has also been reduced to its real value—that of an instrument which has rendered services in the struggle against autocracy, but not an ideal of free political organization. As to the system of philosophy which saw in the State a leader of progress, it was more and more shaken as it became evident that progress is the most effective when it is not checked by State interference. It has thus become obvious that a further advance in social life does not lie in the direction of a further concentration of power and regulative functions in the hands of a governing body, but in the direction of decentralization, both territorial and functional—in a subdivision of public functions with respect both to their sphere of action and to the character of the functions; it is in the abandonment to the initiative of freely constituted groups of all those functions which are now considered as the functions of government.

This current of thought has found its expression not merely in literature, but also to a limited extent in life. The uprise of the Paris Commune, followed by that of the Commune of Cartagena—a movement of which the historical bearing seems to have been quite overlooked—opened a new page of history. If we analyze not only this movement in itself, but also the impression it left in the minds and the tendencies manifested during the communal revolution, we must recognize in it an indication showing that in the future human agglomerations which are more advanced in their social development will try to start an independent life; and that they will endeavor to convert the more backward parts of a nation by example, instead of imposing their opinions by law and force, or submitting themselves to the majority-rule,

which always is a mediocrity-rule. At the same time the
failure of representative government within the Commune
itself proved that self-government and self-administration
must be carried further than in a merely territorial sense.
To be effective they must also be carried into the various
functions of life within the free community. A merely territorial limitation of the sphere of action of government will
not do—representative government being as deficient in a
city as it is in a nation. Life gave thus a further point in
favor of the no-government theory, and a new impulse to
anarchist thought.

Anarchists recognize the justice of both the just-mentioned
tendencies towards economic and political freedom, and see
in them two different manifestations of the very same need
of equality which constitutes the very essence of all struggles mentioned by history. Therefore, in common with all
socialists, the anarchist says to the political reformer: "No
substantial reform in the sense of political equality and no
limitation of the powers of government can be made as long
as society is divided into two hostile camps, and the laborer remains, economically speaking, a slave to his employer." But
to the state socialist we say also: "You cannot modify the
existing conditions of property without deeply modifying at
the same time the political organization. You must limit the
powers of government and renounce parliamentary rule. To
each new economic phase of life corresponds a new political
phase. Absolute monarchy corresponded to the system of
serfdom. Representative government corresponds to capital-
rule. Both, however, are class-rule. But in a society where the
distinction between capitalist and laborer has disappeared,
there is no need of such a government; it would be an an-
achronism, a nuisance. Free workers would require a free
organization, and this cannot have any other basis than free
agreement and free cooperation, without sacrificing the
autonomy of the individual to the all-pervading interference
of the State. The no-capitalist system implies the no-government system."

Meaning thus the emancipation of man from the oppressive powers of capitalism and government as well, the system of anarchism becomes a synthesis of the two powerful currents of thought which characterize our century.

In arriving at these conclusions anarchism proves to be in accordance with the conclusions arrived at by the philosophy of evolution. By bringing to light the plasticity of organization, the philosophy of evolution has shown the admirable adaptability of organisms to their conditions of life, and the ensuing development of such faculties as render more complete both the adaptations of the aggregates to their surroundings and those of each of the constituent parts of the aggregate to the needs of free cooperation. It has familiarized us with the circumstance that throughout organic nature the capacities for life in common grow in proportion as the integration of organisms into compound aggregates becomes more and more complete; and it has enforced thus the opinion already expressed by social moralists as to the perfectibility of human nature. It has shown us that, in the long run of the struggle for existence, "the fittest" will prove to be those who combine intellectual knowledge with the knowledge necessary for the production of wealth, and not those who are now the richest because they, or their ancestors, have been momentarily the strongest.

By showing that the "struggle for existence" must be conceived not merely in its restricted sense of a struggle between individuals for the means of subsistence but in its wider sense of adaptation of all individuals of the species to the best conditions for the survival of the species, as well as for the greatest possible sum of life and happiness for each and all, is has permitted us to deduce the laws of moral science from the social needs and habits of mankind. It has shown us the infinitesimal part played by positive law in moral evolution, and the immense part played by the natural growth of altruistic feelings, which develop as soon as the conditions of life favor their growth. It has thus enforced the opinion of social reformers as to the necessity of modify-

ing the conditions of life for improving man, instead of trying to improve human nature by moral teachings while life
works in an opposite direction. Finally, by studying human
society from the biological point of view, it has come to the
conclusions arrived at by anarchists from the study of history and present tendencies as to further progress being in
the line of socialization of wealth and integrated labor combined with the fullest possible freedom of the individual.

It has happened in the long run of ages that everything
which permits men to increase their production, or even to
continue it, has been appropriated by the few. The land,
which derives its value precisely from its being necessary
for an ever-increasing population, belongs to the few, who
may prevent the community from cultivating it. The coal-
pits, which represent the labor of generations, and which
also derive their value from the wants of the manufacturers
and railroads, from the immense trade carried on and the
density of population, belong again to the few, who have even
the right of stopping the extraction of coal if they choose
to give another use to their capital. The lace-weaving machine, which represents, in its present state of perfection,
the work of three generations of Lancashire weavers, belongs
also to the few; and if the grandsons of the very same
weaver who invented the first lace-weaving machine claim
their right to bring one of these machines into motion, they
will be told "Hands off! this machine does not belong to
you!" The railroads, which mostly would be useless heaps of
iron if not for the present dense population, its industry,
trade, and traffic, belong again to the few—to a few shareholders, who may not even know where the railway is situated
which brings them a yearly income larger than that of a medieval king. And if the children of those people who died
by thousands in digging the tunnels should gather and go—
a ragged and starving crowd—to ask bread or work from the
shareholders, they would be met with bayonets and bullets.

Who is the sophist who will dare to say that such an organization is just? But what is unjust cannot be beneficial to

mankind; and *it is not.* In consequence of this monstrous organization, the son of a workman, when he is able to work, finds no acre to till, no machine to set in motion, unless he agrees to sell his labor for a sum inferior to its real value. His father and grandfather have contributed to drain the field, or erect the factory, to the full extent of their capacities—and nobody can do more than that—but he comes into the world more destitute than a savage. If he resorts to agriculture, he will be permitted to cultivate a plot of land, but on the condition that he gives up part of his product to the landlord. If he resorts to industry, he will be permitted to work, but on the condition that out of the thirty shillings he has produced, ten shillings or more will be pocketed by the owner of the machine. We cry out against the feudal barons who did not permit anyone to settle on the land otherwise than on payment of one quarter of the crops to the lord of the manor; but we continue to do as they did —we extend their system. The forms have changed, but the essence has remained the same. And the workman is compelled to accept the feudal conditions which we call "free contract," because nowhere will he find better conditions. Everything has been appropriated by somebody; he *must* accept the bargain, or starve.

Owing to this circumstance our production takes a wrong turn. It takes no care of the needs of the community; its only aim is to increase the profits of the capitalist. And we have, therefore,—the continuous fluctuations of industry, the crisis coming periodically nearly every ten years, and throwing out of employment several hundred thousand men who are brought to complete misery, whose children grow up in the gutter, ready to become inmates of the prison and workhouse. The workmen being unable to purchase with their wages the riches they are producing, industry must search for markets elsewhere, amidst the middle classes of other nations. It must find markets, in the East, in Africa, anywhere; it must increase, by trade, the number of its serfs in Egypt, in India, on the Congo. But everywhere it finds competitors in other nations which rapidly enter into the same line of industrial development. And wars, continuous wars, must be fought for the supremacy in the world-market—wars for the possession of the East, wars for getting possession of the seas, wars for the right of imposing heavy duties on foreign merchandise. The thunder of European guns never ceases; whole generations are slaughtered from time to time; and we spend in armaments the third of the revenue of our States—a revenue raised, the poor know with what difficulties.

And finally, the injustice of our partition of wealth exercises the most deplorable effect on our morality. Our principles of morality say: "Love your neighbour as yourself"; but let a child follow this principle and take off his coat to give it to the shivering pauper, and his mother will tell him that he must never understand moral principles in their direct sense. If he lives according to them, he will go barefoot, without alleviating the misery around him! Morality is good on the lips, not in deeds. Our preachers say, "Who works, prays," and everyone endeavors to make others work for him. They say, "Never lie!" and politics are a big lie. And we accustom ourselves and our children to live under this double-faced morality, which is hypocrisy, and to conciliate our double-facedness by sophistry. Hypocrisy and sophistry become the very basis of our life. But society cannot live under such a morality. It cannot last so: it must, it will, be changed.

The question is thus no more a mere question of bread. It covers the whole field of human activity. But it has at its bottom a question of social economy, and we conclude: The means of production and of satisfaction of all needs of society, having been created by the common efforts of all, must be at the disposal of all. The private appropriation of requisites for production is neither just nor beneficial. All must be placed on the same footing as producers and consumers of wealth. That will be the only way for society to step out of the bad conditions which have been created by centuries of wars and oppression. That will be the only guarantee for further progress in a direction of equality and freedom, which have always been the real, although unspoken goal of humanity.

II

The views taken in the above as to the combination of efforts being the chief source of our wealth explain why most anarchists see in communism the only equitable solution as to the adequate remuneration of individual efforts. There was a time when a family engaged in agriculture supplemented by a few domestic trades could consider the corn they raised and the plain woolen cloth they wove as productions of their own and nobody else's labor. Even then such a view was not quite correct: there were forests cleared and roads built by common efforts; and even then the family had continually to apply for communal help, as is still the case in so many village communities. But now, in the extremely interwoven state of industry of which each branch supports all others, such an individualistic view can be held no more. If the iron trade and the cotton industry of this country have reached so high a degree of development, they have done so owing to the parallel growth of thousands of other industries, great and small; to the extension of the railway system; to an increase of knowledge among both the skilled engineers and the mass of the workmen; to a certain training in organization slowly developed among producers; and, above all, to the world-trade which has itself grown up, thanks to works executed thousands of miles away. The Italians who died from cholera in digging the Suez Canal or from "tunnel-disease" in the St. Gothard Tunnel have contributed as much towards the enrichment of this country as the British girl who is prematurely growing old in serving a machine at Manchester; and this girl as much as the engineer who made a labor-saving improvement in our machinery. How can we pretend to estimate the exact part of each of them in the riches accumulated around us?

We may admire the inventive genius or the organizing capacities of an iron lord; but we must recognize that all his genius and energy would not realize one-tenth of what they realize here if they were spent in dealing with Mongolian shepherds or Siberian peasants instead of British workmen, British engineers, and trustworthy managers. An English millionaire who succeeded in giving a powerful impulse to a branch of home industry was asked the other day what were, in his opinion, the real causes of his success? His answer was:—"I always sought out the right man for a given branch of the concern, and I left him full independence—maintaining, of course, for myself the general supervision." "Did you never fail to find such men?" was the next question. "Never." "But in the new branches which you introduced you wanted a number of new inventions." "No doubt; we spent thousands in buying patents." This little colloquy sums up, in my opinion, the real case of those industrial undertakings which are quoted by the advocates of "an adequate remuneration of individual efforts" in the shape of millions bestowed on the managers of prosperous industries. It shows in how far the efforts are really "individual." Leaving aside the thousand conditions which sometimes permit a man to show, and sometimes prevent him from showing, his capacities to their full extent, it might be asked in how far the same capacities could bring out the same results, if the very same employer could find no trustworthy managers and no skilled workmen, and if hundreds of inventions were not stimulated by the mechanical turn of mind of so many inhabitants of this country.

The anarchists cannot consider, like the collectivists, that a remuneration which would be proportionate to the hours of labor spent by each person in the production of riches may be an ideal, or even an approach to an ideal, society. Without entering here into a discussion as to how far the exchange value of each merchandise is really measured now by the amount of labor necessary for its production—a separate study must be devoted to the subject—we must say

ANARCHIST COMMUNISM 59

that the collectivist ideal seems to us merely unrealizable in
a society which has been brought to consider the necessaries
for production as a common property. Such a society would
be compelled to abandon the wage-system altogether. It
appears impossible that the mitigated individualism of the
collectivist school could co-exist with the partial communism implied by holding land and machinery in common—
unless imposed by a powerful government, much more
powerful than all those of our own times. The present
wage-system has grown up from the appropriation of the
necessaries for production by the few; it was a necessary
condition for the growth of the present capitalist production;
and it cannot outlive it, even if an attempt be made to pay
to the worker the full value of his produce, and hours-of-
labor-checks be substituted for money. Common possession
of the necessaries for production implies the common enjoyment of the fruits of the common production; and we consider that an equitable organization of society can only arise
when every wage-system is abandoned, and when everybody,
contributing for the common well-being to the full extent
of his capacities, shall enjoy also from the common stock of
society to the fullest possible extent of his needs.

We maintain, moreover, not only that communism is a
desirable state of society, but that the growing tendency of
modern society is precisely towards communism—free communism — notwithstanding the seemingly contradictory
growth of individualism. In the growth of individualism
(especially during the last three centuries) we see merely
the endeavors of the individual towards emancipating himself from the steadily growing powers of capital and the
State. But side by side with this growth we see also,
throughout history up to our own times, the latent struggle
of the producers of wealth to maintain the partial communism
of old, as well as to reintroduce communist principles in a
new shape, as soon as favorable conditions permit it. As soon
as the communes of the tenth, eleventh, and twelfth centuries
were enabled to start their own independent life, they gave

a wide extension to work in common, to trade in common, and to a partial consumption in common. All this has disappeared. But the rural commune fights a hard struggle to maintain its old features, and it succeeds in maintaining them in many places of Eastern Europe, Switzerland, and even France and Germany; while new organizations, based on the same principles, never fail to grow up wherever it is possible.

Notwithstanding the egotistic turn given to the public mind by the merchant-production of our century, the communist tendency is continually reasserting itself and trying to make its way into public life. The penny bridge disappears before the public bridge; and the turnpike road before the free road. The same spirit pervades thousands of other institutions. Museums, free libraries, and free public schools; parks and pleasure grounds; paved and lighted streets, free for everybody's use; water supplied to private dwellings, with a growing tendency towards disregarding the exact amount of it used by the individual; tramways and railways which have already begun to introduce the season ticket or the uniform tax, and will surely go much further in this line when they are no longer private property: all these are tokens showing in what direction further progress is to be expected.

It is in the direction of putting the wants of the individual *above* the valuation of the services he has rendered, or might render, to society; in considering society as a whole, so intimately connected together that a service rendered to any individual is a service rendered to the whole society. The librarian of the British Museum does not ask the reader what have been his previous services to society, he simply gives him the books he requires; and for a uniform fee, a scientific society leaves its gardens and museums at the free disposal of each member. The crew of a lifeboat do not ask whether the men of a distressed ship are entitled to be rescued at a risk of life; and the Prisoners' Aid Society does not inquire what a released prisoner is worth. Here are men in need of a service; they are *fellow* men, and no further rights are required.

And if this very city, so egotistic to-day, be visited by a public calamity—let it be besieged, for example, like Paris in 1871, and experience during the siege a want of food—this very same city would be unanimous in proclaiming that the first needs to be satisfied are those of the children and old, no matter what services they may render or have rendered to society. And it would take care of the active defenders of the city, whatever the degrees of gallantry displayed by each of them. But, this tendency already existing, nobody will deny, I suppose, that, in proportion as humanity is relieved from its hard struggle for life, the same tendency will grow stronger. If our productive powers were fully applied to inceasing the stock of the staple necessities for life; if a modification of the present conditions of property increased the number of producers by all those who are not producers of wealth now; and if manual labor reconquered its place of honor in society, the communist tendencies already existing would immediately enlarge their sphere of application.

Taking all this into account, and still more the practical aspects of the question as to how private property *might* become common property, most of the anarchists maintain that the very next step to be made by society, as soon as the present regime of property undergoes a modification, will be in a communist sense. We are communists. But our communism is not that of the authoritarian school: it is anarchist communism, communism without government, free communism. It is a synthesis of the two chief aims pursued by humanity since the dawn of its history—economic freedom and political freedom.

I have already said that anarchism means no-government. We know well that the word "anarchy" is also used in current phraseology as synonymous with disorder. But that meaning of "anarchy," being a derived one, implies at least two suppositions. It implies, first, that wherever there is no government there is disorder; and it implies, moreover, that order, due to a strong government and a strong police, is always beneficial. Both implications, however, are anything but proved. There is plenty of order—we should say, of harmony—in many branches of human activity where the government, happily, does not interfere. As to the beneficial effects of order, the kind of order that reigned at Naples under the Bourbons surely was not preferable to some disorder started by Garibaldi; while the Protestants of this country will probably say that the good deal of disorder made by Luther was preferable, at any rate, to the order which reigned under the Pope. While all agree that harmony is always desirable, there is no such unanimity about order, and still less about the "order" which is supposed to reign in our modern societies. So that we have no objection whatever to the use of the word "anarchy" as a negation of what has been often described as order.

By taking for our watchword anarchy in its sense of no-government, we intend to express a pronounced tendency of human society. In history we see that precisely those epochs when small parts of humanity broke down the power of their rulers and reassumed their freedom were epochs of the geatest progress, economic and intellectual. Be it the growth of the free cities, whose unrivalled monuments—free work of free associations of workers—still testify to the revival of mind and of the well-being of the citizen; be it the great movement which gave birth to the Reformation—those epochs when the individual recovered some part of his freedom witnessed the greatest progress. And if we carefully watch the present development of civilized nations, we cannot fail to discover in it a marked and ever-growing movement towards limiting more and more the sphere of action of government, so as to leave more and more liberty to the initiative of the individual. After having tried all kinds of government, and endeavored to solve the insoluble problem of having a government "which might compel the individual to obedience, without escaping itself from obedi-

ence to collectivity," humanity is trying now to free itself
from the bonds of any government whatever, and to respond
to its needs of organization by the free understanding between individuals pursuing the same common aims.

Home Rule, even for the smallest territorial unit or group,
becomes a growing need. Free agreement is becoming a substitute for law. And free cooperation a substitute for governmental guardianship. One after the other those activities
which were considered as the functions of government during the last two centuries are disputed; society moves better
the less it is governed. And the more we study the advance
made in this direction, as well as the inadequacy of governments to fulfill the expectations placed in them, the more we
are bound to conclude that humanity, by steadily limiting
the functions of government, is marching towards reducing
them finally to *nil*. We already foresee a state of society
where the liberty of the individual will be limited by no laws,
no bonds—by nothing else but his own social habits and the
necessity, which everyone feels, of finding cooperation, support, and sympathy among his neighbors.

Of course the no-government ethics will meet with at
least as many objections as the no-capital economics. Our
minds have been so nurtured in prejudices as to the provi-
dential functions of government that anarchist ideas *must* be
received with distrust. Our whole education, from childhood to the grave, nurtures the belief in the necessity of a
government and its beneficial effects. Systems of philosophy
have been elaborated to support this view; history has been
written from this standpoint; theories of law have been
circulated and taught for the same purpose. All politics are
based on the same principle, each politician saying to people
he wants to support him: "Give me the governmental
power; I will, I can, relieve you from the hardships of your
present life." All our education is permeated with the same
teachings. We may open any book of sociology, history,
law, or ethics: everywhere we find government, its organization, its deeds, playing so prominent a part that we grow

accustomed to suppose that the State and the political men are everything; that there is nothing behind the big statesmen. The same teachings are daily repeated in the Press. Whole columns are filled up with minutest records of parliamentary debates, of movements of political persons. And, while reading these columns, we too often forget that besides those few men whose importance has been so swollen up as to overshadow humanity, there is an immense body of men—mankind, in fact—growing and dying, living in happiness or sorrow, laboring and consuming, thinking and creating.

And yet, if we revert from the printed matter to our real life, and cast a broad glance on society as it is, we are struck with the infinitesimal part played by government in our life. Millions of human beings live and die without having had anything to do with government. Every day millions of transactions are made without the slighest interference of government; and those who enter into agreements have not the slightest intention of breaking bargains. Nay, those agreements which are not protected by government (those of the exchange, or card debts) are perhaps better kept than any others. The simple habit of keeping one's word, the desire of not losing confidence, are quite sufficient in an overwhelming majority of cases to enforce the keeping of agreements. Of course it may be said that there is still the government which might enforce them if necessary. But without speaking of the numberless cases which could not even be brought before a court, everyone who has the slightest acquaintance with trade will undoubtedly confirm the assertion that, if there were not so strong a feeling of honor in keeping agreements, trade itself would become utterly impossible. Even those merchants and manufacturers who feel not the slightest remorse when poisoning their customers with all kinds of abominable drugs, duly labelled, even they also keep their commercial agreements. But if such a relative morality as commercial honesty exists now under the present conditions, when enrichment is the chief motive, the same feeling will further develop very quickly as soon as robbing someone of the fruits of his labor is no longer the economic basis of our life.

Another striking feature of our century tells in favor of the same no-government tendency. It is the steady enlargement of the field covered by private initiative, and the recent growth of large organizations resulting merely and simply from free agreement. The railway net of Europe—a confederation of so many scores of separate societies—and the direct transport of passengers and merchandise over so many lines which were built independently and federated together, without even so much as a Central Board of European Railways, is a most striking instance of what is already done by mere agreement. If fifty years ago somebody had predicted that railways built by so many separate companies finally would constitute so perfect a net as they do today, he surely would have been treated as a fool. It would have been urged that so many companies, prosecuting their own interests, would never agree without an International Board of Railways, supported by an International Convention of the European States, and endowed with governmental powers. But no such board was resorted to, and the agreement came nevertheless. The Dutch associations of ship and boat owners are now extending their organizations over the rivers of Germany and even to the shipping trade of the Baltic. The numberless amalgamated manufacturers' associations, and the *syndicates* of France, are so many instances in point. If it be argued that many of these organizations are organizations for exploitation, that proves nothing, because, if men pursuing their own egotistic, often very narrow, interests can agree together, better inspired men, compelled to be more closely connected with other groups, will necessarily agree still more easily and still better.

But there also is no lack of free organizations for nobler pursuits. One of the noblest achievements of our century is undoubtedly the Lifeboat Association. Since its first humble start, it has saved no less than thirty-two thousand human lives. It makes appeal to the noblest instincts of man; its activity is entirely dependent upon devotion to the common cause, while its internal organization is entirely based upon the independence of the local committees. The Hospitals Association and hundreds of like organizations, operating on a large scale and covering each a wide field, may also be mentioned under this head. But, while we know everything about governments and their deeds, what do we know about the results achieved by free cooperation? Thousands of volumes have been written to record the acts of governments; the most trifling amelioration due to law has been recorded; its good effects have been exaggerated, its bad effects passed by in silence. But where is the book recording what has been achieved by free cooperation of well-inspired men? At the same time, hundreds of societies are constituted every day for the satisfaction of some of the infinitely varied needs of civilized man. We have societies for all possible kinds of studies—some of them embracing the whole field of natural science, others limited to a small special branch; societies for gymnastics, for shorthand-writing, for the study of a separate author, for games and all kinds of sports, for forwarding the science of maintaining life, and for favoring the art of destroying it; philosophical and industrial, artistic and anti-artistic; for serious work and for mere amusement—in short, there is not a single direction in which men exercise their faculties without combining together for the accomplishment of some common aim. Every day new societies are formed, while every year the old ones aggregate together into larger units, federate across the national frontiers, and cooperate in some common work.

The most striking feature of these numberless free growths is that they continually encroach on what was formerly the domain of the State or the Municipality. A householder in a Swiss village on the banks of Lake Leman belongs now to at least a dozen different societies which supply him with what is considered elsewhere as a function of the municipal government. Free federation of independent communes for temporary or permanent purposes lies at the very bottom of

Swiss life, and to these federations many a part of Switzerland is indebted for its roads and fountains, its rich vineyards, well-kept forests, and meadows which the foreigner admires. And besides these small societies, substituting themselves for the State within some limited sphere, do we not see other societies doing the same on a much wider scale?

One of the most remarkable societies which has recently arisen is undoubtedly the Red Cross Society. To slaughter men on the battle-fields, that remains the duty of the State; but these very States recognize their inability to take care of their own wounded: they abandon the task, to a great extent, to private initiative. What a deluge of mockeries would not have been cast over the poor "Utopist" who should have dared to say twenty-five years ago that the care of the wounded might be left to private societies! "Nobody would go into the dangerous places! Hospitals would all gather where there was no need of them! National rivalries would result in the poor soldiers dying without any help, and so on," —such would have been the outcry. The war of 1871 has shown how perspicacious those prophets are who never believe in human intelligence, devotion, and good sense.

These facts—so numerous and so customary that we pass by without even noticing them—are in our opinion one of the most prominent features of the second half of the nineteenth century. The just-mentioned organisms grew up so naturally, they so rapidly extended and so easily aggregated together, they are such unavoidable outgrowths of the multiplication of needs of the civilized man, and they so well replace State-interference, that we must recognize in them a growing factor of our life. Modern progress is really towards the free aggregation of free individuals so as to supplant government in all those functions which formerly were entrusted to it, and which it mostly performed so badly.

As to parliamentary rule and representative government altogether, they are rapidly falling into decay. The few philosophers who already have shown their defects have only timidly summed up the growing public discontent. It is becoming evident that it is merely stupid to elect a few men and to entrust them with the task of making laws on all possible subjects, of which subjects most of them are utterly ignorant. It is becoming understood that majority rule is as defective as any other kind of rule; and humanity searches and finds new channels for resolving the pending questions. The Postal Union did not elect an international postal parliament in order to make laws for all postal organizations adherent to the Union. The railways of Europe did not elect an international railway parliament in order to regulate the running of the trains and the partition of the income of international traffic. And the Meteorological and Geological Societies of Europe did not elect either meteorological or geological parliaments to plan polar stations, or to establish a uniform subdivision of geological formations and a uniform coloration of geological maps. They proceeded by means of agreement. To agree together they resorted to congresses; but, while sending delegates to their congresses they did not say to them, "Vote about everything you like—we shall obey." They put foreward questions and discussed them first themselves; then they sent delegates acquainted with the special question to be discussed at the congress, and they sent *delegates*—not rulers. Their delegates returned from the congress with no *laws* in their pockets, but with *proposals of agreements*. Such is the way assumed now (the very old way, too) for dealing with questions of public interest—not the way of law-making by means of a representative government.

Representative government has accomplished its historical mission; it has given a mortal blow to court-rule; and by its debates it has awakened public interest in public questions. But to see in it the government of the future socialist society is to commit a gross error. Each economic phase of life implies its own political phase; and it is impossible to touch the very basis of the present economic life—private property —without a corresponding change in the very basis of the political organization. Life already shows in which direction the change will be made. Not in increasing the powers of the State, but in resorting to free organization and free federation in all those branches which are now considered as attributes of the State.

The objections to the above may be easily forseen. It will be said of course: "But wl.at is to be done with those who do not keep their agreements? What with those who are not inclined to work? What with those who would prefer breaking the written laws of society, or—on the anarchist hypothesis—its unwritten customs? Anarchism may be good for a higher humanity,—not for the men of our own times."

First of all, there are two kinds of agreements: there is the free one which is entered upon by free consent, as a free. choice between different courses equally open to each of the agreeing parties. And there is the enforced agreement, imposed by one party upon the other, and accepted by the latter from sheer necessity; in fact, it is no agreement at all; it is a mere submission to necessity. Unhappily, the great bulk of what are now described as agreements belong to the latter category. When a workman sells his labor to an employer and knows perfectly well that some part of the value of his produce will be unjustly taken by the employer; when he sells it without even the slightest guarantee of being employed so much as six consecutive months, it is a sad mockery to call that a free contract. Modern economists may call it free, but the father of poltical economy—Adam Smith—was never guilty of such a misrepresentation. As long as three-quarters of humanity are compelled to enter into agreements of that description, force is of course necessary, both to enforce the supposed agreements and to maintain such a state of things. Force—and a great deal of force —is necessary to prevent the laborers from taking possession of what they consider unjustly appropriated by the few; and force is necessary to continually bring new "uncivilized nations" under the same conditions.

But we do not see the necessity of force for enforcing agreements freely entered upon. We never heard of a penalty imposed on a man who belonged to the crew of a lifeboat and at a given moment preferred to abandon the association. All that his comrades would do with him, if he were guilty of a gross neglect, would probably be to refuse to have anything further to do with him. Nor did we hear of fines imposed on a contributor to the dictionary for a delay in his work, or of *gendarmes* driving the volunteers of Garibaldi to the battlefield. Free agreements need not be enforced.

As to the so-often repeated objection that no one would labor if he were not compelled to do so by sheer necessity, we heard enough of it before the emancipation of slaves in America, as well as before the emancipation of serfs in Russia. And we have had the opportunity of appreciating it at its just value. So we shall not try to convince those who can be convinced only by accomplished facts. As to those who reason, they ought to know that, if it really was so with some parts of humanity at its lowest stages, or if it is so with some small communities, or separate individuals, brought to sheer despair by ill success in their struggle against unfavorable conditions, it is not so with the bulk of the civilized nations. With us, work is a habit, and idleness an artificial growth. Of course, when to be a manual worker means to be compelled to work all one's life long for ten hours a day, and often more, at producing some part of something—a pin's head, for instance; when it means to be paid wages on which a family can live only on the condition of the strictest limitation of all its needs; when it means to be always under the menace of being thrown tomorrow out of employment—and we know how frequent are the industrial crises, and what misery they imply; when it means, in a very great number of cases, premature death in a paupers' infirmary, if not in the workhouse; when to be a manual worker signifies to wear a life-long stamp of inferiority in the eyes of those very people who live on the work of these "hands;" when it always means the renunciation of all those higher enjoyments that science and art give to man—oh, then there is no wonder that everybody—the manual workers

as well—has but one dream: that of rising to a condition
where others would work for him.

Overwork is repulsive to human nature—not work. Overwork for supplying the few with luxury—not work for the
well-being of all. Work is a physiological necessity, a necessity of spending accumulated bodily energy, a necessity which
is health and life itself. If so many branches of useful work
are so reluctantly done now, it is merely because they mean
overwork, or they are improperly organized. But we know—
old Franklin knew it—that four hours of useful work every
day would be more than sufficient for supplying everybody
with the comfort of a moderately well-to-do middle-class
house, if we all gave ourselves to productive work, and if
we did not waste our productive powers as we do waste them
now.

As to the childish question, repeated for fifty years: "Who
would do disagreeable work?" frankly I regret that none of
our *savants* has ever been brought to do it, be it for only one
day in his life. If there is still work which is really disagreeable in itself, it is only because our scientific men have never
cared to consider the means of rendering it less so. They
have always known that there were plenty of starving men
who would do it for a few cents a day.

As to the third—the chief—objection, which maintains the
necessity of a government for punishing those who break the
law of society, there is so much to say about it that it hardly
can be touched incidentally. The more we study the question, the more we are brought to the conclusion that society
itself is responsible for the anti-social deeds perpetrated in
its midst, and that no punishment, no prisons, and no hangmen can diminish the numbers of such deeds; nothing short
of a reorganization of society itself.

Three quarters of all the acts which are brought before
our courts every year have their origin, either directly or indirectly, in the present disorganized state of society with
regard to the production and distribution of wealth—not in
perversity of human nature. As to the relatively few anti-

social deeds which result from anti-social inclinations of separate individuals, it is not by prisons, nor even by resorting to the hangmen, that we can diminish their numbers. By our prisons, we merely multiply them and render them worse. By our detectives, our "price of blood," our executions, and our jails, we spread in society such a terrible flow of basest passions and habits, that he who should realize the effects of these institutions to their full extent would be frightened by what society is doing under the pretext of maintaining morality. We *must* search for other remedies, and the remedies have been indicated long since.

Of course now, when a mother in search of food and shelter for her children must pass by shops filled with the most refined delicacies of refined gluttony; when gorgeous and insolent luxury is displayed side by side with the most execrable misery; when the dog and the horse of a rich man are far better cared for than millions of children whose mothers earn a pitiful salary in the pit or the manufactory; when each "modest" evening dress of a lady represents eight months, or one year, of human labor; when enrichment at somebody else's expense is the avowed aim of the "upper classes," and no distinct boundary can be traced between honest and dishonest means of making money—then force is the only means for maintaining such a state of things. Then an army of policemen, judges, and hangmen becomes a necessary institution.

But if all our children—all children are *our* children—received a sound instruction and education—and we have the means of giving it; if every family lived in a decent home —and they *could* at the present high pitch of our production; if every boy and girl were taught a handicraft at the same time as he or she receives scientific instruction, and *not* to be a manual producer of wealth were considered as a token of inferiority; if men lived in closer contact with one another, and had continually to come into contact on those public affairs which now are vested in the few; and if, in consequence of a closer contact, we were brought to take

as lively an interest in our neighbors' difficulties and pains as
we formerly took in those of our kinsfolk—then we should
not resort to policemen and judges, to prisons and executions.
Anti-social deeds would be nipped in the bud, not punished.
The few contests which would arise would be easily settled
by arbitrators; and no more force would be necessary to impose their decisions than is required now for enforcing the
decisions of the family tribunals of China.

And here we are brought to consider a great question:
what would become of morality in a society which recognized
no laws and proclaimed the full freedom of the individual,
Our answer is plain. Public morality is independent from,
and anterior to, law and religion. Until now, the teachings of
morality have been associated with religious teachings. But
the influence which religious teachings formerly exercised on
the mind has faded of late, and the sanction which morality
derived from religion has no longer the power it formerly
had. Millions and millions grow in our cities who have
lost the old faith. Is it a reason for throwing morality overboard, and for treating it with the same sarcasm as primitive
cosmogony?

Obviously not. No society is possible without certain
principles of morality generally recognized. If everyone grew
accustomed to deceiving his fellow-men; if we never could
rely on each other's promise and words; if everyone treated
his fellow as an enemy, against whom every means of warfare is justifiable—no society could exist. And we see, in
fact, that notwithstanding the decay of religious beliefs, the
principles of morality remain unshaken. We even see irreli-
gious people trying to raise the current standard of morality.
The fact is that moral principles are independent of religious
beliefs: they are anterior to them. The primitive Tchuktchis
have no religion: they have only superstitions and fear of the
hostile forces of nature; and nevertheless we find with them
the very same principles of morality which are taught by
Christians and Buddhists, Mussulmans and Hebrews. Nay,
some of their practices imply a much higher standard of tribal

morality than that which appears in our civilized society.
In fact, each new religion takes its moral principles from
the only real stock of morality—the moral habits which
grow with men as soon as they unite to live together in
tribes, cities, or nations. No animal society is possible without resulting in a growth of certain moral habits of mutual
support and even self-sacrifice for the common well-being.
These habits are a necessary condition for the welfare of the
species in its struggle for life—cooperation of individuals
being a much more important factor in the struggle for the
preservation of the species than the so-much-spoken-of physical struggle between individuals for the means of existence.
The "fittest" in the organic world are those who grow accustomed to life in society; and life in society necessarily implies moral habits. As to mankind, it has during its long
existence developed in its midst a nucleus of social habits,
of moral habits, which cannot disappear as long as human
societies exist. And therefore, notwithstanding the influences
to the contrary which are now at work in consequence of
our present economic relations, the nucleus of our moral
habits continues to exist. Law and religion only formulate
them and endeavor to enforce them by their sanction.

Whatever the variety of theories of morality, all can be
brought under three chief catagories: the morality of religion; the utilitarian morality; and the theory of moral habits
resulting from the very needs of life in society. Each religious morality sanctifies its prescriptions by making them
originate from revelation; and it tries to impress its teachings on the mind by a promise of reward, or punishment,
either in this or in a future life. The utilitarian morality
maintains the idea of reward, but it finds it in man himself.
It invites men to analyze their pleasures, to classify them,
and to give preference to those which are most intense
and most durable. We must recognize, however, that, although it has exercised some influence, this system has been
judged too artificial by the great mass of human beings.
And finally—whatever its varieties—there is the third system

of morality which sees in moral actions—in those actions which are most powerful in rendering men best fitted for life in society—a mere necessity of the individual to enjoy the joys of his brethren, to suffer when some of his brethren are suffering; a habit and a second nature, slowly elaborated and perfected by life in society. That is the morality of mankind; and that is also the morality of anarchism.

Such are, in a very brief summary, the leading principles of anarchism. Each of them hurts many a prejudice, and yet each of them results from an analysis of the very tendencies displayed by human society. Each of them is rich in consequences and implies a thorough revision of many a current opinion. And anarchism is not a mere insight into a remote future. Already now, whatever the sphere of action of the individual, he can act, either in accordance with anarchist principles or on an opposite line. And all that may be done in that direction will be done in the direction to which further development goes. All that may be done in the opposite way will be an attempt to force humanity to go where it will *not* go.

ADDITIONAL NOTE TO "ANARCHIST COMMUNISM"

Kropotkin's earlier writings as to the methods of organizing production and distribution after a revolutionary seizure of property were based on the assumption that there would be sufficiency of goods for each to take what he needed and to work as much as he felt able. After his experience with the Russian Revolution he came to a quite contrary conclusion. He recognized the obstacles to production on a new basis as well as the poverty of the capitalist world and expressed his changed opinion in a postscript to the Russian edition of *Words of a Rebel*, published in 1919. His method for organizing production follows his previous teaching, but his statement of it after the Russian Revolution adds interest to it. (R.N.B.)

* * *

EXTRACT FROM THE POSTSCRIPT OF "WORDS OF A REBEL"

The question of the reconstruction of life by the social revolution has been set forth only in general terms. . . . Unfortunately it is necessary to say that socialists and workingmen in general, having lost hope in the possibility of revolution in the near future, were not interested in the question: What character would it be advisable for the revolution to take? Our comrade Pouget has told us, in *How we will make the Revolution*, how a social revolution could be accomplished in France under the direction of the trade unions; how these unions and the congresses would be able to expropriate the capitalists and organize production on a new basis without the least stoppage of production. It is clear that only the workers through their own organizations would ever be able to achieve this, and though I differ from Pouget in certain details, I recommend this book to all those who understand the inevitability of the social reconstruction which humanity will have to provide for.

In my own studies in England and Scotland I always tried to find out what was the real life of the workers, keeping always in view the following question: What form would the social revolution be able to take to pass without too great a shock from private production to a system of production and exchange organized by the producers and consumers themselves?

My examination of this question brought me to two conclusions. The first is that production and exchange represented an undertaking so complicated that the plans of the state socialists, which lead inevitably to a party directorship, would prove to be absolutely ineffective as soon as they were applied to life. No government would be able to organize production if the workers themselves through their unions did not do it in each branch of industry; for in all production there arise daily thousands of difficulties which no government can solve or foresee. It is certainly impossible to foresee everything. Only the efforts of thousands of intelligences working on the problems can cooperate in the development of a new social system and find the best solutions for the thousands of local needs. . . .

The second conclusion to which I came was that the present economic life in civilized countries is constructed on an erroneous basis. The theory is that the peoples of the world are divided into two categories: those who thanks to their superior education are qualified to direct production, and the others who, because of their limited capacity, are condemned to labor for their employers. The whole course of political economy declares this theory. It is thus that the English employing class has enriched itself. It is thus that other countries, in developing their industry, are enriching themselves at the expense of the backward peoples. But a more profound study of economic life in England and other European countries leads us to another conclusion. It is no longer possible to become enriched in the same way as England has up to now. Not one civilized country wants to remain in the position of furnishing raw materials. All countries aspire to develop manufacturing industry and they are all gradually doing so. . . . The road to the development of the welfare of all peoples lies only in the union of agriculture and industry and not in the sub-division of peoples into industrial and agrarian civilizations. Such sub-division will lead inevitably to incessant wars for the capture of markets and cheap labor for industry. . . .

It follows then that the social revolution, wherever it breaks out, must consider as its first duty the increase of production. The first months of emancipation will inevitably increase consumption of goods and production will diminish. And, furthermore, any country achieving a social revolution will be surrounded by a ring of neighbors either unfriendly or actually enemies. . . . In a word, a revolution will lead inevitably to increased consumption, for a third of the population of all Europe lives in misery and suffers from a lack of clothes and other goods. The demands upon products will increase while production decreases, and finally famine will come. There is only one way of avoiding it. We should understand that as soon as a revolutionary movement begins in any country the only possible way out will consist in the workingmen and peasants from the beginning taking the whole national economy into their hands and organizing it themselves with a view to a rapid increase in production. But they will not be convinced of this necessity except when all responsibility for national economy, today in the hands of a multitude of ministers and committees, is presented in a simple form to each village and city, in every factory and shop, as their own affair, and when they understand that they must direct it themselves.

NOTE FOR "ANARCHIST MORALITY"

This study of the origin and function of what we call "morality" was written for pamphlet publication as a result of an amusing situation. An anarchist who ran a store in England found that his comrades in the movement regarded it as perfectly right to take his goods without paying for them. "To each according to his need" seemed to them to justify letting those who were best able foot the bills. Kropotkin was appealed to, with the result that he not only condemned such doctrine, but was moved to write the comrades this sermon.

Its conception of morality is based on the ideas set forth in *Mutual Aid* and later developed in his *Ethics*. Here they are given specific application to "right and wrong" in the business of social living. The job is done with fine feeling and with acute shafts at the shams of current morality.

Kropotkin sees the source of all so-called moral ideas in primitive superstitions. The real moral sense which guides our social behavior is instinctive, based on the sympathy and unity inherent in group life. Mutual aid is the condition of successful social living. The moral base is therefore the good old golden rule "Do to others as you would have others do to you in the same circumstances,"—which disposed of the ethics of the shopkeeper's anarchist customers.

This natural moral sense was perverted, Kropotkin says, by the superstitions surrounding law, religion and authority, deliberately cultivated by conquerors, exploiters and priests for their own benefit. Morality has therefore become the instrument of ruling classes to protect their privileges.

He defends the morality of killing for the benefit of mankind,—as in the assassination of tyrants,—but never for self. Love and hate he regards as greater social forces for controlling wrong-doing than punishment, which he rejects as useless and evil. Account-book morality,—doing right only to receive a benefit,—he scores roundly, urging instead the satisfactions and joy of "sowing life around you" by giving yourself to the uttermost to your fellow-men. Not of course to do them good, in the spirit of philanthropy, but to be one with them, equal and sharing.

ANARCHIST MORALITY

I

THE history of human thought recalls the swinging of a pendulum which takes centuries to swing. After a long period of slumber comes a moment of awakening. Then thought frees herself from the chains with which those interested—rulers, lawyers, clerics—have carefully enwound her.

She shatters the chains. She subjects to severe criticism all that has been taught her, and lays bare the emptiness of the religious political, legal, and social prejudices amid which she has vegetated. She starts research in new paths, enriches our knowledge with new discoveries, creates new sciences.

But the inveterate enemies of thought—the government, the lawgiver, and the priest—soon recover from their defeat. By degrees they gather together their scattered forces, and remodel their faith and their code of laws to adapt them to the new needs. Then, profiting by the servility of thought and of character, which they themselves have so effectually cultivated; profiting, too, by the momentary disorganization of society, taking advantage of the laziness of some, the greed of others, the best hopes of many, they softly creep back to their work by first of all taking possession of childhood through education.

A child's spirit is weak. It is so easy to coerce it by fear. This they do. They make the child timid, and then they talk to him of the torments of hell. They conjure up before him the sufferings of the condemned, the vengeance of an implacable god. The next minute they will be chattering of the horrors of revolution, and using some excess of the revolutionists to make the child "a friend of order." The priest

1

ANARCHIST MORALITY

81

accustoms the child to the idea of law, to make it obey better
what he calls the "divine law," and the lawyer prates of divine law, that the civil law may be the better obeyed.

And by that habit of submission, with which we are only
too familiar, the thought of the next generation retains this
religious twist, which is at once servile and authoritative;
for authority and servility walk ever hand in hand.

During these slumbrous interludes, morals are rarely discussed. Religious practices and judicial hypocrisy take their
place. People do not criticize, they let themselves be drawn
by habit, or indifference. They do not put themselves out
for or against the established morality. They do their best
to make their actions appear to accord with their *professions*.

All that was good, great, generous or independent in man,
little by little becomes moss-grown; rusts like a disused knife.
A lie becomes a virtue, a platitude a duty. To enrich oneself, to seize one's opportunities, to exhaust one's intelligence,
zeal and energy, no matter how, become the watchwords of
the comfortable classes, as well as of the crowd of poor folk
whose ideal is to appear bourgeois. Then the degradation of
the ruler and of the judge, of the clergy and of the more or
less comfortable classes becomes so revolting that the pendulum begins to swing the other way.

Little by little, youth frees itself. It flings overboard its
prejudices, and it begins to criticize. Thought reawakens,
at first among the few: but insensibly the awakening reaches
the majority. The impulse is given, the revolution follows.

And each time the question of morality comes up again.
"Why should I follow the principles of this hypocritical
morality?" asks the brain, released from religious terrors.
Why should any morality be obligatory?"

Then people try to account for the moral sentiment that
they meet at every turn without having explained it to
themselves. And they will never explain it so long as they
believe it a privilege of human nature, so long as they do not
descend to animals, plans and rocks to understand it. They
seek the answer, however, in the science of the hour.

And, if we may venture to say so, the more the basis of conventional morality, or rather of the hypocrisy that fills its place is sapped, the more the moral plane of society is raised. It is above all at such times, precisely when folks are criticizing and denying it, that moral sentiment makes the most progress. It is then that it grows, that it is raised and refined.

Years ago the youth of Russia were passionately agitated by this very question. "I will be immoral!" a young nihilist came and said to his friend, thus translating into action the thoughts that gave him no rest. "I will be immoral, and why should I not? Because the Bible wills it? But the Bible is only a collection of Babylonian and Hebrew traditions, traditions collected and put together like the Homeric poems, or as is being done still with Basque poems and Mongolian legends. Must I then go back to the state of mind of the half civilized peoples of the East?

"Must I be moral because Kant tells me of a categoric imperative, of a mysterious command which comes to me from the depths of my own being and bids me be moral? But why should this 'categoric imperative' exercise a greater authority over my actions than that other imperative, which at times may command me to get drunk. A word, nothing but a word, like the words 'Providence,' or 'Destiny,' invented to conceal our ignorance.

"Or perhaps I am to be moral to oblige Bentham, who wants me to believe that I shall be happier if I drown to save a passerby who has fallen into the river than if I watched him drown?

"Or perhaps because such has been my education? Because my mother taught me morality? Shall I then go and kneel down in a church, honor the Queen, bow before the judge I know for a scountrel, simply because our mothers, our good ignorant mothers, have taught us such a pack of nonsense?

"I am prejudiced,—like everyone else. I will try to rid myself of prejudice! Even though immorality be distasteful, I will yet force myself to be immoral, as when I was

a boy I forced myself to give up fearing the dark, the church-
yard, ghosts and dead people—all of which I had been taught
to fear.

"It will be immoral to snap a weapon abused by religion;
I will do it, were it only to protect against the hyprocrisy imposed on us in the name of a word to which the name morality has been given!"

Such was the way in which the youth of Russia reasoned
when they broke with old-world prejudices, and unfurled this
banner of nihilist or rather of anarchist philosophy: to bend
the knee to no authority whatsoever, however respected; to
accept no principle so long as it is unestablished by reason.

Need we add, that after pitching into the waste-paper
basket the teachings of their fathers, and burning all systems of
morality, the nihilist youth developed in their midst a nucleus
of moral customs, infinitely superior to anything that their
fathers had practiced under the control of the "Gospel," of
the "Conscience," of the "Categoric Imperative," or of the
"Recognized Advantage" of the utilitarian. But before answering the question, "Why am I to be moral?" let us see
if the question is well put; let us analyze the motives of
human action.

II

When our ancestors wished to account for what led
men to act in one way or another, they did so in a very
simple fashion. Down to the present day, certain catholic
images may be seen that represent this explanation. A man
is going on his way, and without being in the least aware
of it, carries a devil on his left shoulder and an angel on his
right. The devil prompts him to do evil, the angel tries to
keep him back. And if the angel gets the best of it and the
man remains virtuous, three other angels catch him up and
carry him to heaven. In this way everything is explained
wondrously well.

Old Russian nurses full of such lore will tell you never
to put a child to bed without unbuttoning the collar of its

shirt. A warm spot at the bottom of the neck should be left bare, where the guardian angel may nestle. Otherwise the devil will worry the child even in its sleep.

These artless conceptions are passing away. But though the old words disappear, the essential idea remains the same.

Well brought up folks no longer believe in the devil, but as their ideas are no more rational than those of our nurses, they do but disguise devil and angel under a pedantic wordiness honored with the name of philosophy. They do not say "devil" now-a-days, but "the flesh," or "the passions." The "angel" is replaced by the words "conscience" or "soul," by "reflection of the thought of a divine creator" or "the Great Architect," as the Free-Masons say. But man's action is still represented as the result of a struggle between two hostile elements. And a man is always considered virtuous just in the degree to which one of these two elements—the soul or conscience—is victorious over the other—the flesh or passions.

It is easy to understand the astonishment of our great-grandfathers when the English philosophers, and later the Encyclopedists, began to affirm in opposition to these primitive ideas that the devil and the angel had nothing to do with human action, but that all acts of man, good or bad, useful or baneful, arise from a single motive: the lust for pleasure.

The whole religious confraternity, and, above all, the numerous sects of the pharisees shouted "immorality." They covered the thinkers with insult, they excommunicated them. And when later on in the course of the century the same ideas were again taken up by Bentham, John Stuart Mill, Tchernischevsky, and a host of others, and when these thinkers began to affirm and prove that egoism, or the lust for pleasure, is the true motive of all our actions, the maledictions redoubled. The books were banned by a conspiracy of silence; the authors were treated as dunces.

And yet what can be more true than the assertion they made?

Here is a man who snatches its last mouthful of bread from a child. Every one agrees in saying that he is a horrible egoist, that he is guided solely by self-love.

But now here is another man, whom every one agrees to recognize as virtuous. He shares his last bit of bread with the hungry, and strips off his coat to clothe the naked. And the moralists, sticking to their religious jargon, hasten to say that this man carries the love of his neighbor to the point of self-abnegation, that he obeys a wholly different passion from that of the egoist. And yet with a little reflection we soon discover that however great the difference between the two actions in their result for humanity, the motive has still been the same. It is the quest of pleasure.

If the man who gives away his last shirt found no pleasure in doing so, he would not do it. If he found pleasure in taking bread from a child, he would do that but this is distasteful to him. He finds pleasure in giving, and so he gives. If it were not inconvenient to cause confusion by employing in a new sense words that have a recognized meaning, it might be said that in both cases the men acted under the impulse of their egoism. Some have actually said this, to give prominence to the thought and precision to the idea by presenting it in a form that strikes the imagination, and at the same time to destroy the myth which asserts that these two acts have two different motives. They have the same motive, the quest of pleasure, or the avoidance of pain, which comes to the same thing.

Take for example the worst of scoundrels: a Thiers, who massacres thirty-five thousand Parisians, or an assassin who butchers a whole family in order that he may wallow in debauchery. They do it because for the moment the desire of glory or of money gains in their minds the upper hand of every other desire. Even pity and compassion are extinguished for the moment by this other desire, this other thirst. They act almost automatically to satisfy a craving of their nature. Or again, putting aside the stronger passions, take the petty man who deceives his friends, who lies at every step to get out of somebody the price of a pot of beer, or from sheer love of brag, or from cunning. Take the employer who cheats his workmen to buy jewels for his wife or his mistress. Take any petty scoundrel you like. He again only obeys an impulse. He seeks the satisfaction of a craving, or he seeks to escape what would give him trouble.

We are almost ashamed to compare such petty scoundrels with one who sacrifices his whole existence to free the oppressed, and like a Russian nihilist mounts the scaffold. So vastly different for humanity are the results of these two lives; so much do we feel ourselves drawn towards the one and repelled by the other.

And yet were you to talk to such a martyr, to the woman who is about to be hanged, even just as she nears the gallows, she would tell you that she would not exchange either her life or her death for the life of the petty scoundrel who lives on the money stolen from his work-people. In her life, in the struggle against monstrous might, she finds her highest joys. Everything else outside the struggle, all the little joys of the bourgeois and his little troubles seem to her so contemptible, so tiresome, so pitiable! "You do not live, you vegetate," she would reply; "I have lived."

We are speaking of course of the deliberate, conscious acts of men, reserving for the present what we have to say about that immense series of unconscious, all but mechanical acts, which occupy so large a portion of our life. In his deliberate, conscious acts man always seeks what will give him pleasure.

One man gets drunk, and every day lowers himself to the condition of a brute because he seeks in liquor the nervous excitement that he cannot obtain from his own nervous system. Another does not get drunk; he takes no liquor, even though he finds it pleasant, because he wants to keep the freshness of his thoughts and the plentitude of his powers, that he may be able to taste other pleasures which he prefers to drink. But how does he act if not like the judge of good living who, after glancing at the menu of an elaborate dinner, rejects one dish that he likes very well to eat his fill of another that he likes better.

When a woman deprives herself of her last piece of bread to give it to the first comer, when she takes off her own scanty rags to cover another woman who is cold, while she herself shivers on the deck of a vessel, she does so because she would suffer infinitely more in seeing a hungry man, or a woman starved with cold, than in shivering or feeling hungry herself. She escapes a pain of which only those who have felt it know the intensity.

When the Australian, quoted by Guyau, wasted away beneath the idea that he has not yet revenged his kinsman's death; when he grows thin and pale, a prey to the consciousness of his cowardice, and does not return to life till he has done the deed of vengeance, he performs this action, a heoric one sometimes, to free himself of a feeling which possesses him, to regain that inward peace which is the highest of pleasures.

When a troupe of monkeys has seen one of its members fall in consequence of a hunter's shot, and comes to besiege his tent and claim the body despite the threatening gun; when at length the Elder of the band goes right in, first threatens the hunter, then implores him, and finally by his lamentations induces him to give up the corpse, which the groaning troupe carry off into the forest, these monkeys obey a feeling of compassion stronger than all considerations of personal security. This feeling in them exceeds all others. Life itself loses its attraction for them while they are not sure whether they can restore life to their comrade or not. This feeling becomes so oppressive that the poor brutes do everything to get rid of it.

When the ants rush by thousands into the flames of the burning ant-hill, which that evil beast, man, has set on fire, and perish by hundreds to rescue their larvæ, they again obey a craving to save their offspring. They risk everything for the sake of bringing away the larvæ that they have brought up with more care than many women bestow on their children.

To seek pleasure, to avoid pain, is the general line of action (some would say law) of the organic world. Without this quest of the agreeable, life itself would be impossible. Organisms would disintegrate, life cease.

Thus whatever a man's actions and line of conduct may be, he does what he does in obedience to a craving of his nature. The most repulsive actions, no less than actions which are indifferent or most attractive, are all equally dictated by a need of the individual who performs them. Let him act as he may, the individual acts as he does because he finds a pleasure in it, or avoids, or thinks he avoids, a pain.

Here we have a well-established fact. Here we have the essence of what has been called the egoistic theory.

Very well, are we any better off for having reached this general conclusion?

Yes, certainly we are. We have conquered a truth and destroyed a prejudice which lies at the root of all prejudices. All materialist philosophy in its relation to man is implied in this conclusion. But does it follow that all the actions of the individual are indifferent, as some have hastened to conclude? This is what we have now to see.

III

We have seen that men's actions (their deliberate and conscious actions, for we will speak afterwards of unconscious habits) all have the same origin. Those that are called virtuous and those that are designated as vicious, great devotions and petty knaveries, acts that attract and acts that repel, all spring from a common source. All are performed in answer to some need of the individual's nature. All have for their end the quest of pleasure, the desire to avoid pain.

We have seen this in the last section, which is but a very succinct summary of a mass of facts that might be brought forward in support of this view.

It is easy to understand how this explanation makes those still imbued with religious principles cry out. It leaves no room for the supernatural. It throws over the idea of an immortal soul. If man only acts in obedience to the needs of his nature, if he is, so to say, but a "conscious automaton," what becomes of the immortal soul? What of immortality, that last refuge of those who have known too few pleasures and too many sufferings, and who dream of finding some compensation in another world?

It is easy to understand how people who have grown up in prejudice and with but little confidence in science, which has so often deceived them, people who are led by feeling rather than thought, reject an explanation which takes from them their last hope.

IV

Mosaic, Buddhist, Christian and Mussulman theologians have had recourse to devine inspiration to distinguish between good and evil. They have seen that man, be he savage or civilized, ignorant or learned, perverse or kindly and honest, always knows if he is acting well or ill, especially always knows if he is acting ill. And as they have found no explanation of this general fact, they have put it down to divine inspiration. Metaphysical philosophers, on their side, have told us of conscience, of a mystic "imperative," and, after all, have changed nothing but the phrases.

But neither have known how to estimate the very simple and very striking fact that animals living in societies are also able to distinguish between good and evil, just as man does. Moreover, their conceptions of good and evil are of the same nature as those of man. Among the best developed representatives of each separate class,—fish, insects, birds, mammals,—they are even identical.

Forel, that inimitable observer of ants, has shown by a mass of observations and facts that when an ant who has her crop well filled with honey meets other ants with empty stomachs, the latter immediately ask her for food. And amongst these little insects it is the duty of the satisfied ant to disgorge the honey that her hungry friends may also be satisfied. Ask the ants if it would be right to refuse food to other ants of the same ant-hill when one has had one's share. They will answer, by actions impossible to mistake, that it would be extremely wrong. So selfish an ant would be more harshly treated than enemies of another species. If such a thing happens during a battle between two different species, the ants would stop fighting to fall upon their selfish comrade. This fact has been proved by experiments which exclude all doubt.

Or again, ask the sparrows living in your garden if it is right not to give notice to all the little society when some crumbs are thrown out, so that all may come and share in the meal. Ask them if that hedge sparrow has done right in stealing from his neighbor's nest those straws he had picked up, straws which the thief was too lazy to go and collect himself. The sparrows will answer that he is very wrong, by flying at the robber and pecking him.

Or ask the marmots if it is right for one to refuse access to his underground storehouse to other marmots of the same colony. They will answer that it is very wrong, by quarrelling in all sorts of ways with the miser.

Finally, ask primitive man if it is right to take food in the tent of a member of the tribe during his absence. He will answer that, if the man could get his food for himself, it was very wrong. On the other hand, if he was weary or in want, he ought to take food where he finds it; but in such a case, he will do well to leave his cap or his knife, or even a bit of knotted string, so that the absent hunter may know on his return that a friend has been there, not a robber. Such a precaution will save him the anxiety caused by the possible presence of a marauder near his tent.

Thousands of similar facts might be quoted, whole books might be written, to show how identical are the conceptions of good and evil amongst men and the other animals.

The ant, the bird, the marmot, the savage have read neither Kant nor the Fathers of the Church nor even Moses. And yet all have the same idea of good and evil. And if you reflect for a moment on what lies at the bottom of this idea, you will see directly that what is considered as *good* among ants, marmots, and Christian or atheist moralists is that which is *useful* for the preservation of the race; and that which is considered *evil* is that which is *hurtful* for race preservation. Not for the individual, as Bentham and Mill put it, but fair and good for the whole race.

The idea of good and evil has thus nothing to do with religion or a mystic conscience. It is a natural need of animal races. And when founders of religions, philosophers, and moralists tell us of divine or metaphysical entities, they are only recasting what each ant, each sparrow practises in its little society.

Is this useful to society? Then it is good. Is this hurful? Then it is bad.

This idea may be extremely restricted among inferior animals, it may be enlarged among the more advanced animals; but its essence always remains the same.

Among ants it does not extend beyond the ant-hill. All sociable customs, all rules of good behavior are applicable only to the individuals in that one ant-hill, not to any others. One ant-hill will not consider another as belonging to the same family, unless under some exceptional circumstances, such as a common distress falling upon both. In the same way the sparrows in the Luxembourg Gardens in Paris, though they will mutually aid one another in a striking manner, will fight to the death with another sparrow from the Monge Square who may dare to venture into the Luxembourg. And the savage will look upon a savage of another tribe as a person to whom the usages of his own tribe do not apply. It is even allowable to sell to him, and to sell is always to rob the buyer more or less; buyer or seller, one or other is always "sold." A Tchoutche would think it a crime to sell to the members of his tribe: to them he gives without any reckoning. And civilized man, when at last he understands the relations between himself and the simplest Papuan, close relations, though imperceptible at the first glance, will extend his principles of solidarity to the whole human race, and even to the animals. The idea enlarges, but its foundation remains the same.

On the other hand, the conception of good or evil varies according to the degree of intelligence or of knowledge acquired. There is nothing unchangeable about it.

Primitive man may have thought it very right—that is, useful to the race—to eat his aged parents when they became a charge upon the community—a very heavy charge in the main. He may have also thought it useful to the community to kill his new-born children, and only keep two or three in each family, so that the mother could suckle them until they were three years old and lavish more of her tenderness upon them.

In our days ideas have changed, but the means of subsistence are no longer what they were in the Stone Age. Civilized man is not in the position of the savage family who have to choose between two evils: either to eat the aged parents or else all to get insufficient nourishment and soon find themselves unable to feed both the aged parents and the young children. We must transport ourselves into those ages, which we can scarcely call up in our mind, before we can understand that in the circumstances then existing, half-savage man may have reasoned rightly enough.

Ways of thinking may change. The estimate of what is useful or hurtful to the race changes, but the foundation remains the same. And if we wished to sum up the whole philosophy of the animal kingdom in a single phrase, we should see that ants, birds, marmots, and men are agreed on one point.

The morality which emerges from the observation of the whole animal kingdom may be summed up in the words: "Do to others what you would have them to to you in the same circumstances.

And it adds: "Take note that this is merely a piece of *advice*; but this advice is the fruit of the long experience of animals in society. And among the great mass of social animals, man included, it has become *habitual* to act on this principle. Indeed without this no society could exist, no race could have vanquished the natural obstacles against which it must struggle."

Is it really this very simple principle which emerges from the observation of social animals and human societies? Is it applicable? And how does this principle pass into a habit and continually develop? This is what we are now going to see.

V

The idea of good and evil exists within humanity itself. Man, whatever degree of intellectual development he may have attained, however his ideas may be obscured by prejudices and personal interest in general, considers as good that which is useful to the society wherein he lives, and as evil that which is hurtful to it.

But whence comes this conception, often so vague that it can scarcely be distinguished from a feeling? There are millions and millions of human beings who have never reflected about the human race. They know for the most part only the clan or family, rarely the nation, still more rarely mankind. How can it be that they should consider what is useful for the human race as good, or even attain a feeling of solidarity with their clan, in spite of all their narrow, selfish interests?

This fact has greatly occupied thinkers at all times, and it continues to occupy them still. We are going in our turn to give our view of the matter. But let us remark in passing that though the *explanations* of the fact may vary, the fact itself remains none the less incontestable. And should our explanation not be the true one, or should it be incomplete, the fact with its consequences to humanity will still remain. We may not be able fully to explain the origin of the planets revolving round the sun, but the planets revolve none the less, and one of them carries us with it in space.

We have already spoken of the religious explanation. If man distinguishes between good and evil, say theologians, it is God who has inspired him with this idea. Useful or hurtful is not for him to inquire; he must merely obey the fiat of his creator. We will not stop at this explanation, fruit of the ignorance and terrors of the savage. We pass on.

Others have tried to explain the fact by *law*. It must have been law that developed in man the sense of just and unjust, right and wrong. Our readers may judge of this explanation for themselves. They know that law has merely utilized the social feelings of man, to slip in, among the moral precepts he accepts, various mandates useful to an exploiting minority, to which his nature refuses obedience. Law has perverted the feeling of justice instead of developing it. Again let us pass on.

Neither let us pause at the explanation of the Utilitarians. They will have it that man acts morally from self-interest, and they forget his feelings of solidarity with the whole race, which exist, whatever be their origin. There is some truth in the Utilitarian explanation. But it is not the whole truth. Therefore, let us go further.

It is again to the thinkers of the eighteenth century that we are indebted for having guessed, in part at all events, the origin of the moral sentiment.

In a fine work, *The Theory of Moral Sentiment,* left to slumber in silence by religious prejudice, and indeed but little known even among anti-religious thinkers, Adam Smith has laid his finger on the true origin of the moral sentiment. He does not seek it in mystic religious feelings; he finds it simply in the feeling of sympathy.

You see a man beat a child. You know that the beaten child suffers. Your imagination causes you yourself to suffer the pain inflicted upon the child; or perhaps its tears, its little suffering face tell you. And if you are not a coward, you rush at the brute who is beating it and rescue it from him.

This example by itself explains almost all the moral sentiments. The more powerful your imagination, the better you can picture to yourself what any being feels when it is made to suffer, and the more intense and delicate will your moral sense be. The more you are drawn to put yourself in the place of the other person, the more you feel the pain inflicted upon him, the insult offered him, the injustice of which he is a victim, the more will you be urged to act so that you may prevent the pain, insult, or injustice. And the more you are accustomed by circumstances, by those surrounding you, or by the intensity of your own thought and your own imagination, to *act* as your thought and imagination urge, the more will the moral sentiment grow in you, the more will it become habitual.

This is what Adam Smith develops with a wealth of examples. He was young when he wrote this book which is far superior to the work of his old age upon political economy. Free from religious prejudice, he sought the explanation of morality in a physical fact of human nature, and this is why official and non-official theological prejudice has put the treatise on the Black List for a century.

Adam Smith's only mistake was not to have understood that this same feeling of sympathy in its habitual stage exists among animals as well as among men.

The feeling of solidarity is the leading characteristic of all animals living in society. The eagle devours the sparrow, the wolf devours the marmot. But the eagles and the wolves respectively aid each other in hunting, the sparrow and the marmot unite among themselves against the beasts and birds of prey so effectually that only the very clumsy ones are caught. In all animal societies solidarity is a natural law of far greater importance than that struggle for existence, the virtue of which is sung by the ruling classes in every strain that may best serve to stultify us.

When we study the animal world and try to explain to ourselves that struggle for existence maintained by each living being against adverse circumstances and against its enemies, we realize that the more the principles of solidarity and equality are developed in an animal society and have become habitual to it, the more chance has it of surviving and coming triumphantly out of the struggle against hardships and foes. The more thoroughly each member of the society feels his solidarity with each other member of the society, the more completely are developed in all of them those two qualities which are the main factors of all progress: courage on the one hand, and on the other, free individual initiative. And on the contrary, the more any animal society or little group of animals loses this feeling of solidarity—which may chance as the result of exceptional scarcity or else of exceptional plenty—the more do the two other factors of progress, courage and individual initiative, diminish. In the end they disappear, and the society falls into decay and sinks before its foes. Without mutual confidence no struggle is possible; there is no courage, no initiative, no solidarity—and no victory! Defeat is certain.

We can prove with a wealth of examples how in the animal and human worlds the law of mutual aid is the law of progress, and how mutual aid with the courage and individual initiative which follow from it secures victory to the species most capable of practising it.

Now let us imagine this feeling of solidarity acting during the millions of ages which have succeeded one another since the first beginnings of animal life appeared upon the globe. Let us imagine how this feeling little by little became a habit, and was transmitted by heredity from the simplest microscopic organism to its descendants—insects, birds, reptiles, mammals, man—and we shall comprehend the origin of the moral sentiment, which is a necessity to the animal, like food or the organ for digesting it.

Without going further back and speaking of complex animals springing from colonies of extremely simple little beings, here is the origin of the moral sentiment. We have been obliged to be extremely brief in order to compress this great question within the limits of a few pages, but enough

has already been said to show that there is nothing mysterious
or sentimental about it. Without this solidarity of the individual with the species, the animal kingdom would never
have developed or reached its present perfection. The most
advanced being upon the earth would still be one of those
tiny specks swimming in the water and scarcely perceptible
under a microscope. Would even this exist? For are not
the earliest aggregations of cellules themselves an instance of
association in the struggle?

VI

Thus by an unprejudiced observation of the animal kingdom, we reach the conclusion that wherever society exists at
all, this principle may be found: *Treat others as you would
like them to treat you under similar circumstances.*

And when we study closely the evolution of the animal
world, we discover that the aforesaid principle, translated
by the one word *Solidarity,* has played an infinitely larger
part in the development of the animal kingdom than all the
adaptations that have resulted from a struggle between individuals to acquire personal advantages.

It is evident that in human societies a still greater degree
of solidarity is to be met with. Even the societies of monkeys
highest in the animal scale offer a striking example of practical solidarity, and man has taken a step further in the same
direction. This and this alone has enabled him to preserve
his puny race amid the obstacles cast by nature in his way,
and to develop his intelligence.

A careful observation of those primitive societies still remaining at the level of the Stone Age shows to what a great
extent the members of the same community practise solidarity among themselves.

This is the reason why practical solidarity never ceases;
not even during the worst periods of history. Even when
temporary circumstances of domination, servitude, exploitation cause the principle to be disowned, it still lives deep

in the thoughts of the many, ready to bring about a strong recoil against evil institutions, a revolution. If it were otherwise society would perish.

For the vast majority of animals and men this feeling remains, and must remain an acquired habit, a principle always present to the mind even when it is continually ignored in action.

It is the whole evolution of the animal kingdom speaking in us. And this evolution has lasted long, very long. It counts by hundreds of millions of years.

Even if we wished to get rid of it we could not. It would be easier for a man to accustom himself to walk on all fours than to get rid of the moral sentiment. It is anterior in animal evolution to the upright posture of man.

The moral sense is a natural faculty in us like the sense of smell or of touch.

As for law and religion, which also have preached this principle, they have simply filched it to cloak their own wares, their injunctions for the benefit of the conqueror, the exploiter, the priest. Without this principle of solidarity, the justice of which is so generally recognized, how could they have laid hold on men's minds?

Each of them covered themselves with it as with a garment; like authority which made good its position by posing as the protector of the weak against the strong.

By flinging overboard law, religion and authority, mankind can regain possession of the moral principle which has been taken from them. Regain that they may criticize it, and purge it from the adulterations wherewith priest, judge and ruler have poisoned it and are poisoning it yet.

Besides this principle of treating others as one wishes to be treated oneself, what is it but the very same principle as equality, the fundamental principle of anarchism? And how can any one manage to believe himself an anarchist unless he practises it?

We do not wish to be ruled. And by this very fact, do we not declare that we ourselves wish to rule nobody? We do not wish to be deceived, we wish always to be told nothing but the truth. And by this very fact, do we not declare that we ourselves do not wish to deceive anybody, that we promise to always tell the truth, nothing but the truth, the whole truth? We do not wish to have the fruits of our labor stolen from us. And by that very fact, do we not declare that we respect the fruits of others' labor?

By what right indeed can we demand that we should be treated in one fashion, reserving it to ourselves to treat others in a fashion entirely different? Our sense of equality revolts at such an idea.

Equality in mutual relations with the solidarity arising from it, this is the most powerful weapon of the animal world in the struggle for existence. And equality is equity.

By proclaiming ourselves anarchists, we proclaim beforehand that we disavow any way of treating others in which we should not like them to treat us; that we will no longer tolerate the inequality that has allowed some among us to use their strength, their cunning or their ability after a fashion in which it would annoy us to have such qualities used against ourselves. Equality in all things, the synonym of equity, this is anarchism in very deed. It is not only against the abstract trinity of law, religion, and authority that we declare war. By becoming anarchists we declare war against all this wave of deceit, cunning, exploitation, depravity, vice—in a word, inequality—which they have poured into all our hearts. We declare war against their way of acting, against their way of thinking. The governed, the deceived, the exploited, the prostitute, wound above all else our sense of equality. It is in the name of equality that we are determined to have no more prostituted, exploited, deceived and governed men and women.

Perhaps it may be said—it has been said sometimes—"But if you think that you must always treat others as you would be treated yourself, what right have you to use force under any circumstances whatever? What right have you to level a cannon at any barbarous or civilized invaders of your country? What right have you to dispossess the exploiter? What right to kill not only a tyrant but a mere viper?"

What right? What do you mean by that singular word, borrowed from the law? Do you wish to know if I shall feel conscious of having acted well in doing this? If those I esteem will think I have done well? Is this what you ask? If so the answer is simple.

Yes, certainly! Because we ourselves should ask to be killed like venomous beasts if we went to invade Burmese or Zulus who have done us no harm. We should say to our son or our friend: "Kill me, if I ever take part in the invasion!"

Yes, certainly! Because we ourselves should ask to be dispossessed, if giving the lie to our principles, we seized upon an inheritance, did it fall from on high, to use it for the exploitation of others.

Yes, certainly! Because any man with a heart asks beforehand that he may be slain if ever he becomes venomous; that a dagger may be plunged into his heart if ever he should take the place of a dethroned tyrant.

Ninety-nine men out of a hundred who have a wife and children would try to commit suicide for fear they should do harm to those they love, if they felt themselves going mad. Whenever a good-hearted man feels himself becoming dangerous to those he loves, he wishes to die before he is so.

Perovskaya and her comrades killed the Russian Czar. And all mankind, despite the repugnance to the spilling of blood, despite the sympathy for one who had allowed the serfs to be liberated, recognized their right to do as they did. Why? Not because the act was generally recognized as *useful*; two out of three still doubt if it were so. But because it was felt that not for all the gold in the world would Perovskaya and her comrades have consented to become tyrants themselves. Even those who know nothing of the drama are certain that it was no youthful bravado, no palace conspiracy, no attempt to gain power. It was hatred of tyranny, even to the scorn of self, even to the death.

"These men and women," it was said, "had conquered the

right to kill;" as it was said of Louise Michel, "*She* had the right to rob." Or again, "*They* have the right to steal," in speaking of those terrorists who lived on dry bread, and stole a million or two of the Kishineff treasure.

Mankind has never refused the right to use force on those who have conquered that right, be it exercised upon the barricades or in the shadow of a cross-way. But if such an act is to produce a deep impression upon men's minds, *the right must be conquered*. Without this, such an act whether useful or not will remain merely a brutal fact, of no importance in the progress of ideas. People will see in it nothing but a displacement of force, simply the substitution of one exploiter for another.

VII

We have hitherto been speaking of the conscious, deliberate actions of man, those performed intentionally. But side by side with our conscious life we have an unconscious life which is very much wider. Yet we have only to notice how we dress in the morning, trying to fasten a button that we know we lost last night, or stretching out our hand to take something that we ourselves have moved away, to obtain an idea of this unconscious life and realize the enormous part it plays in our existence.

It makes up three-fourths of our relations with others. Our ways of speaking, smiling, frowning, getting heated or keeping cool in a discussion, are unintentional, the result of habits, inherited from our human or pre-human ancestors (only notice the likeness in expression between an angry man and an angry beast), or else consciously or unconsciously acquired.

Our manner of acting towards others thus tends to become habitual. To treat others as he would wish to be treated himself becomes with man and all sociable animals, simply a habit. So much so that a person does not generally even ask himself how he must act under such and such circumstances. It is only when the circumstances are exceptional, in some complex case or under the impulse of strong passion that he hesitates, and a struggle takes place between the various portions of his brain—for the brain is a very complex organ, the various portions of which act to a certain degree independently. When this happens, the man substitutes himself in imagination for the person opposed to him; he asks himself if he would like to be treated in such a way, and the better he has identified himself with the person whose dignity or interests he has been on the point of injuring, the more moral will his decision be. Or maybe a friend steps in and says to him: "Fancy yourself in his place; should you have suffered from being treated by him as he has been treated by you?" And this is enough.

Thus we only appeal to the principle of equality in moments of hesitation, and in ninety-nine cases out of a hundred act morally from habit.

It must have been obvious that in all we have hitherto said, we have not attempted to enjoin anything. We have simply set forth the manner in which things happen in the animal world and amongst mankind.

Formerly the church threatened men with hell to moralize them, and she succeeded in demoralizing them instead. The judge threatens with imprisonment, flogging, the gallows, in the name of those social principles he has filched from society; and he demoralizes them. And yet the very idea that the judge may disappear from the earth at the same time as the priest causes authoritarians of every shade to cry out about peril to society.

But we are not afraid to forego judges and their sentences. We forego sanctions of all kinds, even obligations to morality. We are not afraid to say: "Do what you will; act as you will"; because we are persuaded that the great majority of mankind, in proportion to their degree of enlightenment and the completeness with which they free themselves from existing fetters will behave and act always in a direction useful to society just as we are persuaded beforehand that a child will one day walk on its two feet and not on all fours, simply because it is born of parents belonging to the genus *homo*.

All we can do is to give advice. And again while giving it we add: "This advice will be valueless if your own experience and observation do not lead you to recognize that it is worth following."

When we see a youth stooping and so contracting his chest and lungs, we advise him to straighten himself, hold up his head and open his chest. We advise him to fill his lungs and take long breaths, because this will be his best safeguard against consumption. But at the same time we teach him physiology that he may understand the functions of the lungs, and himself choose the posture he knows to be the best.

And this is all we can do in the case of morals. We have only a right to give advice, to which we add: "Follow it *if* it seems good to you."

But while leaving to each the right to act as he thinks best; while utterly denying the right of society to punish anyone in any way for any anti-social act he may have committed, we do not forego our own capacity to love what seems to us good and to hate what seems to us bad. Love and hate; for only those who know how to hate know how to love. We keep this capacity; and as this alone serves to maintain and develop the moral sentiments in every animal society, so much the more will it be enough for the human race.

We only ask one thing, to eliminate all that impedes the free development of these two feelings in the present society, all that perverts our judgment:—the State, the church, exploitation; judges, priests, governments, exploiters.

Today when we see a Jack the Ripper murder one after another some of the poorest and most miserable of women, our first feeling is one of hatred.

If we had met him the day when he murdered that woman who asked him to pay her for her slum lodging, we should have put a bullet through his head, without reflecting that the bullet might have been better bestowed in the brain of the owner of that wretched den.

But when we recall to mind all the infamies which have brought him to this; when we think of the darkness in which he prowls, haunted by images drawn from indecent books or thoughts suggested by stupid books, our feeling is divided. And if some day we hear that Jack is in the hands of some judge who has slain in cold blood a far greater number of men, women and children than all the Jacks together; if we see him in the hands of one of those deliberate maniacs, then all our hatred of Jack the Ripper will vanish. It will be transformed into hatred of a cowardly and hypocritical society and its recognized representatives. All the infamies of a Ripper disappear before that long series if infamies committed in the name of law. It is these we hate.

At the present day our feelings are continually thus divided. We feel that all of us are more or less, voluntarily or involuntarily, abettors of this society. We do not dare to hate. Do we even dare to love? In a society based on exploitation and servitude human nature is degraded.

But as servitude disappears we shall regain our rights. We shall feel within ourselves strength to hate and to love, even in such complicated cases as that we have just cited.

In our daily life we do already give free scope to our feelings of sympathy or antipathy; we are doing so every moment. We all love moral strength, we all despise moral weakness and cowardice. Every moment our words, looks, smiles express our joy in seeing actions useful to the human race, those which we think good. Every moment our looks and words show the repugnance we feel towards cowardice, deceit, intrigue, want of moral courage. We betray our disgust, even when under the influence of a worldly education we try to hide our contempt beneath those lying appearances which will vanish as equal relations are established among us.

This alone is enough to keep the conception of good and ill at a certain level and to communicate it one to another.

It will be still more efficient when there is no longer judge or priest in society, when moral principles have lost their obligatory character and are considered merely as relations between equals.

Moreover in proportion to the establishment of these relations, a loftier moral conception will arise in society. It is this conception which we are about to analyze.

VIII

Thus far our analysis has only set forth the simple principles of equality. We have revolted and invited others to revolt against those who assume the right to treat their fellows otherwise than they would be treated themselves; against those who, not themselves wishing to be deceived, exploited, prostituted or ill-used, yet behave thus to others. Lying, and brutality are repulsive we have said, not because they are disapproved by codes of morality, but because such conduct revolts the sense of equality in everyone to whom equality is not an empty word. And above all does it revolt him who is a true anarchist in his way of thinking and acting.

If nothing but this simple, natural, obvious principle were generally applied in life, a very lofty morality would be the result; a morality comprising all that moralists have taught.

The principle of equality sums up the teachings of moralists. But it also contains something more. This something more is respect for the individual. By proclaiming our morality of equality, or anarchism, we refuse to assume a right which moralists have always taken upon themselves to claim, that of mutilating the individual in the name of some ideal. We do not recognize this right at all, for ourselves or anyone else.

We recognize the full and complete liberty of the individual; we desire for him plentitude of existence, the free development of all his faculties. We wish to impose nothing upon him; thus returning to the principle which Fourier placed in opposition to religious morality when he said:

"Leave men absolutely free. Do not mutilate them as religions have done enough and to spare. Do not fear even their passions. In a *free* society these are not dangerous."

Provided that you yourself do not abdicate your freedom; provided that you yourself do not allow others to enslave you; and provided that to the violent and anti-social passions of this or that person you oppose your equally vigorous social passions, then you have nothing to fear from liberty.

We renounce the idea of mutilating the individual in the name of any ideal whatsoever. All we reserve to ourselves is the frank expression of our sympathies and antipathies towards what seems to us good or bad. A man deceives his friends. It is his bent, his character to do so. Very well, it is our character, our bent to despise liars. And as this is our character, let us be frank. Do not let us rush and press him to our bosom or cordially shake hands with him, as is sometimes done today. Let us vigorously oppose our active passion to his.

This is all we have the right to do, this is all the duty we have to perform to keep up the principle of equality in society. It is the principle of equality in practice.

But what of the murderer, the man who debauches children? The murderer who kills from sheer thirst for blood is excessively rare. He is a madman to be cured or avoided. As for the debauchee, let us first of all look to it that society does not pervert our children's feelings, then we shall have little to fear from rakes.

All this it must be understood is not *completely* applicable until the great sources of moral depravity—capitalism, religion, justice, government—shall have ceased to exist. But the greater part of it may be put in practice from this day forth. It is in practice already.

And yet if societies knew only this principle of equality; if each man practised merely the equity of a trader, taking care all day long not to give others anything more than he was receiving from them, society would die of it. The very principle of equality itself would disappear from our relations. For, if it is to be maintained, something grander, more lovely, more vigorous than mere equity must perpetually find a place in life.

And this greater than justice is here.

Until now humanity has never been without large natures overflowing with tenderness, with intelligence, with good-will, and using their feeling, their intellect, their active force in the service of the human race without asking anything in return.

This fertility of mind, of feeling or of good-will takes all possible forms. It is in the passionate seeker after truth, who renounces all other pleasures to throw his energy into the search for what he believes true and right contrary to the affirmations of the ignoramuses around him. It is in the inventor who lives from day to day forgetting even his food, scarcely touching the bread with which perhaps some woman devoted to him feeds him like a child, while he follows out the intention he thinks destined to change the face of the world. It is in the ardent revolutionist to whom the joys of art, of science, even of family life, seem bitter, so long as they cannot be shared by all, and who works despite misery and persecution for the regeneration of the world. It is in the youth who, hearing of the atrocities of invasion, and taking literally the heroic legends of patriotism, inscribes himself in a volunteer corps and marches bravely through snow and hunger until he falls beneath the bullets. It was in the Paris street arab, with his quick intelligence and bright choice of aversions and sympathies, who ran to the ramparts with his little brother, stood steady amid the rain of shells, and died murmuring: "Long live the Commune!" It is in the man who is revolted at the sight of a wrong without waiting to ask what will be its result to himself, and when all backs are bent stands up to unmask the iniquity and brand the exploiter, the petty despot of a factory or great tyrant of an empire. Finally it is in all those number-less acts of devotion, less striking and therefore unknown and almost always misprized, which may be continually observed, especially among women, if we will take the trouble to open our eyes and notice what lies at the very foundation of human life, and enables it to enfold itself one way or another in spite of the exploitation and oppression it undergoes.

Such men and women as these, some in obscurity, some within a larger arena, create the progress of mankind. And mankind is aware of it. This is why it encompasses such lives with reverence, with myths. It adorns them, makes them the subject of its stories, songs, romances. It adores in them the courage, goodness, love and devotion which are lacking in most of us. It transmits their memory to the young. It recalls even those who have acted only in the narrow circle of home and friends, and reveres their memory in family tradition.

Such men and women as these make true morality, the only morality worthy the name. All the rest is merely equality in relations. Without their courage, their devotion, humanity would remain besotted in the mire of petty calculations. It is such men and women as these who prepare the morality of the future, that which will come when our children have ceased to *reckon*, and have grown up to the idea that the best use for all energy, courage and love is to expend it where the need of such a force is most strongly felt.

Such courage, such devotion has existed in every age. It is to be met with among sociable animals. It is to be found among men, even during the most degraded epochs.

And religions have always sought to appropriate it, to turn it into current coin for their own benefit. In fact if religions are still alive, it is because—ignorance apart—they have always appealed to this very devotion and courage. And it is to this that revolutionists appeal.

The moral sentiment of duty which each man has felt in his life, and which it has been attempted to explain by every sort of mysticism, the unconsciously anarchist Guyau says, "is nothing but a superabundance of life, which demands to be exercised, to give itself; at the same time, it is the consciousness of a power."

All accumulated force creates a pressure upon the obstacles placed before it. *Power* to act is *duty* to act. And all this moral "obligation" of which so much has been said or written is reduced to the conception: *the condition of the maintenance of life is its expansion.*

"The plant cannot prevent itself from flowering. Sometimes to flower means to die. Never mind, the sap mounts all the same," concludes the young anarchist philosopher.

It is the same with the human being when he is full of force and energy. Force accumulates in him. He expands his life. He gives without calculation, otherwise he could not live. If he must die like the flower when it blooms, never mind. The sap rises, if sap there be.

Be strong. Overflow with emotional and intellectual energy, and you will spread your intelligence, your love, your energy of action broadcast among others! This is what all moral teaching comes to.

IX

That which mankind admires in a truly moral man is his energy, the exuberance of life which urges him to give his intelligence, his feeling, his action, asking nothing in return.

The strong thinker, the man overflowing with intellectual life, naturally seeks to diffuse his ideas. There is no pleasure in thinking unless the thought is communicated to others. It is only the mentally poverty-stricken man, who after he has painfully hunted up some idea, carefully hides it that later on he may label it with his own name. The man of powerful intellect runs over with ideas; he scatters them by the handful. He is wretched if he cannot share them with others, cannot scatter them to the four winds, for in this is his *life.*

The same with regard to feeling. "We are not enough for ourselves: we have more tears than our own sufferings claim, more capacity for joy than our own existence can justify," says Guyau, thus summing up the whole question of morality in a few admirable lines, caught from nature. The solitary being is wretched, restless, because he cannot share his thoughts and feelings with others. When we feel some great pleasure, we wish to let others know that we exist, we feel, we love, we live, we struggle, we fight.

At the same time, we feel the need to exercise our will, our active energy. To act, to work has become a need for the vast majority of mankind. So much so that when absurd conditions divorce a man or woman from useful work, they invent something to do, some futile and senseless obligations whereby to open out a field for their active energy. They invent a theory, a religion, a "social duty"—to persuade themselves that they are doing something useful. When they dance, it is for a charity. When they ruin themselves with expensive dresses, it is to keep up the position of the aristocracy. When they do nothing, it is on principle.

"We *need* to help our fellows, to lend a hand to the coach laboriously dragged along by humanity; in any case, we buzz round it," says Guyau. This need of lending a hand is so great that it is found among all sociable animals, however low in the scale. What is all the enormous amount of activity spent uselessly in politics every day but an expression of the need to lend a hand to the coach of humanity, or at least to buzz around it.

Of course this "fecundity of will," this thirst for action, when accompanied by poverty of feeling and an intellect incapable of *creation*, will produce nothing but a Napoleon I or a Bismarck, wiseacres who try to force the world to progress backwards. While on the other hand, mental fertility destitute of well developed sensibility will bring forth such barren fruits as literary and scientific pedants who only hinder the advance of knowledge. Finally, sensibility unguided by large intelligence will produce such persons as the woman ready to sacrifice everything for some brute of a man, upon whom she pours forth all her love.

If life is to be really fruitful, it must be so at once in intelligence, in feeling and in will. This fertility in every direction is *life;* the only thing worthy the name. For one moment of this life, those who have obtained a glimpse of it give years of vegetative existence. Without this overflowing life, a man is old before his time, an impotent being, a plant that withers before it has ever flowered.

"Let us leave to latter-day corruption this life that is no life," cries youth, the true youth full of sap that longs to live and scatter life around. Every time a society falls into decay, a thrust from such youth as this shatters ancient economic, and political and moral forms to make room for the up-springing of a new life. What matter if one or another fall in the struggle! Still the sap rises. For youth to live is to blossom whatever the consequences! It does not regret them.

But without speaking of the heroic periods of mankind, taking every-day existence, is it life to live in disagreement with one's ideal?

Now-a-days it is often said that men scoff at the ideal. And it is easy to understand why. The word has so often been used to cheat the simple-hearted that a reaction is inevitable and healthy. We too should like to replace the word "ideal," so often blotted and stained, by a new word more in conformity with new ideas.

But whatever the word, the fact remains; every human being has his ideal. Bismarck had his—however strange—; a government of blood and iron. Even every philistine has his ideal however low.

But besides these, there is the human being who has conceived a loftier ideal. The life of a beast cannot satisfy him. Servility, lying, bad faith, intrigue, inequality in human relations fill him with loathing. How can he in his turn become servile, be a liar, and intriguer, lord it over others? He catches a glimpse of how lovely life might be if better relations existed among men; he feels in himself the power to succeed in establishing these better relations with those he may meet on his way. He conceives what is called an ideal.

Whence comes this ideal? How is it fashioned by heredity

on one side and the impressions of life on the other? We know not. At most we could tell the story of it more or less truly in our own biographies. But it is an actual fact—variable, progressive, open to outside influences but always living. It is a largely unconscious feeling of what would give the greatest amount of vitality, of the joy of life.

Life is vigorous, fertile, rich in sensation only on condition of answering to this feeling of the ideal. Act *against* this feeling, and you feel your life bent back on itself. It is no longer at one, it loses its vigor. Be untrue often to your ideal and you will end by paralyzing your will, your active energy. Soon you will no longer regain the vigor, the spontaneity of decision you formerly knew. You are a broken man.

Nothing mysterious in all this, once you look upon a human being as a compound of nervous and cerebral centers acting independently. Waver between the various feelings striving within you, and you will soon end by breaking the harmony of the organism; you will be a sick person without will. The intensity of your life will decrease. In vain will you seek for compromises. Never more will you be the complete, strong, vigorous being you were when your acts were in accordance with the ideal conceptions of your brain.

There are epochs in which the moral conception changes entirely. A man perceives that what he had considered moral is the deepest immorality. In some instances it is a custom, a venerated tradition, that is fundamentally immoral. In others we find a moral system framed in the interests of a single class. We cast them over-board and raise the cry "Down with morality!" It becomes a duty to act "immorally."

Let us welcome such epochs for they are epochs of criticism. They are an infallible sign that thought is working in society. A higher morality has begun to be wrought out.

What this morality will be we have sought to formulate, taking as our basis the study of man and animal.

We have seen the kind of morality which is even now shaping itself in the ideas of the masses and of the thinkers. This morality will issue no commands. It will refuse once and for all to model individuals according to an abstract idea, as it will refuse to mutilate them by religion, law or government. It will leave to the individual man full and perfect liberty. It will be but a simple record of facts, a science. And this science will say to man: "If you are not conscious of strength within you, if your energies are only just sufficient to maintain a colorless, monotonous life, without strong impressions, without deep joys, but also without deep sorrows, well then, keep to the simple principles of a just equality. In relations of equality you will find probably the maximum of happiness possible to your feeble energies.

"But if you feel within you the strength of youth, if you wish to live, if you wish to enjoy a perfect, full and overflowing life—that is, know the highest pleasure which a living being can desire—be strong, be great, be vigorous in all you do.

"Sow life around you. Take heed that if you deceive, lie, intrigue, cheat, you thereby demean yourself, belittle yourself, confess your own weakness beforehand, play the part of the slave of the harem who feels himself the inferior of his master. Do this if it so pleases you, but know that humanity will regard you as petty, contemptible and feeble, and will treat you as such. Having no evidence of your strength, it will act towards you as one worthy of pity—and pity only. Do not blame humanity if of your own accord you thus paralyze your energies. Be strong on the other hand, and once you have seen unrighteousness and recognized it as such—inequity in life, a lie in science, or suffering inflicted by another —rise in revolt against the iniquity, the lie or the injustice.

"Struggle! To struggle is to live, and the fiercer the struggle the intenser the life. Then you will have lived; and a few hours of such life are worth years spent vegetating.

"Struggle so that all may live this rich, overflowing life. And be sure that in this struggle you will find a joy greater than anything else can give."

This is all that the science of morality can tell you. Yours is the choice.

NOTE FOR "ANARCHISM: ITS PHILOSOPHY AND IDEAL"

This lecture, reprinted and widely distributed in many languages as a pamphlet, answers the question as to whether anarchism has a philosophy, and what that philosophy is. Kropotkin answers the criticism that anarchism is merely destructive, by tracing analogies with the natural sciences, in which he shows that progress takes place by violent changes in the equilibruim established at any period, followed by new adaptations, and a new harmony arising out of the reacting parts. An ever-changing equilibruim rather than forms fixed by law is the harmony he regards as natural. This natural growth of society he sees balked by powerful minorities, holding it in bonds made for their advantage.

Against them he pits the power of the aroused workers who see the appropriation of their labor and their liberties, but who are prevented from a revolutionary seizure of land and wealth by diversion to war and the mistakes in policy of the socialist movement.

To bring the workers' revolutionary movement to the anarchist conception of free federation, and to arouse the initiative of the people to a seizure of property he regards as essential to restoring the natural process of growth. "Variety is life, uniformity is death," is a principle which applies to the revolutionary movement as to all of life. Complete individual liberty is of course the goal. To aid in developing these natural tendencies is the practical task of anarchism. These are not dreams for a distant future, nor a stage to be reached when other stages are gone through, but processes of life about us everywhere which we may either advance or hold back.

ANARCHISM: ITS PHILOSOPHY AND IDEAL

THOSE who are persuaded that anarchism is a collection of visions relating to the future, and an unconscious striving towards the destruction of all present civilization, are still very numerous. To clear the ground of such prejudices as maintain this view we should have to enter into many details which it would be difficult to cover briefly.

Anarchists have been spoken of so much lately that part of the public has at last taken to reading and discussing our doctrines. Sometimes men have even given themselves the trouble to reflect, and at the present time we have at least gained the admission that anarchists have an ideal. Their ideal is even found too beautiful, too lofty for a society not composed of superior beings.

But is it not pretentious on my part to speak of a philosophy, when according to our critics our ideas are but dim visions of a distant future? Can anarchism pretend to possess a philosophy when it is denied that socialism has one?

This is what I am about to answer with all possible precision of clearness. I begin by taking a few elementary illustrations borrowed from natural sciences. Not for the purpose of deducing our social ideas from them—far from it; but simply the better to set off certain relations which are easier grasped in phenomena verified by the exact sciences than in examples taken only from the complex facts of human societies.

What especially strikes us at present in exact sciences is the profound modification which they are undergoing in the whole of their conceptions and interpretations of the facts of the universe.

There was a time when man imagined the earth placed in

the center of the universe. Sun, moon, planets and stars seemed to roll round our globe; and this globe inhabited by man represented for him the center of creation. He himself—the superior being on his planet—was the elected of his Creator. The sun, the moon, the stars were made for him—towards him was directed all the attention of a God who watched the least of his actions, arrested the sun's course for him, launched his showers or his thunderbolts on fields and cities to recompense the virtue or punish the crimes of mankind. For thousands of years man thus conceived the universe.

An immense change in all conceptions of the civilized part of mankind was produced in the sixteenth century when it was demonstrated that far from being the center of the universe, the earth was only a grain of sand in the solar system—a ball much smaller even than the other planets —that the sun itself, though immense in comparison to our little earth, was but a star among many other countless stars which we see shining in the skies and swarming in the milkyway. How small man appeared in comparison to this immensity without limits, how ridiculous his pretentions! All the philosophy of that epoch, all social and religious conceptions, felt the effects of this transformation in cosmogony. Natural science, whose present development we are so proud of, only dates from that time.

But a change much more profound and with far wider-reaching results is being effected at the present time in the whole of the sciences, and anarchism is but one of the many manifestations of this evolution.

Take any work on astronomy of the last century. You will no longer find in it our tiny planet placed in the center of the universe. But you will meet at every step the idea of a central luminary—the sun—which by its powerful attraction governs our planetary world. From this central body radiates a force guiding the course of the planets, and maintaining the harmony of the system. Issued from a central agglomeration, planets have, so to say, budded from it. They owe their birth to this agglomeration; they owe everything to the radiant star that represents it still: the rhythm of their movements, their orbits set at wisely regulated distances, the life that animates them and adorns their surfaces. And when any perturbation disturbs their course and makes them deviate from their orbits, the central body re-establishes order in the system; it assures and perpetuates its existence.

This conception, however, is also disappearing as the other one did. After having fixed all their attention on the sun and the large planets, astronomers are beginning to study now the infinitely small ones that people the universe. And they discover that the interplanetary and interstellar spaces are peopled and crossed in all imaginable directions by little swarms of matter, invisible, infinitely small when taken separately, but all-powerful in their numbers.

It is to these infinitely tiny bodies that dash through space in all directions with giddy swiftness, that clash with one another, agglomerate, disintegrate, everywhere and always, it is to them that today astronomers look for an explanation of the origin of our solar system, the movements that animate its parts, and the harmony of their whole. Yet another step, and soon universal gravitation itself will be but the result of all the disordered and incoherent movements of these infinitely small bodies—of oscillations of atoms that manifest themselves in all possible directions. Thus the center, the origin of force, formerly transferred from the earth to the sun, now turns out to be scattered and disseminated. It is everywhere and nowhere. With the astronomer, we perceive that solar systems are the work of infinitely small bodies; that the power which was supposed to govern the system is itself but the result of the collision among those infinitely tiny clusters of matter, that the harmony of stellar systems is harmony only because it is an adaptation, a resultant of all these numberless movements uniting, completing, equilibrating one another.

The whole aspect of the universe changes with this new conception. The idea of force governing the world, pre-established law, preconceived harmony, disappears to make room for the harmony that Fourier had caught a glimpse of: the one which results from the disorderly and incoherent movements of numberless hosts of matter, each of which goes its own way and all of which hold each in equilibrium.

If it were only astronomy that were undergoing this change! But no; the same modification takes place in the philosophy of all sciences without exception; those which study nature as well as those which study human relations.

In physical sciences, the entities of heat, magnetism, and electricity disappear. When a physicist speaks today of a heated or electrified body, he no longer sees an inanimate mass, to which an unknown force should be added. He strives to recognize in this body and in the surrounding space, the course, the vibrations of infinitely small atoms which dash in all directions, vibrate, move, live, and by their vibrations, their shocks, their life, produce the phenomena of heat, light, magnetism or electricity.

In sciences that treat of organic life, the notion of species and its variations is being substituted by a notion of the variations of the individual. The botanist and zoologist study the individual—his life, his adaptations to his surroundings. Changes produced in him by the action of drought or damp, heat or cold, abundance or poverty of nourishment, of his more or less sensitiveness to the action of exterior surroundings will originate species; and the variations of species are now for the biologist but resultants—a given sum of variations that have been produced in each individual separately. A species will be what the individuals are, each undergoing numberless influences from the surroundings in which they live, and to which they correspond each in his own way.

And when a physiologist speaks now of the life of a plant or of an animal, he sees an agglomeration, a colony of millions of separate individuals rather than a personality, one and invisible. He speaks of a federation of digestive, sensual, nervous organs, all very intimately connected with one another, each feeling the consequence of the well-being or indisposition of each, but each living its own life. Each organ, each part of an organ in its turn is composed of independent cellules which associate to struggle against conditions unfavorable to their existence. The individual is quite a world of federations, a whole universe in himself.

And in this world of aggregated beings the physiologist sees the autonomous cells of blood, of the tissues, of the nerve-centers; he recognizes the millions of white corpuscles who wend their way to the parts of the body infected by microbes in order to give battle to the invaders. More than that: in each microscopic cell he discovers today a world of autonomous organisms, each of which lives its own life, looks for well-being for itself and attains it by grouping and associating itself with others. In short, each individual is a cosmos of organs, each organ is a cosmos of cells, each cell is a cosmos of infinitely small ones. And in this complex world, the well-being of the whole depends entirely on the sum of well-being enjoyed by each of the least miscroscopic particles of organized matter. A whole revolution is thus produced in the philosophy of life.

But it is especially in psychology that this revolution leads to consequences of great importance.

Quite recently the psychologist spoke of man as an entire being, one and indivisible. Remaining faithful to religious tradition, he used to class men as good and bad, intelligent and stupid, egotists and altruists. Even with materialists of the eighteenth century, the idea of a soul, of an indivisible entity, was still upheld.

But what would we think today of a psychologist who would still speak like this! The modern psychologist sees in a man a multitude of separate faculties, autonomous tendencies, equal among themselves, performing their functions independently, balancing, opposing one another continually. Taken as a whole, man is nothing but a resultant, always changeable, of all his divers faculties, of all his autonomous tendencies, of brain cells and nerve centers. All are related so closely to one another that they each react on all the others, but they lead their own life without being subordinated to a central organ—the soul.

Without entering into further details you thus see that a profound modification is being produced at this moment in the whole of natural sciences. Not that this analysis is extended to details formerly neglected. No! the facts are not new, but the way of looking at them is in course of evolution. And if we had to characterize this tendency in a few words, we might say that if formerly science strove to study the results and the great sums (integrals, as mathematicians say), today it strives to study the infinitely small ones—the individuals of which those sums are composed and in which it now recognizes independence and individuality at the same time as this intimate aggregation.

As to the harmony that the human mind discovers in nature, and which harmony is on the whole but the verification of a certain stability of phenomena, the modern man of science no doubt recognizes it more than ever. But he no longer tries to explain it by the action of laws conceived according to a certain plan pre-established by an intelligent will.

What used to be called "natural law" is nothing but a certain relation among phenomena which we dimly see, and each 'law" takes a temporary character of causality; that is to say: *If* such a phenomenon is produced under such conditions, such another phenomenon will follow. No law placed outside the phenomena: each phenomenon governs that which follows it—not law.

Nothing preconceived in what we call harmony in Nature. The chance of collisions and encounters has sufficed to establish it. Such a phenomenon will last for centuries because the adaptation, the equilibrium it represents has taken centuries to be established; while such another will last but an instant if that form of momentary equilibrium was born in an instant. If the planets of our solar system do not collide with one another and do not destroy one another every day, if they last millions of years, it is because they represent an equilibrium that has taken millions of centuries to establish as a resultant of millions of blind forces. If continents are not continually destroyed by volcanic shocks it is because they have taken thousands and thousands of centuries to build up, molecule by molecule, and to take their present shape. But lightning will only last an instant; because it represents a momentary rupture of the equilibrium, a sudden redistribution of force.

Harmony thus appears as a temporary adjustment established among all forces acting upon a given spot—a provisory adaptation. And that adjustment will only last under one condition: that of being continually modified; of representing every moment the resultant of all conflicting actions. Let but one of those forces be hampered in its action for some time and harmony disappears. Force will accumulate its effect, it *must* come to light, it must exercise its action, and if other forces hinder its manifestation it will not be annihilated by that, but will end by upsetting the present adjustment, by destroying harmony, in order to find a new form of equilibrium and to work to form a new adaptation. Such is the eruption of a volcano, whose imprisoned force ends by breaking the petrified lavas which hindered them to pour forth the gases, the molten lavas, and the incandescent ashes. Such, also, are the revolutions of mankind.

An analogous transformation is being produced at the same time in the sciences that treat of man. Thus we see that history, after having been the history of kingdoms, tends to become the history of nations and then the study of individuals. The historian wants to know how the members, of which such a nation was composed, lived at such a time, what their beliefs were, their means of existence, what ideal of society was visible to them, and what means they possessed to march towards this ideal. And by the action of all those forces, formerly neglected, he interprets the great historical phenomena.

So the man of science who studies jurisprudence is no longer content with such or such a code. Like the ethnologist he wants to know the genesis of the institutions that succeed one another; he follows their evolution through ages, and in this study he applies himself far less to written law than to local customs—to the "customary law" in which the constructive genius of the unknown masses has found expression in all times. A wholly new science is being elaborated in this direction and promises to upset established conceptions we learned at school, succeeding in interpreting history in the same manner as natural sciences interpret the phenomena of nature.

And, finally, political economy, which was at the beginning a study of the wealth of *nations,* becomes today a study of the wealth of *individuals.* It cares less to know if such a nation has or has not a large foreign trade; it wants to be assured that bread is not wanting in the peasant's or worker's cottage. It knocks at all doors—at that of the palace as well as that of the hovel—and asks the rich as well as the poor: Up to what point are your needs satisfied both for necessities and luxuries?

And as it discovers that the most pressing needs of nine-tenths of each nation are not satisfied, it asks itself the question that a physiologist would ask himself about a plant or an animal:—"Which are the means to satisfy the needs of all with the least loss of power? How can a society guarantee to each, and consequently to all, the greatest sum of satisfaction?" It is in this direction that economic science is being transformed; and after having been so long a simple statement of phenomena interpreted in the interest of a rich minority, it tends to become a science in the true sense of the word—a physiology of human societies.

While a new philosophy—a new view of knowledge taken as a whole—is thus being worked out, we may observe that a different conception of society, very different from that which now prevails, is in process of formation. Under the name of anarchism, a new interpretation of the past and present life of society arises, giving at the same time a forecast as regards its future, both conceived in the same spirit as the above mentioned interpretation in natural sciences. Anarchism, therefore, appears as a constituent part of the new philosophy, and that is why anarchists come in contact on so many points with the greatest thinkers and poets of the present day.

In fact it is certain that in proportion as the human mind frees itself from ideas inculcated by minorities of priests, military chiefs and judges, all striving to establish their domination, and of scientists paid to perpetuate it, a conception of society arises in which there is no longer room for those dominating minorities. A society entering into possession of the social capital accumulated by the labor of preceding generations, organizing itself so as to make use of this capital in the interests of all, and constituting itself without reconstituting the power of the ruling minorities. It comprises in its midst an infinite variety of capacities, temperaments and individual energies: it excludes none. It even calls for struggles and contentions; because we know that periods of contests, so long as they were freely fought out without the weight of constituted authority being thrown on one side of the balance, were periods when human genius took its mightiest flights and achieved the greatest aims. Acknowledging, as a fact, the equal rights of its members to the treasures accumulated in the past, it no longer recognizes a division between exploited and exploiters, governed and governors, dominated and dominators, and it seeks to establish a certain harmonious compatibility in its midst—not by subjecting all its members to an authority that is fictitiously supposed to represent society, not by trying to establish uniformity, but by urging all men to develop free initiative, free action, free association.

It seeks the most complete development of individuality combined with the highest development of voluntary association in all its aspects, in all possible degrees, for all imaginable aims; ever changing, ever modified associations which carry in themselves the elements of their durability and constantly assume new forms which answer best to the multiple aspirations of all.

A society to which pre-established forms, crystallized by law, are repugnant; which looks for harmony in an ever-changing and fugitive equilibrium between a multitude of varied forces and influences of every kind, following their own course,—these forces themselves promoting the energies which are favorable to their march towards progress, towards the liberty of developing in broad daylight and counterbalancing one another.

This conception and ideal of society is certainly not new. On the contrary, when we analyze the history of popular institutions—the clan, the village community, the guild and even the urban commune of the middle ages in their first stages,—we find the same popular tendency to constitute a society according to this idea; a tendency, however, always trammelled by domineering minorities. All popular movements bore this stamp more or less, and with the Anabaptists and their forerunners in the ninth century we already find the same ideas clearly expressed in the religious language which was in use at that time. Unfortunately, till the end of the last century, this ideal was always tainted by a theocratic spirit. It is only nowadays that the conception of society deduced from the observation of social phenomena is rid of its swaddling-clothes.

It is only today that the ideal of a society where each governs himself according to his own will (which is evidently a result of the social influences borne by each) is affirmed in its economic, political and moral aspects at one and the same time, and that this ideal presents itself based on the necessity of communism, imposed on our modern societies by the eminently social character of our present production.

In fact, we know full well today that it is futile to speak of liberty as long as economic slavery exists.

"Speak not of liberty—poverty is slavery!" is not a vain

formula; it has penetrated into the ideas of the great working-class masses; it filters through all the present literature; it even carries those along who live on the poverty of others, and takes from them the arrogance with which they formerly asserted their rights to exploitation.

Millions of socialists of both hemispheres already agree that the present form of capitalistic social appropriation cannot last much longer. Capitalists themselves feel that it must go and dare not defend it with their former assurance. Their only argument is reduced to saying to us: "You have invented nothing better!" But as to denying the fatal consequences of the present forms of property, as to justifying their right to property, they cannot do it. They will practise this right as long as freedom of action is left to them, but without trying to base it on an idea. This is easily understood.

For instance, take the town of Paris—a creation of so many centuries, a product of the genius of a whole nation, a result of the labor of twenty or thirty generations. How could one maintain to an inhabitant of that town who works every day to embellish it, to purify it, to nourish it, to make it a center of thought and art—how could one assert before one who produces this wealth that the palaces adorning the streets of Paris belong in all justice to those who are the legal proprietors today, when we are all creating their value, which would be *nil* without us?

Such a fiction can be kept up for some time by the skill of the people's educators. The great battalions of workers may not even reflect about it; but from the moment a minority of thinking men agitate the question and submit it to all, there can be no doubt of the result. Popular opinion answers: "It is by spoliation that they hold these riches!"

Likewise, how can the peasant be made to believe that the bourgeois or manorial land belongs to the proprietor who has a legal claim, when a peasant can tell us the history of each bit of land for ten leagues around? Above all, how make him believe that it is useful for the nation that Mr. So-and-so keeps a piece of land for his park when so many neighboring peasants would be only too glad to cultivate it?

And, lastly, how make the worker in a factory, or the miner in a mine, believe that factory and mine equitably belong to their present masters, when worker and even miner are beginning to see clearly through scandal, bribery, pillage of the State and the legal theft, from which great commercial and industrial property are derived?

In fact the masses have never believed in sophisms taught by economists, uttered more to confirm exploiters in their rights than to convert the exploited; Peasants and workers, crushed by misery and finding no support in the well-to-do classes, have let things go, save from time to time, when they have affirmed their rights by insurrection. And if workers ever thought that the day would come when personal appropriation of capital would profit all by turning it into a stock of wealth to be shared by all, this illusion is vanishing like so many others. The worker perceives that he has been disinherited, and that disinherited he will remain, unless he has recourse to strikes or revolts to tear from his masters the smallest part of riches built up by his own efforts—that is to say, in order to get that little, he already must impose on himself the pangs of hunger and face imprisonment, if not exposure to imperial, royal, or republican fusillades.

But a greater evil of the present system becomes more and more marked; namely, that in a system based on private appropriation, all that is necessary to life and to production —land, housing, food and tools—having once passed into the hands of a few, the production of necessities that would give well-being to all is continually hampered. The worker feels vaguely that our present technical power could give abundance to all, but he also perceives how the capitalistic system and the State hinder the conquest of this well-being in every way.

Far from producing more than is needed to assure material riches, we do not produce enough. When a peasant covets the parks and gardens of industrial filibusters, round which judges and police mount guard—when he dreams of covering them with crops which, he knows, would carry abundance to the villages whose inhabitants feed on bread hardly washed down with sloe wine—he understands this.

The miner, forced to be idle three days a week, thinks of the tons of coal he might extract and which are sorely needed in poor households.

The worker whose factory is closed, and who tramps the streets in search of work, sees bricklayers out of work like himself, while one-fifth of the population of Paris live in insanitary hovels; he hears shoe-makers complain of want of work, while so many people need shoes—and so on.

In short, if certain economists delight in writing treatises on over-production, and in explaining each industrial crisis by this cause, they would be much at a loss if called upon to name a single article produced by France in greater quantities than are necessary to satisfy the needs of the whole population. It is certainly not corn: the country is obliged to import it. It is not wine either: peasants drink but little wine, and substitute sloe wine in its stead, and the inhabitants of towns have to be content with adulterated stuff. It is evidently not houses: millions still live in cottages of the most wretched description, with one or two apertures. It is not even good or bad books, for they are still objects of luxury in the villages. Only one thing is produced in quantities greater than needed,—it is the budget-devouring individual. But such merchandise is not mentioned in lectures by political economists, although those individuals possess all the attributes of merchandise, being ever ready to sell themselves to the highest bidder.

What economists call over-production is but a production that is above the purchasing power of the worker, who is reduced to poverty by capital and State. Now, this sort of over-production remains fatally characteristic of the present capitalist production, because workers cannot buy with their salaries what they have produced and at the same time copiously nourish the swarm of idlers who live upon their work.

The very essence of the present economic system is that the worker can never enjoy the well-being he has produced, and that the number of those who live at his expense will always augment. The more a country is advanced in industry, the more this number grows. Inevitably, industry is directed, and will have to be directed, not towards what is needed to satisfy the needs of all, but towards that which, at a given moment, brings in the greatest temporary profit to a few. Of necessity, the abundance of some will be based on the poverty of others, and the straitened circumstances of the greater number will have to be maintained at all costs, that there may be hands to sell themselves for a part only of that which they are capable of producing; without which private accumulation of capital is impossible!

These characteristics of our economic system are its very essence. Without them, it cannot exist; for who would sell his labor power for less than it is capable of bringing in if he were not forced thereto by the threat of hunger?

And those essential traits of the system are also its most crushing condemnation.

As long as England and France were pioneers of industry in the midst of nations backward in their technical development, and as long as neighbors purchased their wools, their cotton goods, their silks, their iron and machines, as well as a whole range of articles of luxury, at a price that allowed them to enrich themselves at the expense of their clients,— the worker could be buoyed up by hope that he, too, would be called upon to appropriate an ever and ever larger share of the booty to himself. But these conditions are disappearing. In their turn, the backward nations have become great producers of cotton goods, wools, silks, machines and articles of luxury. In certain branches of industry they have even taken the lead, and not only do they struggle with the pioneers of industry and commerce in distant lands, but they even compete with those pioneers in their own countries. In a few years Germany, Switzerland, Italy, the United States, Russia and Japan have become great industrial countries. Mexico, the Indies, even Serbia, are on the march—and what will it be when China begins to imitate Japan in manufacturing for the world's market?

The result is that industrial crises, the frequency and duration of which are always augmenting, have passed into a chronic state in many industries.

All is linked, all holds together under the present economic system, and all tends to make the fall of the industrial and mercantile system under which we live inevitable. Its duration is but a question of time that may already be counted by years and no longer by centuries. A question of time—and energetic attack on our part! Idlers do not make history: they suffer it!

That is why such powerful minorities constitute themselves in the midst of civilized nations, and loudly ask for the return to the community of all riches accumulated by the work of preceding generations. The holding in common of lands, mines, factories, inhabited houses, and means of transport is already the watch-word of these imposing factions, and repression—the favorite weapon of the rich and powerful—can no longer do anything to arrest the triumphal march of the spirit of revolt. And if millions of workers do not rise to seize the land and factories from the monopolists by force, be sure it is not for want of desire. They but wait for a favorable opportunity—a chance, such as presented itself in 1848, when they will be able to start the destruction of the present economic system, with the hope of being supported by an international movement.

We have already obtained the unanimous assent of those who have studied the subject, that a society, having recovered the possession of all riches accumulated in its midst, can liberally assure abundance to all in return for four or five hours effective and manual work a day, as far as regards production. If everyone, from childhood, learned whence came the bread he eats, the house he dwells in, the book he studies, and so on; and if each one accustomed himself to complete mental work by manual labor in some branch of manufacture,—society could easily perform this task, to say nothing of the further simplification of production which a more or less near future has in store for us.

In fact, it suffices to recall for a moment the present terrible waste to conceive what a civilized society can produce with but a small quantity of labor if all share in it, and what grand works might be undertaken that are out of the question today. Unfortunately, the metaphysics called political economy has never troubled about that which should have been its essence—economy of labor.

There is no longer any doubt as regards the possibility of wealth in a communist society, armed with our present machinery and tools. Doubts only arise when the question at issue is whether a society can exist in which man's actions are not subject to State control; whether, to reach well-being, it is not necessary for European communities to sacrifice the little personal liberty they have reconquered at the cost of so many sacrifices during this century? A section of socialists believe that it is impossible to attain such a result without sacrificing personal liberty on the altar of State. Another section, to which we belong, believes, on the contrary, that it is only by the abolition of the State, by the conquest of perfect liberty by the individual, by free agreement, association, and absolute free federation that we can reach communism—the possession in common of our social inheritance, and the production in common of all riches.

That is the question outweighing all others at present, and socialism *must* solve it, on pain of seeing all its efforts endangered and all its ulterior development paralyzed.

Let us, therefore, analyze it with all the attention it deserves.

If every socialist will carry his thoughts back to an earlier date, he will no doubt remember the host of prejudices aroused in him when, for the first time, he came to the idea that abolishing the capitalist system and private appropriation of land and capital had become an historical necessity.

The same feelings are today produced in the man who for the first time hears that the abolition of the State, its laws, its entire system of management, governmentalism and centralization, also becomes an historical necessity: that the abolition of the one without the abolition of the other is materially impossible. Our whole education—made, be it noted, by church and State, in the interests of both—revolts at this conception.

Is it less true for that? And shall we allow our belief in the State to survive the host of prejudices we have already sacrificed for our emancipation?

To begin with, if man, since his origin, has always lived in societies, the State is but one of the forms of social life, quite recent as far as regards European societies. Men lived thousands of years before the first States were constituted; Greece and Rome existed for centuries before the Macedonian and Roman Empires were built up, and for us modern Europeans the centralized States date but from the sixteenth century. It was only then, after the defeat of the free medieval communes had been completed that the mutual insurance company between military, judicial, landlord, and capitalist authority which we call "State," could be fully established.

It was only in the sixteenth century that a mortal blow was dealt to ideas of local independence, to free union and organization, to federation of all degrees among sovereign groups, possessing all functions now seized upon by the State. It was only then that the alliance between church and the nascent power of royalty put an end to an organization, based on the principle of federation, which had existed from the ninth to the fifteenth century, and which had produced in Europe the great period of free cities of the middle ages.

We know well the means by which this association of lord, priest, merchant, judge, soldier, and king founded its domination. It was by the annihilation of all free unions: of village communities, guilds, trades unions, fraternities, and medieval cities. It was by confiscating the land of the communes and the riches of the guilds. It was by the absolute and ferocious prohibition of all kinds of free agreement between men. It was by massacre, the wheel, the gibbet, the sword, and the fire that church and State established their domination, and that they succeeded henceforth to reign over an incoherent agglomeration of "subjects" who had no more direct union among themselves.

It is only recently that we began to reconquer, by struggle, by revolt, the first steps of the right of association that was freely practised by the artisans and the tillers of the soil through the whole of the middle ages.

And, already now, Europe is covered by thousands of voluntary associations for study and teaching, for industry, commerce, science, art, literature, exploitation, resistance to exploitation, amusement, serious work, gratification and self-denial, for all that makes up the life of an active and thinking being. We see these societies rising in all nooks and corners of all domains: political, economic, artistic, intellectual. Some are as shortlived as roses, some hold their own for several decades, and all strive—while maintaining the independence of each group, circle, branch, or section—to federate, to unite, across frontiers as well as among each nation; to cover all the life of civilized men with a net, meshes of which are intersected and interwoven. Their numbers can already be reckoned by tens of thousands, they comprise millions of adherents—although less than fifty years have elapsed since church and State began to tolerate a few of them—very few, indeed.

These societies already begin to encroach everywhere on the functions of the State, and strive to substitute free action of volunteers for that of a centralized State. In England we see insurance companies arise against theft; societies for coast defense, volunteer societies for land defense, which the State endeavors to get under its thumb, thereby making them instruments of domination, although their original aim was to do without the State. Were it not for church and State, free societies would have already conquered the whole of the immense domain of education. And, in spite of all difficulties, they begin to invade this domain as well, and make their influence already felt.

And when we mark the progress already accomplished in that direction, in spite of and against the State, which tries by all means to maintain its supremacy of recent origin; when we see how voluntary societies invade everything and are only impeded in their development by the State, we are forced to recognize a powerful *tendency,* a latent force in modern society. And we ask ourselves this question: If five, ten, or twenty years hence—it matters little—the workers succeed by revolt in destroying the said mutual insurance societies of landlords, bankers, priests, judges, and soldiers; if the people become masters of their destiny for a few months, and lay hands on the riches they have created, and which belong to them by right—will they really begin to reconstitute that blood-sucker, the State? Or will they not rather try to organize from the simple to the complex according to mutual agreement and to the infinitely varied, ever-changing needs of each locality, in order to secure the possession of those riches for themselves, to mutually guarantee one another's life, and to produce what will be found necessary for life?

Will they follow the dominant tendency of the century, towards decentralization, home rule and free agreement; or will they march contrary to this tendency and strive to reconstitute demolished authority?

Educated men tremble at the idea that society might some day be without judges, police or jailers.

But frankly, do you need them as much as you have been told in musty books? Books written, be it noted, by scientists who generally know well what has been written before them, but, for the most part, absolutely ignore the people and their everyday life.

If we can wander, without fear, not only in the streets of Paris, which bristle with police, but especially in rustic walks where you rarely meet passers-by, is it to the police that we owe this security? or rather to the absence of people who care to rob or murder us? I am evidently not speaking of the one who carries millions about him. That one—a recent trial tells us—is soon robbed, by preference in places where there are as many policemen as lamp-posts. No, I speak of the man who fears for his life and not for his purse filled with ill-gotten sovereigns. Are his fears real?

Besides, has not experience demonstrated quite recently that Jack the Ripper performed his exploits under the eye of the London police—a most active force—and that he only left off killing when the population of Whitechapel itself began to give chase to him?

And in our everyday relations with our fellow-citizens, do you think that it is really judges, jailers, and police that hinder anti-social acts from multiplying? The judge, ever ferocious, because he is a maniac of law, the accuser, the informer, the police spy, all those interlopers that live from hand to mouth around the law courts, do they not scatter demoralization far and wide into society? Read the trials, glance behind the scenes, push your analysis further than the exterior façade of law courts, and you will come out sickened.

Have not prisons—which kill all will and force of character in man, which enclose within their walls more vices than are met with on any other spot of the globe—always been universities of crime? Is not the court of a tribunal a school of ferocity? And so on.

When we ask for the abolition of the State and its organs we are always told that we dream of a society composed of men better than they are in reality. But no; a thousand times, no. All we ask is that men should not be made worse than they are, by such institutions!

If by following the very old advice given by Bentham you begin to think of the fatal consequences—direct, and especially indirect—of legal coercion, then, like Tolstoy, like us, you will begin to hate the use of coercion, and you will begin to say that society possesses a thousand other means for preventing anti-social acts. If it neglects those means today, it is because, being educated by church and State, our cowardice and apathy of spirit hinder our seeing clearly on this point. When a child has committed a fault, it is so easy to punish it: that puts an end to all discussions! It is so easy to hang a man—especially when there is an executioner who is paid so much for each execution—and it relieves us of thinking of the cause of crimes.

It is often said that anarchists live in a world of dreams to come, and do not see the things which happen today. We see them only too well, and in their true colors, and that is what makes us carry the hatchet into the forest of prejudices that besets us.

Far from living in a world of visions and imagining men better than they are, we see them as they are; and that is why we affirm that the best of men is made essentially bad by the exercise of authority, and that the theory of the "balancing of powers" and "control of authorities" is a hypocritical formula, invented by those who have seized power, to make the "sovereign people," whom they despise, believe that the people themselves are governing. It is because we know men that we say to those who imagine that men would devour one another without those governors: "You reason like the king, who, being sent across the frontier, called out, 'What will become of my poor subjects without me?'"

Ah, if men were those superior beings that the utopians of authority like to speak to us of, if we could close our eyes to reality and live like them in a world of dreams and illusions as to the superiority of those who think themselves called to power, perhaps we also should do like them; perhaps we also should believe in the virtues of those who govern.

If the gentlemen in power were really so intelligent and so devoted to the public cause, as panegyrists of authority love to represent, what a pretty government and paternal utopia we should be able to construct! The employer would never be the tyrant of the worker; he would be the father! The factory would be a palace of delight, and never would masses of workers be doomed to physical deterioration. A judge would not have the ferocity to condemn the wife and children of the one whom he sends to prison to suffer years of hunger and misery and to die some day of anemia; never would a public prosecutor ask for the head of the accused for the unique pleasure of showing off his oratorical talent; and nowhere would we find a jailer or an executioner to do the bidding of judges who have not the courage to carry out their sentences themselves.

Oh, the beautiful utopia, the lovely Christmas dream we can make as soon as we admit that those who govern represent a superior caste, and have hardly any or no knowledge of simple mortals' weaknesses! It would then suffice to make them control one another in hierarchical fashion, to let them exchange fifty papers, at most, among different administrators, when the wind blows down a tree on the national road. Or, if need be, they would have only to be valued at their proper worth, during elections, by those same masses of mortals which are supposed to be endowed with all stupidity in their mutual relations but become wisdom itself when they have to elect their masters.

All the science of government, imagined by those who govern, is imbibed with these utopias. But we know men too well to dream such dreams. We have not two measures for the virtues of the governed and those of the governors; we know that we ourselves are not without faults and that the best of us would soon be corrupted by the exercise of power. We take men for what they are worth,—and that is why we hate the government of man by man, and why we work with all our might—perhaps not strong enough—to put an end to it.

But it is not enough to destroy. We must also know how to build, and it is owing to not having thought about it that the masses have always been led astray in all their revolutions. After having demolished they abandoned the care of reconstruction to the middle-class people who possessed a more or less precise conception of what they wished to realize, and who consequently reconstituted authority to their own advantage.

That is why anarchism, when it works to destroy authority in all its aspects, when it demands the abrogation of laws and the abolition of the mechanism that serves to impose them, when it refuses all hierarchical organization and preaches free agreement, at the same time strives to maintain and enlarge the precious kernel of social customs without which no human or animal society can exist. Only instead of demanding that those social customs should be maintained through the authority of a few, it demands it from the continued action of all.

Communist customs and institutions are of absolute necessity for society, not only to solve economic difficulties, but also to maintain and develop social customs that bring men in contact with one another. They must be looked to for establishing such relations between men that the interest of each should be the interest of all; and this alone can unite men instead of dividing them.

In fact when we ask ourselves by what means a certain moral level can be maintained in a human or animal society, we find only three such means: the repression of anti-social acts; moral teaching; and the practice of mutual help itself. And as all three have already been put to the test of practice, we can judge them by their effects.

As to the impotence of repression—it is sufficiently demonstrated by the disorder of present society and by the necessity of a revolution that we all desire or feel inevitable. In the domain of economy, coercion has led us to industrial servitude; in the domain of politics to the State; that is to say, to the destruction of all ties that formerly existed among citizens, and to the nation, which becomes nothing but an incoherent mass of obedient *subjects* of a central authority.

Not only has a coercive system contributed and powerfully aided to create all the present economic, political, and social evils, but it has given proof of its absolute impotence to raise the moral level of societies; it has not even been able to maintain it at the level it had already reached. If a benevolent fairy could only reveal to our eyes all the crimes that are committed every day, every minute, in a civilized society, under cover of the unknown, or the protection of law itself,—society would shudder at that terrible state of affairs. The authors of the greatest political crimes, like those of Napoleon III's *coup d'état,* or the bloody week in May after the fall of the Commune of 1871, never are arraigned.

Practised for centuries, repression has so badly succeeded that it has but led us into a blind alley from which we can only issue by carrying torch and hatchet into the institutions of our authoritarian past.

Far be it from us not to recognize the importance of the second factor, moral teaching—especially that which is unconsciously transmitted in society and results from the whole of the ideas and comments emitted by each of us on facts and events of everyday life. But this force can only act on society under one condition, that of not being crossed by a mass of contradictory immoral teachings resulting from the practise of institutions.

In that case, its influence is *nil* or baneful. Take Christian morality: what other teaching could have had more hold on minds than that spoken in the name of a crucified God, and could have acted with all its mystical force, all its poetry of martyrdom, its grandeur in forgiving executioners? And yet the institution was more powerful than the religion. Soon Christianity—a revolt against imperial Rome—was conquered by that same Rome; it accepted its maxims, customs, and language. The Christian church accepted the Roman law as its own, and as such—allied to the State—it became in history the most furious enemy of all semi-communist institutions, to which Christianity appealed at its origin.

Can we for a moment believe that moral teaching, patronized by circulars from ministers of public instruction, would have the creative force that Christianity has not had? And what could the verbal teaching of truly social men do, if it were counteracted by the whole teaching derived from institutions based, as our present institutions of property and State are, upon unsocial principles?

The third element alone remains—*the institution itself,* acting in such a way as to make social acts a state of habit and instinct. This element—history proves it—has never missed its aim, never has it acted as a double-bladed sword; and its influence has only been weakened when custom strove to become immovable, crystallized to become in its turn a religion not to be questioned when it endeavored to absorb the individual, taking all freedom of action from him and compelling him to revolt against that which had become, through its crystallization, an enemy to progress.

In fact, all that was an element of progress in the past or an instrument of moral and intellectual improvement of the human race is due *to the practice of mutual aid,* to the customs that recognized the equality of men and brought them to ally, to unite, to associate for the purpose of producing and consuming, to unite for purposes of defense, to federate and to recognize no other judges in fighting out their differences than the arbitrators they took from their own midst.

Each time these institutions, issued from popular genius, when it had reconquered its liberty for a moment,—each time these institutions developed in a new direction, the moral level of society, its material well-being, its liberty, its intellectual progress, and the affirmation of individual originality made a step in advance. And, on the contrary, each time that in the course of history, whether following upon a foreign conquest, or whether by developing authoritarian prejudices, men become more and more divided into governors and governed, exploiters and exploited, the moral level fell, the well-being of the masses decreased in order to insure riches to a few, and the spirit of the age declined.

History teaches us this, and from this lesson we have learned to have confidence in free communist institutions to raise the moral level of societies, debased by the practice of authority.

Today we live side by side without knowing one another. We come together at meetings on an election day: we listen to the lying or fanciful professions of faith of a candidate, and we return home. The State has the care of all questions of public interest; the State alone has the function of seeing that we do not harm the interests of our neighbor, and, if it fails in this, of punishing us in order to repair the evil.

Our neighbor may die of hunger or murder his children,— it is no business of ours; it is the business of the policeman. You hardly know one another, nothing unites you, everything tends to alienate you from one another, and finding no better way, you ask the Almighty (formerly it was a God, now it is the State) to do all that lies within his power to stop anti-social passions from reaching their highest climax.

In a communist society such estrangement, such confidence in an outside force, could not exist. Communist organizations cannot be left to be constructed by legislative bodies called parliaments, municipal or communal councils. It must be the work of all, a natural growth, a product of the constructive genius of the great mass. Communism cannot be imposed from above; it could not live even for a few months if the constant and daily cooperation of all did not uphold it. It must be free.

It cannot exist without creating a continual contact between all for the thousands and thousands of common transactions; it cannot exist without creating local life, independent in the smallest unities—the block of houses, the street, the district, the commune. It would not answer its purpose if it did not cover society with a network of thousands of associations to satisfy its thousand needs: the necessaries of life, articles of luxury, of study, enjoyment, amusements. And such associations cannot remain narrow and local; they must necessarily tend (as is already the case with learned societies, cyclist clubs, humanitarian societies and the like) to become international.

And the sociable customs that communism—were it only partial at its origin—must inevitably engender in life, would already be a force incomparably more powerful to maintain and develop the kernel of sociable customs than all repressive machinery.

This, then, is the form—sociable institution—of which we ask the development of the spirit of harmony that church and State had undertaken to impose on us—with the sad result we know only too well. And these remarks contain our answer to those who affirm that communism and anarchism cannot go together. They are, you see, a necessary complement to one another. The most powerful development of individuality, of individual originality—as one of our comrades has so well said,—can only be produced when the first needs of food and shelter are satisfied; when the struggle for existence against the forces of nature has been simplified; when man's time is no longer taken up entirely by the meaner side of daily subsistence,—then only, his intelligence, his artistic taste, his inventive spirit, his genius, can develop freely and ever strive to greater achievements.

Communism is the best basis for individual development and freedom; not that individualism which drives man to the war of each against all—this is the only one known up till now,—but that which represents the full expansion of man's faculties, the superior development of what is original in him, the greatest fruitfulness of intelligence, feeling and will.

Such being our ideal, what does it matter to us that it cannot be realized at once!

Our first duty is to find out by an analysis of society, its characteristic *tendencies* at a given moment of evolution and to state them clearly. Then, to act according to those tendencies in our relations with all those who think as we do. And, finally, from today and especially during a revolutionary period, work for the destruction of the institutions, as well as the prejudices that impede the development of such tendencies.

That is all we can do by peaceable or revolutionary methods, and we know that by favoring those tendencies we con--

tribute to progress, while those who resist them impede the march of progress.

Nevertheless men often speak of stages to be travelled through, and they propose to work to reach what they consider to be the nearest station and only *then* to take the highroad leading to what they recognize to be a still higher ideal.

But reasoning like this seems to me to misunderstand the true character of human progress and to make use of a badly chosen military comparison. Humanity is not a rolling ball, nor even a marching column. It is a whole that evolves simultaneously in the multitude of millions of which it is composed. And if you wish for a comparison you must rather take it in the laws of organic evolution than in those of an inorganic moving body.

The fact is that each phase of development of a society is a resultant of all the activities of the intellects which compose that society; it bears the imprint of all those millions of wills. Consequently whatever may be the stage of development that the twentieth century is preparing for us, this future state of society will show the effects of the awakening of libertarian ideas which is now taking place. And the depth with which this movement will be impressed upon twentieth-century institutions will depend on the number of men who will have broken today with authoritarian prejudices, on the energy they will have used in attacking old institutions, on the impression they will make on the masses, on the clearness with which the ideal of a free society will have been impressed on the minds of the masses.

Now it is the workers' and peasants' initiative that all parties—the socialist authoritarian party included—have always stifled, wittingly or not, by party discipline. Committees, centers, ordering everything; local organs having but to obey, "so as not to put the unity of the organization in danger." A whole teaching, in a word; a whole false history, written to serve that purpose, a whole incomprehensible pseudo-science of economics, elaborated to this end.

Well, then, those who will work to break up these super-annuated tactics, those who will know how to rouse the spirit of initiative in individuals and in groups, those who will be able to create in their mutual relations a movement and a life based on the principles of free understanding—those that will understand that *variety, conflict even, is life and that uniformity is death,*—they will work, not for future centuries, but in good earnest for the next revolution, for our own times.

We need not fear the dangers and "abuses" of liberty. It is only those who do nothing who make no mistakes. As to those who only know how to obey, they make just as many, and more mistakes than those who strike out their own path in trying to act in the direction their intelligence and their social education suggest to them. The ideal of liberty of the individual—if it is incorrectly understood owing to surroundings where the notion of solidarity is insufficiently accentuated by institutions—can certainly lead isolated men to acts that are repugnant to the social sentiments of humanity. Let us admit that it does happen: is it, however, a reason for throwing the principle of liberty overboard? Is it a reason for accepting the teaching of those masters who, in order to prevent "digressions," re-establish the censure of an enfranchised press and guillotine advanced parties to maintain uniformity and discipline—that which, when all is said, was in 1793 the best means of insuring the triumph of reaction?

The only thing to be done when we see anti-social acts committed in the name of liberty of the individual, is to repudiate the principle of "each for himself and God for all," and to have the courage to say aloud in anyone's presence what we think of such acts. This can perhaps bring about a conflict; but conflict is life itself. And from the conflict will arise an appreciation of those acts far more just than all those appreciations which could have been produced under the influence of old-established ideas.

It is evident that so profound a revolution producing itself in people's minds cannot be confined to the domain of ideas without expanding to the sphere of action.

Consequently, the new ideas have provoked a multitude of acts of revolt in all countries, under all possible conditions: first, individual revolt against capital and State; then collective revolt—strikes and working-class insurrections—both preparing, in men's minds as in actions, a revolt of the masses, a revolution. In this, socialism and anarchism have only followed the course of evolution, which is always accomplished by force-ideas at the approach of great popular risings.

That is why it would be wrong to attribute the monopoly of acts of revolt to anarchism. And, in fact, when we pass in review the acts of revolt of the last quarter of a century, we see them proceeding from all parties.

In all Europe we see a multitude of risings of working masses and peasants. Strikes, which were once "a war of folded arms," today easily turning to revolt, and sometimes taking the proportions of vast insurrections. In the new and old worlds it is by the dozen that we count the risings of strikers having turned to revolts.

If you wish, like us, that the entire liberty of the individual and, consequently, his life be respected, you are necessarily brought to repudiate the government of man by man, whatever shape it assumes; you are forced to accept the principles of anarchism that you have spurned so long. You must then search with us the forms of society that can best realize that ideal and put an end to all the violence that rouses your indignation.

NOTE FOR "MODERN SCIENCE AND ANARCHISM"

The effort to give anarchism a scientific foundation, based on the methods of the natural sciences, was Kropotkin's chief concern,—and in so far as he succeeded, his most significant achievement. In this pamphlet, published both in French and English at about the same time, he described the principles of anarchism in relation to the tendencies away from metaphysics and toward physics. As much of the discussion concerned controversial philosophic questions and writers no longer of interest to the general reader, that portion is omitted. Kropotkin quoted them only to demolish them,—and it is hardly necessary to repeat the battle. The chapter on the "Means of Action" is reprinted for its compact statement, although it is not closely related to the main thesis of the booklet.

One paragraph of the pamphlet is the key to it: "Anarchism is a world-wide concept based upon a mechanical explanation of all phenomena, embracing the whole of nature. . . . Its method of investigation is that of the exact natural sciences. . . . Its aim is to construct a synthetic philosophy comprehending in one generalization all the phenomena of nature."

Kropotkin revised the original work, and it was published in 1913, but only in a French edition. The revision brought the controversial material up to date, but added nothing to the main thesis, which is the only matter of interest to the general reader.

MODERN SCIENCE AND ANARCHISM

ANARCHISM like socialism is general, and like every other social movement, has not of course developed out of science or out of some philosophical school. The social sciences are still very far removed from the time when they shall be as exact as are physics and chemistry. Even in meteorology we cannot yet predict the weather a month or even one week in advance. It would be unreasonable, therefore, to expect of the young social sciences, which are concerned with phenomena much more complex than winds and rain, that they should foretell social events with any approach to certainty. Besides, it must not be forgotten that men of science, too, are but human, and that most of them either belong by descent to the possessing classes and are steeped in the prejudices of their class, or else are in the actual service of the government. Not out of the universities therefore does anarchism come.

Like socialism in general, and like all other social movements, anarchism was born *among the people;* and it will continue to be full of life and creative power only as long as it remains a thing of the people.

At all times two tendencies were continually at war in human society. On the one hand, the masses were developing in the form of customs a number of institutions which were necessary to make social life at all possible—to insure peace amongst men, to settle any disputes that might arise, and to help one another in everything requiring cooperative effort. The savage clan at its earliest stage, the village community, the hunters', and later on, the industrial guilds of the free town-republics of the middle ages, the beginnings of international law that these cities worked out to settle their mutual relations in those early periods, and many other institutions,—were elaborated, not by legislators, but by the creative power of the people.

And at all times, too, there appeared sorcerers, prophets, priests and heads of military organizations, who endeavored to establish and to strengthen their authority over the people. They supported one another, concluded alliances in order that they might reign over the people, hold them in subjection and compel them to work for the masters.

Anarchism is obviously the representative of the first tendency—that is, of the creative, constructive power of the people themselves who aimed at developing institutions of common law in order to protect them from the power-seeking minority. By means of the same popular creative power and constructive activity, based upon modern science and technique, anarchism tries now as well to develop institutions which would insure a free evolution of society. In this sense, therefore, anarchists and governmentalists have existed through all historic times.

Then again it always happened that institutions—even those established originally with the object of securing equality, peace and mutual aid—in the course of time became petrified, lost their original meaning, came under the control of the ruling minority, and became in the end a constraint upon the individual in his endeavors for further development. Then men would rise against these institutions. But while some of these discontented endeavored to throw off the yoke of the old institutions—of caste, commune or guild —only in order that they themselves might rise over the rest and enrich themselves at their expense, others aimed at a modification of the institutions in the interest of all, especially in order to shake off the authority which had fixed its hold upon society. All really serious reformers—political, religious, and economic—have belonged to this class. And among them there always appeared persons who, without waiting for the time when all their fellow-countrymen, or even a majority of them, shall have become imbued with the same views, moved onward in the struggle against oppression, in mass where it was possible, and single-handed where it could not be done otherwise. These were the revolutionists, and them too we meet at all times.

But the revolutionists themselves generally appeared under two different aspects. Some of them in rising against the established authority endeavored not to abolish it but to take it in their own hands. In place of the authority which had become oppressive, these reformers sought to create a new one, promising that if they exercised it they would have the interests of the people dearly at heart, and would ever represent the people themselves. In this way, however, the authority of the Cæsars was established in Imperial Rome, the power of the church rose in the first centuries after the fall of the Roman Empire, and the tyranny of dictators grew up in the medieval communes at the time of their decay. On the same tendency, too, the kings and the czars availed themselves to constitute their power at the end of the feudal period. The belief in an emperor "for the people," that is, Cæsarism, has not died out even yet.

But all the while another tendency was ever manifest. At all times, beginning with ancient Greece, there were persons and popular movements that aimed not at the substitution of one government for another, but at the abolition of authority altogether. They proclaimed the supreme rights of the individual and the people, and endeavored to free popular institutions from forces which were foreign and harmful to them, in order that the unhampered creative genius of the people might remould these institutions in accordance with the new requirements. In the history of the ancient Greek republics, and especially in that of the medieval commonwealths, we find numerous examples of this struggle. In this sense, therefore, Jacobinists and anarchists have existed at all times among reformers and revolutionists.

In past ages there were even great popular movements of this latter (anarchist) character. Many thousands of people then rose against authority—its tools, its courts and its laws

—and proclaimed the supreme rights of man. Discarding all written laws, the promoters of these movements endeavored to establish a new society based on equality and labor and on the government of each by his own conscience. In the Christian movement against Roman law, Roman government, Roman morality (or, rather, Roman immorality), which began in Judea in the reign of Augustus, there undoubtedly existed much that was essentially anarchistic. Only by degrees it degenerated into an ecclesiastical movement, modeled upon the ancient Hebrew church and upon Imperial Rome itself, which killed the anarchistic germ, assumed Roman governmental forms, and became in time the chief bulwark of government authority, slavery, and oppression.

Likewise, in the Anabaptist movement (which really laid the foundation for the Reformation) there was a considerable element of anarchism. But, stifled as it was by those of the reformers who, under Luther's leadership, joined the princes against the revolting peasants, it died out after wholesale massacres of the peasants had been carried out in Holland and Germany. Thereupon the moderate reformers degenerated by degrees into those compromisers between conscience and government who exist today under the name of Protestants.

Anarchism consequently, to summarize, owes its origin to the constructive, creative activity of the people, by which all institutions of communal life were developed in the past, and to a protest—a revolt against the external force which had thrust itself upon these institutions; the aim of this protest being to give new scope to the creative activity of the people in order that it might work out the necessary institutions with fresh vigor.

In our own time anarchism arose from the same critical and revolutionary protest that called forth socialism in general. Only that some of the socialists, having reached the negation of capital and of our social organization based upon the exploitation of labor, went no further. They did not denounce what in our oponion constitutes the chief bulwark of capital; namely, government and its chief supports: centralization, law (always written by a minority in the interest of that minority), and courts of justice (established mainly for the defense of authority and capital).

Anarchism does not exclude these institutions from its criticism. It attacks not only capital, but also the main sources of the power of capitalism: law, authority, and the State.

But, though anarchism, like all other revolutionary movements, was born among the people—in the struggles of real life, and not in the philosopher's studio,—it is none the less important to know what place it occupies among the various scientific and philosophic streams of thought now prevalent: what is its relation to them; upon which of them principally does it rest; what method it employs in its researches—in other words, to which school of philosophy of law it belongs, and to which of the now existing tendencies in science it has the greatest affinity.

THE PLACE OF ANARCHISM IN MODERN SCIENCE

Anarchism is a world-concept based upon a mechanical explanation of all phenomena, embracing the whole of nature —that is, including in it the life of human societies and their economic, political, and moral problems. Its method of investigation is that of the exact natural sciences, and, if it pretends to be scientific, every conclusion it comes to must be verified by the method by which every scientific conclusion must be verified. Its aim is to construct a synthetic philosophy comprehending in one generalization all the phenomena of nature—and therefore also the life of societies.

It is therefore natural that to most of the questions of modern life anarchism should give new answers, and hold with regard to them a position differing from those of all political and to a certain extent of all socialistic parties which have not yet freed themselves from the metaphysical fictions of old.

Of course the elaboration of a complete mechanical world-conception has hardly been begun in its sociological part—in that part, that is, which deals with the life and the evolution of societies. But the little that has been done undoubtedly bears a marked though often not fully conscious character. In the domain of philosophy of law, in the theory of morality, in political economy, in history, both of nations and institutions, anarchism has already shown that it will not content itself with metaphysical conclusions, but will seek in every case a basis in the realm of natural science.

In the same way as the metaphysical conceptions of a Universal Spirit, or of a Creative Force in Nature, the Incarnation of the Idea, Nature's Goal, the Aim of Existence, the Unknowable, Mankind (conceived as having a separate spiritualized existence), and so on—in the same way as all these have been brushed aside by the materialist philosophy of today, while the embryos of generalizations concealed beneath these misty terms are being translated into the concrete language of natural sciences,—so we proceed in dealing with the facts of social life. Here also we try to sweep away the metaphysical cobwebs, and to see what embryos of generalizations—if any—may have been concealed beneath all sorts of misty words.

When the metaphysicians try to convince the naturalist that the mental and moral life of man develops in accordance with certain "In-dwelling Laws of the Spirit," the latter shrugs his shoulders and continues his physiological study of the phenomena of life, of intelligence, and of emotions and passions, with a view to showing that they can all be resolved into chemical and physical phenomena. He endeavors to discover the natural laws on which they are based. Similarly, when the anarchists are told, for instance, that every development consists of a thesis, an antithesis, and a synthesis; or that "the object of law is the establishment of justice, which represents the realization of the highest idea;" or, again, when they are asked what, in their opinion, is "the object of life?", they, too, simply shrug their shoulders and wonder how, at the present state of development of natural science, old-fashioned people can still be found who continue to believe in "words" like these and still express themselves in the language of primitive anthropomorphism (the conception of nature as a thing governed by a being endowed with human attributes). Anarchists are not to be deceived by sonorous phrases, because they know that these words simply conceal either ignorance—that is, uncompleted investigation—or, what is much worse, mere superstition. They therefore pass on and continue their study of past and present social ideas and institutions according to the scientific method of induction. And in doing so they find of course that the development of social life is incomparably more complicated, and incomparably more interesting for practical purposes, than we should be led to believe if we judged by metaphysical formulæ.

We have heard much of late about "the dialectic method," which was recommended for formulating the socialist ideal. Such a method we do not recognize, neither would the modern natural sciences have anything to do with it. "The dialectic method" reminds the modern naturalist of something long since passed—of something outlived and now happily forgotten by science. The discoveries of the nineteenth century in mechanics, physics, chemistry, biology, physical psychology, anthropology, psychology of nations, etc., were made —not by the dialectic method, but by the natural-scientific method, the method of induction and deduction. And since man is part of nature, and since the life of his "spirit", personal as well as social, is just as much a phenomenon of nature as is the growth of a flower or the evolution of social life amongst the ants and the bees, there is no cause for suddenly changing our method of investigation when we pass from the flower to man, or from a settlement of beavers to a human town.

The inductive method has proved its merits so well, that the nineteenth century, which has applied it, has caused science to advance more in a hundred years than it had advanced

during the two thousand years that went before. And when
in the second half of the century this method began to be
applied to the investigation of human society, no point was
ever reached where it was found necessary to abandon it and
again adopt medieval scholasticism. Besides, when philistine
naturalists, seemingly basing their arguments on "Darwinism," began to teach, "Crush whoever is weaker than yourself,
such is the law of nature," it was easy for us to prove first,
that this was *not* Darwin's conclusion, and by the same scientific method to show that these scientists were on the
wrong path; that no such law exists: that the life of animals
teaches us something entirely different, and that their conclusions were absolutely unscientific. They were just as
unscientific as for instance the assertion that the inequality
of wealth is a law of nature, or that capitalism is the most
advantageous form of social life calculated to promote progress. Precisely this natural-scientific method applied to economic facts, enables us to prove that the so-called "laws" of
middle-class sociology, including also their political economy,
are not laws at all, but simply guesses, or mere assertions
which have never been verified at all.

Moreover every investigation bears fruit only when it has
a definite aim—when it is undertaken for the purpose of ob-
taining an answer to a definite and clearly-worded question.
And it is the more fruitful the more clearly the explorer
sees the connection that exists between his problem and his
general concept of the universe. The better he understands
the importance of the problem in the general concept, the
easier will the answer be. The question then which anarchism puts to itself may be stated thus: "What forms of
social life assure to a given society, and then to mankind
generally, the greatest amount of happiness, and hence also
the greatest amount of vitality?" "What forms of social
life are most likely to allow this amount of happiness to grow
and to develop, quantitatively as well as qualitatively,—
that is, to become more complete and more varied?" (from
which, let us note in passing, a definition of *progress* is

derived). The desire to promote evolution in this direction determines the scientific as well as the social and artistic activity of the anarchist. And this activity, in its turn, precisely on account of its falling in with the development of society in this direction, becomes a source of increased vitality, vigor, sense of oneness with mankind and it best vital forces.

It therefore becomes a source of increased vitality and happiness for the individual.

THE ANARCHIST IDEAL AND THE PRECEDING REVOLUTIONS

Anarchism originated, as has already been said, from the demands of practical life.

At the time of the great French Revolution of 1789-1793, Godwin had the opportunity of himself seeing how the govermental authority created during the revolution and by the revolution itself acted as a retarding force upon the revolutionary movement. And he knew too what was then taking place in England, under cover of Parliament,—the confiscation of public lands, the kidnapping of poor workhouse children by factory agents and their deportation to weavers' mills, where they perished wholesale. He understood that a government, even the government of the "One and Undivided" Jacobinist Republic would not bring about the necessary revolution; that the revolutionary government itself, from the very fact of its being a guardian of the State, and of the privileges every State has to defend, was an obstacle to emancipation; that to insure the success of the revolution, people ought to part, first of all, with their belief in law, authority, uniformity, order, property, and other superstitions inherited by us from our servile past. And with this purpose in view he wrote *Political Justice*.

The theorist of anarchism who followed Godwin—Proudhon—had himself lived through the Revolution of 1848 and had seen with his own eyes the crimes perpetrated by the revolutionary republican government, and the impotence of state socialism. Fresh from the impressions of what he had witnessed, Proudhon penned his admirable works, *A General Idea of the Social Revolution* and *Confessions of a Revolutionist*, in which he boldly advocated the abolition of the State and proclaimed anarchism.

And finally the idea of anarchism reappeared again in the International Working Men's Association, after the revolution that was attempted in the Paris Commune of 1871. The eyes of many were opened by the complete failure of the Council of the Commune and its incapacity to act as a revolutionary body—although it consisted, in due proportion, of representatives of every revolutionary faction of the time—and, on the other hand, by the incapacity of the London General Council of the International and its ludicrous and even harmful pretension to direct the Paris insurrection by orders sent from England. They led many members of the International, including Bakunin, to reflect upon the harmfulness of every kind of authority, of government—even when it had been as freely elected as that of the Commune and the International Working Men's Association. A few months later the resolution, passed by the same General Council of the Association at a secret conference held in London in 1871 instead of at an annual congress, made the dangers of having a government in the International still more evident. By this dire resolution they decided to turn the entire labor movement into another channel and to convert it from an economic revolutionary movement—from a direct struggle of the workingmen's organizations against capitalism—into an elective parliamentary and political movement. This decision led to open revolt on the part of the Italian, Spanish, Swiss, and partly also of the Belgian Federations against the London General Council, and out of this rebellion modern anarchism subsequently developed.

Every time, then, the anarchist movement sprang up in response to the lessons of actual life and originated from the practical tendencies of events. And, under the impulse thus given it, anarchism set to work out its theoretic, scientific basis. Scientific—not in the sense of adopting an incomprehensible terminology, or by clinging to ancient metaphysics, but in the sense of finding a basis for its principles in the natural sciences of the time, and of becoming one of their departments.

At the same time it worked out its ideal. No struggle can be successful if it does not render itself a clear and concise account of its aim. No destruction of the existing order is possible, if at the time of the overthrow, or of the struggle leading to the overthrow, the idea of what is to take the place of what is to be destroyed is not always present in the mind. Even the theoretical criticism of the existing conditions is impossible, unless the critic has in his mind a more or less distinct picture of what he would have in place of the existing state. Consciously or unconsciously, the *ideal,* the conception of something better is forming in the mind of everyone who criticizes social institutions.

This is even more the case with a man of action. To tell people, "First let us abolish autocracy or capitalism, and then we will discuss what to put in its place," means simply to deceive oneself and others. And *power* is never created by deception. The very man who deprecates ideals and sneers at them always has, nevertheless, some ideal of what he would like to take the place of what he is attacking. Among those who work for the abolition—let us say, of autocracy—some inevitably think of a constitution like that of England or Germany, while others think of a republic, either placed under the powerful dictatorship of their own party or modeled after the French empire-republic, or, again, of a federal republic as in the United States.

And when people attack capitalism, they always have a certain conception, a vague or definite idea, of what they hope to see in the place of capitalism: State capitalism, or some sort of state communism, or a federation of free communist association for the production, the exchange, and the consumption of commodities.

Every party thus has its ideal of the future, which serves

it as a criterion in all events of political and economic life, as well as a basis for determining its proper modes of action. Anarchism, too, has conceived its own ideal; and this very ideal has led it to find its own immediate aims and its own methods of action different from those of all other political parties and also to some extent from those of the socialist parties which have retained the old Roman and ecclesiastic ideals of governmental organization.

It is seen from the foregoing that a variety of considerations, historical, ethnological, and economic, have brought the anarchists to conceive a society very different from what is considered as an ideal by the authoritarian political parties. The anarchists conceive a society in which all the mutual relations of its members are regulated, not by laws, not by authorities, whether self-imposed or elected, but by mutual agreements between the members of that society and by a sum of social customs and habits—not petrified by law, routine, or superstition, but continually developing and continually readjusted in accordance with the ever-growing requirements of a free life stimulated by the progress of science, invention, and the steady growth of higher ideals.

No ruling authorities, then. No government of man by man; no crystallization and immobility, but a continual evolution—such as we see in nature. Free play for the individual, for the full development of his individual gifts—*for his individualization*. In other words, no actions are *imposed* upon the individual by a fear of punishment; none is required from him by society, but those which receive his free acceptance. *In a society of equals* this would be quite sufficient for preventing those unsociable actions that might be harmful to other individuals and to society itself, and for favoring the steady moral growth of that society.

This is the conception developed and advocated by the anarchists.

Of course, up till now no society has existed which would have realized these principles in full, although the striving towards a partial realization of such principles has always been at work in mankind. We may say, therefore, that anarchism is a certain *ideal* of society and that this ideal is different from the ideal of society which has hitherto been advocated by most philosophers, scientists, and leaders of political parties, who pretended to rule mankind and to govern men.

But it would not be fair to describe such a conception as a Utopia, because the word "Utopia" in our current language conveys the idea of something that *cannot* be realized.

Taken in its usual current sense, therefore, the word "Utopia" ought to be limited to those conceptions only which are based on merely theoretical reasonings as to what is *desirble* from the writers' point of view, but not on what *is already developing* in human agglomerations. Such were, for instance, the Utopias of the Catholic Empire of the Popes, the Napoleonic Empire, the Messianism of Mickiewicz, and so in. But it cannot be applied to a conception of society which is based, as anarchism is, on an analysis of *tendencies of an evolution that is already going on in society,* and on *inductions* therefrom as to the future—those tendencies which have been, as we saw, for thousands of years the mainspring for the growth of sociable habits and customs, known in science under the name of customary law, and which affirm themselves more and more definitely in modern society.

When we look into the origin of the anarchist conception of society, we see that it has had a double origin: the criticism, on the one side, of the hierachical organizations and the authoritarian conceptions of society; and on the other side, the analysis of the tendencies that are seen in the progressive movements of mankind, both in the past, and still more so at the present time.

GROWTH OF ANARCHIST IDEAS

From the remotest, stone-age antiquity, men must have realized the evils that resulted from letting some of them acquire personal authority—even if they were the most intelligent, the bravest, or the wisest. Consequently they developed in the primitive clan, the village community, the medieval guild (neighbors' guilds, arts and crafts' guilds, traders', hunters', and so on), and finally in the free medieval city, such institutions as enabled them to resist the encroachments upon their life and fortunes both of those strangers who conquered them, and of those clansmen of their own who endeavored to establish their personal authority. The same popular tendency was self evident in the religious movements of the masses in Europe during the earlier portions of the Reform movement and its Hussite and Anabaptist forerunners. At a much later period, namely in 1793, the same current of thought and of action found its expression in the strikingly independent, freely federated activity of the "Sections" of Paris and all great cities and many small "Communes" during the French Revolution. And later still, the labor combinations which developed in England and France, notwithstanding Draconic laws, as soon as the factory system began to grow up, were an outcome of the same popular resistance to the growing power of the few —the capitalists in this case.

These were the main popular anarchist currents which we know of in history, and it is self-evident that these movements could not but find their expression in literature. So they did, beginning with Lao-tse in China, and some of the earliest Greek philosophers (Aristippus and the Cynics; Zeno and some of the Stoics). However, being born in the masses, and not in any centers of learning, these popular movements, both when they were revolutionary and when they were deeply constructive, found little sympathy among the learned men—far less than the authoritarian hierarchical tendencies.

It was Godwin, in his *Enquiry Concerning Political Justice,* who stated in 1793 in a quite definite form the political and economic principles of anarchism. He did not use the word "anarchism" itself, but he very forcibly laid down its principles, boldly attacking the laws, proving the uselessness of the State, and maintaining that only with the abolition of courts would true *justice*—the only real foundation of all society—become possible. As regards property, he openly advocated communism.

Proudhon was the first to use the word "an-archy" (no-government) and to submit to a powerful criticism the fruitless efforts of men to give themselves such a government as would prevent the rich ones from dominating the poor, and at the same time always remain under the control of the governed ones. The repeated attempts of France, since 1793, at giving herself such a constitution, and the failure of the Revolution of 1848, gave him rich material for his criticism.

Being an enemy of all forms of state socialism, of which the communists of those years (the forties and fifties of the nineteenth century) represented a mere subdivision, Proudhon fiercely attacked all such attempts; and taking Robert Owen's system of labor checks representing hours of labor, he developed a conception of *mutualism*, in which any sort of political government would be useless.

The values of all the commodities being measured by the amount of labor necessary to produce them, all the exchanges between the producers could be carried on by means of a national bank, which would accept payment in labor checks —a clearing house establishing the daily balance of exchanges between the thousands of branches of this bank.

The services exchanged by different men would thus be *equivalent;* and as the bank would be able to lend the labor checks' money without interest, and every association would be able to borrow it on payment of only one per cent or less to cover the administration costs, capital would lose its pernicious power; it could be used no more as an instrument of exploitation.

Proudhon gave to the system of mutualism a very full development in connection with his anti-government and anti-state ideas; but it must be said that the mutualist portion of his program had already been developed in England by Willian Thompson (he was a mutualist prior to his becoming a communist) and the English followers of Thompson—John Gray (1825, 1831) and J. F. Bray (1839).

In the United States, the same direction was represented by Josiah Warren, who, after having taken part in Robert Owen's colony, "New Harmony," turned against communism, and in 1827 founded, in Cincinnati, a "store" in which goods were exchanged on the principle of time-value and labor checks. Such institutions remained in existence up till 1865 under the names of "equity stores," "equity village," and "house of equity."

The same ideas of labor-value and exchange at labor-cost were advocated in Germany, in 1843 and 1845, by Moses Hess and Karl Grün; and in Switzerland by Wilhelm Marr, who opposed the authoritarian communist teachings of Weitling.

On the other side, in opposition to the strongly authoritarian communism of Weitling, which had found a great number of adherents among workingmen in Germany, there appeared in 1845 the work of a German Hegelian, Max Stirner (Johann Kaspar Schmidt was his real name), *The Ego and His Own*, which was lately rediscovered, so to say, by J. H. Mackay, and very much spoken of in anarchist circles as a sort of manifesto of the individualist anarchists.

Stirner's work is a revolt against both the State and the new tyranny which would have been imposed upon man if authoritarian communism were introduced. Reasoning on Hegelian metaphysical lines, Stirner preaches, therefore, the rehabilitation of the "I" and the supremacy of the individual; and he comes in this way to advocate complete "a-moralism" (no morality) and an "association of egoists."

It is easy to see, however,—as has been indicated more than once by anarchist writers, and lately by the French professor, V. Basch, in an interesting work, *Anarchist Individualism: Max Stirner* (1904, in French)—that this sort of individualism, aiming as it does at the "full development," not of all members of society, but of those only who would be considered as the most gifted ones, without caring for the right of full development for *all*—is merely a disguised return towards the now-existing education-monopoly of the few. It simply means a "right to their full development" for the privileged minorities. But, as such monopolies cannot be maintained otherwise than under the protection of a monopolist legislation and an organized coercion by the State, the claims of these individualists necessarily end in a return to the state idea and to that same coercion which they so fiercely attack themselves. Their position is thus the same as that of Spencer, and of all the so-called "Manchester school" of economists, who also begin by a severe criticism of the State and end in its full recognition in order to maintain the property monopolies, of which the State is the necessary stronghold.

Such was the growth of anarchist ideas, from the French Revolution and Godwin to Proudhon. The next step was made within the great "International Working Men's Association," which so much inspired the working-classes with hope, and the middle classes with terror, in the years 1868-1870—just before the Franco-German War.

That this association was not founded by Marx, or any other personality, as the hero-worshippers would like us to believe, is self-evident. It was the outcome of the meeting, at London, in 1862, of a delegation of French workingmen who had come to visit the Second International Exhibition, with representatives of British Trade Unions and radicals who received that delegation.

ANARCHISM AND THE FREE COMMUNE

With the Franco-German War came the crushing defeat of France, the provisory government of Gambetta and Thiers, and the Commune of Paris, followed by similar attempts at Saint Etienne in France, and at Barcelona and Cartagena in Spain. And these popular insurrections brought into evidence what the *political* aspect of a social revolution ought to be.

Not a democratic republic, as was said in 1848, but *the free, independent Communist Commune.*

The Paris Commune itself suffered from the confusion of ideas as to the economic and political steps to be taken by the revolution, which prevailed, as we saw, in the international. Both the Jacobinists and the communalists—*i.e.* the centralists and the federalists—were represented in the uprising, and necessarily they came into conflict with each other. The most warlike elements were the Jacobinists and the Blanquists, but the economic, communist ideals of Babeuf had already faded among their middle-class leaders. They treated the economic question as a secondary one, which would be attended to later on, *after* the triumph of the Commune, and this idea prevailed. But the crushing defeat which soon followed, and the bloodthirsty revenge taken by the middle class, proved once more that the triumph of a popular commune was materially impossible without a parallel triumph of the people in the economic field.

For the Latin nations, the Commune of Paris, followed by similar attempts at Cartagena and Barcelona, settled the ideas of the revolutionary proletariat.

This was the form that the social revolution must take— the independent commune. Let all the country and all the world be against it; but once its inhabitants have decided that they *will* communalize the consumption of commodities, their exchange, and their production, *they must realize it among themselves.* And in so doing, they will find such forces as never could be called into life and to the service of a great cause, if they attempted to take in the sway of the revolution the whole country including its most backward or indifferent regions. Better to fight such strongholds of reaction openly than to drag them as so many chains rivetted to the feet of the fighter.

More than that. We made one step more. We understood that if no central government was needed to rule the independent communes, if the national government is thrown overboard and national unity is obtained by free federation, then a central *municipal* government becomes equally useless and noxious. The same federative principle would do within the commune.

The uprising of the Paris Commune thus brought with it the solution of a question which tormented every true revolutionist. Twice had France tried to bring about some sort of socialist revolution by imposing it through a central government more or less disposed to accept it: in 1793-94, when she tried to introduce *l'égalité de fait*—real, economic equality —by means of strong Jacobinist measures; and in 1848, when she tried to impose a "Democratic Socialist Republic." And each time she failed. But now a new solution was indicated: the free commune must do it on its own territory, and with this grew up a new ideal—anarchism.

We understood then that at the bottom of Proudhon's *Idée Générale sur la Revolution au Dix-neuvième Siècle* (unfortunately not yet translated into English) lay a deeply *practical* idea—that of anarchism. And in the Latin countries the thought of the more advanced men began to work in this direction.

Alas! in Latin countries only: in France, in Spain, in Italy, in the French-speaking part of Switzerland, and the Wallonic part of Belgium. The Germans, on the contrary, drew from their victory over France quite another lesson and quite different ideals—the worship of the centralized State.

The centralized State, hostile even to national tendencies of independence; the power of centralization and a strong central authority—these were the lessons they drew from the victories of the German Empire, and to these lessons they cling even now, without understanding that this was only a victory of a military mass, of the universal obligatory military service of the Germans over the recruiting system of the French and over the rottenness of the second Napoleonic Empire approaching a revolution which would have benefitted mankind, if it had not been hindered by the German invasion.

In the Latin countries, then, the lesson of the Paris and

the Cartagena communes laid the foundations for the development of anarchism. And the authoritarian tendencies of the General council of the International Working Men's Association, which soon became evident and worked fatally against the unity of action of the great association, still more reinforced the anarchist current of thought. The more so as that council, led by Marx, Engels, and some French Blanquist refugees— all pure Jacobinists—used its powers to make a *coup d'état* in the International. It substituted in the program of the association parliamentary political action *in lieu* of the economic struggle of labor against capital, which hitherto had been the essence of the International. And in this way it provoked an open revolt against its authority in the Spanish, Italian, Jurassic, and East Belgian Federations, and among a certain section of the English Internationalists.

BAKUNIN AND THE STATE

In Mikhail Bakunin, the anarchist tendency, now growing within the International, found a powerful, gifted, and inspired exponent; while round Bakunin and his Jura friends gathered a small circle of talented young Italians and Spaniards, who further developed his ideas. Largely drawing upon his wide knowledge of history and philosophy, Bakunin established in a series of powerful pamphlets and letters the leading principles of modern anarchism.

The complete abolition of the State, with all its organization and ideals, was the watchword he boldly proclaimed. The State has been in the past a historical necessity which grew out of the authority won by the religious castes. But its complete extinction is now, in its turn, a historical necessity because the State represents the negation of liberty and spoils even what is undertakes to do for the sake of general well-being. All legislation made within the State, even when it issues from the so-called universal suffrage, has to be repudiated because it always has been made with regard to the interests of the privileged classes. Every nation, every region, every commune must be absolutely free to organize itself, politically and economically, as it likes, so long as it is not a menace to its neighbors. "Federalism" and "autonomy" are not enough. These are only words, used to mask the State authority. Full independence of the communes, their free federation, and the social revolution within the communes—this was, he proved, the ideal now rising before our civilization from the mists of the past. The individual understands that he will be really free in proportion only as all the others round him become free.

As to his economic conceptions, Bakunin was at heart a communist; but, in common with his federalist comrades of the International, and as a concession to the antagonism to communism that the authoritarian communists had inspired in France, he described himself as a "collectivist anarchist." But, of course, he was not a "collectivist" in the sense of Vidal or Pecqueur, or of their modern followers, who simply aim at "state capitalism;" he understood it in the abovementioned sense of *not* determining in advance what form of distribution the producers should adopt in their different groups—whether the communist solution, or the labor checks, or equal salaries, or any other method. And with these views, he was an ardent preacher of the social revolution, the near approach of which was foreseen then by all socialists, and which he foretold in fiery words.

The State is an institution which was developed for the very purpose of establishing monopolies in favor of the slave and serf owners, the landed proprietors, canonic and laic, the merchant guilds and the money-lenders, the kings, the military commanders, the noblemen, and finally, in the nineteenth century, the industrial capitalist, whom the State supplied with "hands" driven away from the land. Consequently the State would be, to say the least, a useless institution, once these monopolies ceased to exist. *Life would be simplified,* once the mechanism created for the exploitation of the poor by the rich would have been done away with.

The idea of independent communes for the territorial organization, and of federations of trade unions for the organization of men in accordance with their different functions, gave a *concrete* conception of society regenerated by a social revolution. There remained only to add to these two modes of organization a third, which we saw rapidly developing during the last fifty years, since a little liberty was conquered in this direction: the thousands upon thousands of free combines and societies growing up everywhere for the satisfaction of all possible and imaginable needs, economic, sanitary, and educational; from mutual protection, for the propaganda of ideas, for art, for amusement, and so on. All of them covering each other, and all of them always ready to meet the new needs by new organizations and adjustments.

More than that. It begins to be understood now that if human societies go on devoloping on these lines, coercion and punishment must necessarily fall into decay. The greatest obstacle to the maintenance of a certain moral level in our present societies lies in the absence of social equality. Without *real* equality, the sense of justice can never be universally developed, because *justice implies the recognition of equality;* while in a society in which the principles of justice would not be contradicted at every step by the existing inequalities of rights and possibilities of development, they would be bound to spread and to enter into the habits of the people.

In such a case the individual would be *free,* in the sense that his freedom would not be limited any more by *fear:* by the fear of a social or a mystical punishment, or by obedience, either to other men reputed to be his superiors, or to mystical and metaphysical entities—which leads in both cases to intellectual servility (one of the greatest curses of mankind) and to the lowering of the moral level of men.

In free surroundings based upon equality, man might with full confidence let himself be guided by his own reason (which, of course, by necessity, would bear the stamp of his social surroundings). And he might also attain the full development of his individuality; while the "individualism" considered now by middle-class intellectuals as the *means* for the development of the better-gifted individuals, is, as every one may himself see, the chief *obstacle* to this development. Not only because, with a low productivity, which is kept at a low level by capitalism and the State, the immense majority of gifted men have neither the leisure nor the chance to develop their higher gifts; but also because those who have that leisure are recognized and rewarded by the present society on the condition of never going "too far" in their criticisms of that society, and especially never going over to acts that may lead to its destruction, or even to a serious reform. Those only are allowed to attain a certain "development of their individualities" who are not dangerous in this respect—those who are merely "interesting," but not dangerous to the Philistine.

The anarchists, we have said, build their previsions of the future upon those data which are supplied by the observation of life at the present time.

Thus, when we examine into the tendencies that have prevailed in the life of civilized countries since the end of the eighteenth century, we certainly do not fail to see how strong the centralizing and authoritarian tendency was during that time, both among the middle classes and those workingmen who have been educated in the ideas of the middle classes and now strive to enter the ranks of their present rulers and exploiters.

But at the same time it is a fact that the anti-centralist and anti-militarist ideas, as well as the ideas of a free understanding, grow stronger and stronger nowadays both among the workingmen and the better educated and more or less intellectually free portions of the middle classes—especially in Western Europe.

I have shown, indeed, elsewhere (in *The Conquest of Bread* and in *Mutual Aid*) how strong at the present time is the tendency to constitute freely, *outside the State and the churches,* thousands upon thousands of free organizations for all sorts of needs: economic (agreements between the railway companies, the labor syndicates, trusts of employers, agricultural cooperation, cooperation for export, etc.), political, intellectual, artistic, educational, and so on. What formerly belonged without a shadow of doubt to the functions of the State, or the church, enters now into the domain of free organization.

This tendency develops with a striking rapidity under our very eyes. It was sufficient that a breath of emancipation should have slightly limited the powers of church and State in their never-satisfied tendency towards further extension—and voluntary organizations have already germinated by the thousand. And we may be sure that every new limitation that may be imposed upon State and church—the two inveterate enemies of freedom—will still further widen the sphere of action of the free organizations.

Future progress lies in this direction, and anarchism works precisely that way.

ECONOMIC VIEWS OF ANARCHISM

Passing now to the economic views of anarchists, three different conceptions must be distinguished.

So long as socialism was understood in its wide, generic, and true sense—as an effort to *abolish* the exploitation of labor by capital—the anarchists were marching hand-in-hand with the socialists of that time. But they were compelled to separate from them when the socialists began to say that there is no possibility of *abolishing* capitalist exploitation within the lifetime of our generation: that *during that phase of economic evolution which we are now living through* we have only to *mitigate* the exploitation, and to impose upon the capitalists certain legal limitations.

Contrarily to this tendency of the present-day socialists, we maintain that already now, without waiting for the coming of new phases and forms of the capitalist exploitation of labor, we must work for its *abolition*. We must, already now, tend to transfer all that is needed for production—the soil, the mines, the factories, the means of communication,

and the means of existence, too—from the hands of the
individual capitalist into those of the communities of producers and consumers.

As for the *political* organization—*i. e.*, the forms of the
commonwealth in the midst of which an economic revolution could be accomplished—we entirely differ from all the
sections of state socialists in that we do not see in the system
of *state capitalism*, which is now preached under the name of
collectivism, a solution of the social question. We see in the
organization of the posts and telegraphs, in the State railways,
and the like—which are represented as illustrations of a society without capitalists—nothing but a new, perhaps improved, but still undesirable form of the wage system. We
even think that such a solution of the social problem would
so much run against the present libertarian tendencies of
civilized mankind, that it simply would be unrealizable.

We maintain that the State organization, having been the
force to which the minorities resorted for establishing and
organizing their power over the masses, cannot be the force
which will serve to destroy these privileges. The lessons of
history tell us that a new form of economic life always calls
forth a new form of political organization; and a socialist
society (whether communist or collectivist) cannot be an
exception to this rule. Just as the churches cannot be utilized
for freeing man from his old superstitions, and just as the
feeling of human solidarity will have to find other channels
for its expression besides the churches, so also the economic
and political liberation of man will have to create new forms
for its expression in life, instead of those established by the
State.

Consequently, the chief aim of anarchism is to awaken
those constructive powers of the laboring masses of the people
which at all great moments of history came forward to accomplish the necessary changes, and which, aided by the now
accumulated knowledge, will accomplish the change that is
called forth by all the best men of our own time.

This is also why the anarchists refuse to accept the functions of legislators or servants of the State. We know that the social revolution will not be accomplished by means of *laws*. Laws can only *follow* the accomplished facts; and even if they honestly do follow them—which usually is *not* the case—a law remains a dead letter so long as there are not on the spot the living forces required for making of the *tendencies* expressed in the law an accomplished *fact*.

On the other hand, since the times of the International Working Men's Association, the anarchists have always advised taking an active part in those workers' organizations which carry on the *direct* struggle of labor against capital and its protector,—the State.

Such a struggle, they say, better than any other indirect means, permits the worker to obtain some temporary improvements in the present conditions of work, while it opens his eyes to the evil that is done by capitalism and the State that supports it, and wakes up his thoughts concerning the possibility of organizing consumption, production, and exchange without the intervention of the capitalist and the State.

REMUNERATION OF LABOR

The opinions of the anarchists concerning the form which *the remuneration of labor* may take in a society freed from the yoke of capital and State still remain divided.

To begin with, all are agreed in repudiating the new form of the wage system which would be established if the State became the owner of all the land, the mines, the factories, the railways, and so on, and the great organizer and manager of agriculture and all the industries. If these powers were added to those which the State already possesses (taxes, defence of the territory, subsidized religions, etc.), we should create a new tyranny even more terrible than the old one.

The greater number of anarchists accept the communist solution. They see that the only form of communism that would be acceptable in a civilized society is one which would exist without the continual interference of government, *i.e.*, the anarchist form. And they realize also that an anarchist society of a large size would be impossible, unless it would begin by guaranteeing to all its members a certain minimum of well-being produced in common. Communism and anarchism thus complete each other.

However, by the side of this main current there are those who see in anarchism a rehabilitation of individualism.

This last current is, in our opinion, a survival from those times when the power of production of food-stuffs and of all industrial commodities had not yet reached the perfection they have attained now. In those times communism was truly considered as equivalent to general poverty and misery, and well-being was looked at as something which is accessible to a very small number only. But this quite real and extremely important obstacle to communism exists no more. Owing to the immense productivity of human labor which has been reached nowadays in all directions—agricultural and industrial—it is quite certain, on the contrary, that a very high degree of well-being can easily be obtained in a few years by communist work.

Be this as it may, the individualist anarchists subdivide into two branches. There are, first, the pure individualists, in the sense of Max Stirner, who have lately gained some support in the beautiful poetical form of the writings of Nietzsche. But we have already said once how metaphysical and remote from real life is this "self-assertion of the individual;" how it runs against the feelings of equality of most of us; and how it brings the would-be "individualists" dangerously near to those who imagine themselves to represent a "superior breed"—those to whom we owe the State, the church, modern legislation, the police, militarism, imperialism, and all other forms of oppression.

The other branch of individualist anarchists comprises the *mutualists*, in the sense of Proudhon. However, there will always be against this system the objection that it could hardly be compatible with a system of common ownership of land and the necessaries for production. Communism in the possession of land, factories, etc. and individualism in production are too contradictory to coexist in the same society— to say nothing of the difficulty of estimating the *market* value or the *selling* value of a product by the average time that is necessary, or the time that was actually used, in producing it. To bring men to agree upon such an estimation of their work would already require a deep penetration of the communist principle into their ideas—at least, for all produce of first necessity. And if a community introduced, as a further concession to individualism, a higher payment for skilled work, or chances of promotion in a hierarchy of functionaries, this would reintroduce all those inconveniences of the present wage system which are combatted now by the workers.

To some extent the same remark applies to the American anarchist individualists who were represented in the fifties by S. P. Andrews and W. Greene, later on by Lysander Spooner, and now are represented by Benjamin Tucker, the well-known editor of the New York *Liberty*. Their ideas are partly those of Proudhon, but partly also those of Herbert Spencer. They start from the principle that the only law which is obligatory for the anarchist is to mind his own business, and not to meddle with that of others; that each individual and each group has the *right* to oppress all mankind—if they have the *force* to do so; and that if this only law, of minding one's own business, had received a *general* and *complete* application, it would offer no danger, because the rights of each individual would have been limited by the equal rights of all others.

But to reason in this way is to pay, in our opinion, too large a tribute to metaphysical dialectics, and to ignore the facts of real life. It is impossible to conceive a society in which the affairs of any one of its members would not concern many others members, if not all; still less a society in which a continual contact between its members would not have established an interest of every one towards all others, which would render it *impossible* to act without thinking of the effects which our actions may have on others.

This is why Tucker, like Spencer, after his admirable criticism of the State and a vigorous defense of the rights of the individual, comes to recognize the right of *defense* of its members by the State. But it was precisely by assuming the function of "defense" of its weaker members that the State in its historical evolution developed all its *aggressive* functions, which Spencer and Tucker have so brilliantly criticized.

This contradiction is probably the reason why anarchist individualism, while it finds followers amongst the middle-class intellectuals, does not spread amongst the workers. It must be said, however, that it renders a real service in preventing the anarchist communists from making too many concessions to the old idea of State officialism. Old ideas are so difficult to get rid of.

As to anarchist communism, it is certain that this solution wins more and more ground nowadays among those workingmen who try to get a clear conception as to the forthcoming revolutionary action. The syndicalist and trade union movements, which permit the workingmen to realize their solidarity and to feel the community of their interests much better than any elections, prepare the way for these conceptions And it is hardly too much to hope that when some serious movement for the emancipation of labor begins in Europe and America, attempts will be made, at least in the Latin countries, in the anarchist-communist direction — much deeper than anything that was done by the French nation in 1793-94.

ANARCHISM AND THE LAW

When we are told that Law (written with a capital letter) "is the objectification of Truth;" or that "the principles underlying the development of Law are the same as those underlying the development of the human spirit;"

or that "Law and Morality are identical and differ only form-
ally;" we feel as little respect for these assertions as does
Mephistopheles in Goethe's *Faust*. We are aware that those
who make such seemingly profound statements as these have
expended much thought upon these questions. But they
have taken a wrong path; and hence we see in these high-
flown sentences mere attempts at unconscious generalization
based upon inadequate foundations and confused moreover
by words chosen to hypnotize men by their obscurity. In
olden times they tried to give "Law" a divine origin; later
they began to seek a metaphysical basis for it; now, however,
we are able to study its anthropological origin. And, availing
ourselves of the results obtained by the anthropological school,
we take up the study of social customs, beginning with those
of the primitive savages, and trace the origin and the development of the laws at different epochs.

In this way we come to the conclusion already expressed,
namely, that all laws have a twofold origin, and in this very
respect differ from those institutions established by custom
which are generally recognized as the moral code of a given
society at a given time. Law confirms and crystallizes these
customs, but while doing so it takes advantage of this fact
to establish (for the most part in a disguised form) the
germs of slavery and class distinction, the authority of priest
and warrior, serfdom and various other institutions, in the
interests of the armed and would-be ruling minority. In
this way a yoke has imperceptibly been placed upon man,
of which he could only rid himself by means of subsequent
bloody revolutions. And this is the course of events down
to the present moment—even in contemporary "labor legislation" which, along with "protection of labor," covertly
introduces the idea of *compulsory* State arbitration in case of
strikes, a *compulsory* working day of so many hours, military
exploitation of the railroads during strikes, legal sanction
for the dispossession of the peasants in Ireland, and so on.
And this will continue to be so as long as *one* portion of

society goes on framing laws for *all* society, and thereby strengthens the power of the State, which forms the chief support of capitalism.

It is plain, therefore, why anarchism,—although the anarchists, more than any legislators, aspire to *Justice,* which is equivalent to *Equality,* and impossible without it,—has from the time of Godwin rejected all written *laws.*

When, however, we are told that by rejecting law we reject all morality, we answer that the very wording of this objection is to us strange and incomprehensible. It is as strange and incomprehensible to us as it would be to every naturalist engaged in the study of the phenomena of morality. In answer to this argument, we ask: "What do you really mean? Can you not translate your statements into comprehensible language?"

Now, what does a man who takes his stand on "universal law" really mean? Does he mean that *there is* in all men the conception that one ought not to do to another what he would not have done to himself—that it would be better even to return good for evil? If so, well and good. Let us, then, study the origin of these moral ideas in man, and their course of development. Let us extend our studies also to prehuman times. Then, we may analyze to what extent the idea of *Justice* implies that of *Equality.* The question is an important one, because only those who regard *others* as their equals can accept the rule, "Do not to others what you would not have done to yourself." The landlord and the slave-owner, who did not look upon "the serf" and the negro as their equals, did not recognize "the universal law" as applicable to these unhappy members of the human family. And then, if this observation of ours be correct, we shall see whether it is at all possible to inculcate morality while teaching the doctrine of inequality.

We shall finally analyze, as Mark Guyau did, the facts of self-sacrifice. And then we shall consider what has most promoted the development in man of moral feelings—first, of those which are expressed in the commandment concerning our neighbor, and then of the other feelings which lead to self-sacrifice; and after this consideration we shall be able to deduce from our study exactly what social conditions and what institutions promise the best results for the future. Is this development promoted by religion, and to what extent? Is it promoted by inequality—economic and political—and by a division into classes? Is it promoted by law? By punishment? By prisons? By the judge? The jailer? The hangman?

Let us study all this in detail, and then only may we speak again of morality and moralization by means of laws, law courts, jailers, spies, and police. But we had better give up using the sonorous words which only conceal the superficiality of our semi-learning. In their time the use of these words was, perhaps, unavoidable—their application could never have been useful. But now that we are able to approach the study of burning social questions in exactly the same manner as the gardener and the physiologist take up the study of the conditions most favorable for the growth of a plant—let us do so!

ECONOMIC LAWS

Likewise, when certain economists tell us that "in a perfectly free market the price of commodities is measured by the amount of labor socially necessary for their production," we do not take this assertion on faith because it is made by certain authorities or because it may seem to us "tremendously socialistic." It may be so, we say. But do you not notice that by this very statement you maintain that value and the necessary labor *are proportional to each other*—just as the speed of a falling body is proportional to the number of seconds it has been falling? Thus you maintain a *quantitative relation* between these two magnitudes; whereas a quantitative relation can be proved *only* by quantitative measurements. To confine yourself to the remark that the exchange-value of commodities "generally" increases when a greater expenditure of labor is required, and then to assert that *therefore* the two quantities are proportional to each other, is to make as great a mistake as the man who would assert that the quantity of rainfall is measured by the fall of the barometer below its average height. He who first observed that, generally speaking, when the barometer is falling a greater amount of rain falls than when it is rising; or, that there is a certain relation between the speed of a falling stone and the height from which it fell—that man surely made a scientific discovery. But the person who would come after him and assert that the amount of rainfall is *measured* by the fall of the barometer below its average height, or that the space through which a falling body has passed is *proportional* to the time of fall and is measured by it,—that person would not only talk nonsense, but would prove by his very words that the method of scientific research is absolutely strange to him; that his work is unscientific, full as it may be of scientific expressions. The absence of data is clearly no excuse. Hundreds if not thousands of similar relationships are known to science in which we see the dependence of one magnitude upon another—for example, the recoil of a cannon depending upon the quantity of powder in the charge, or the growth of a plant depending upon the amount of heat or light received by it. But no scientific man will presume to affirm the proportion of these magnitudes without having investigated their relations quantitatively, and still less would he represent this proportion as a scientific *law*. In most instances the dependence is very complex—as it is, indeed, in the theory of value. The necessary amount of labor and value are by no means proportional.

The same remark refers to almost every economic doctrine that is current to-day in certain circles and is being presented with wonderful naiveté as an invariable law. We not only find most of these so-called laws grossly erroneous, but maintain also that those who believe in them will themselves become convinced of their error as soon as they come to see the necessity of verifying their quantitative deductions by quantitative investigation.

Moreover, the whole of political economy appears to us in a different light from that in which it is seen by modern economists of both the middle-class and the social-democratic camps. The scientific method (the inductive method of natural sciences) being utterly unknown to them, they fail to give themselves any definite account of what constitutes "a law of nature," although they delight in using the term. They do not know—or if they know they continually forget —that every law of nature has a *conditional* character. In fact every natural law always means this: "*If* certain conditions in nature are at work, certain things will happen." "*If* one line intersects another, forming right angles on both its sides at the crossing point, the consequences will be such and such." "*If* two bodies are acted upon by such movements only as exist in interstellar space, and there is not, within measurable distance of them, a third body or a fourth body acting upon the two, then their centers of gravity will approach each other at a certain speed (the law of gravitation)." And so on. In every case there is an "*if*"—a condition.

In consequence of this, all the so-called laws and theories of political economy are in reality no more than statements of the following nature: "Granting that there are always in a country a considerable number of people who cannot subsist a month, or even a fortnight, without earning a salary and accepting for that purpose the conditions of work imposed upon them by the State, or offered to them by those whom the State recognizes as owners of land, factories, railways, etc., then the results will be so and so."

So far academic political economy has been only an enumeration of what happens under the just-mentioned conditions—without distinctly stating the conditions themselves. And then, having described *the facts* which arise in our society under these conditions, they represent to us these *facts* as rigid, *inevitable economic laws*. As to socialist political economy, although it criticizes some of these deductions, or explains others somewhat differently,—it has not yet been original enough to find a path of its own. It still follows in the old grooves, and in most cases repeats the very same mistakes. And yet, in our opinion, political economy must have an entirely different problem in view. It ought to occupy with respect to human societies a place in science similar to that held by physiology in relation to plants and animals. It must become *the physiology of society.* It should aim at *studying the needs of society and the various means, both hitherto used and available under the present state of scientific knowledge, for their satisfaction.* It should try to analyze how far the present means are expedient and satisfactory, economic or wasteful; and then, since the ultimate end of every science (as Bacon had already stated) is obviously prediction and practical application to the demands of life, it should concern itself with the discovery of means *for the satisfaction of these needs with the smallest possible waste of labor and with the greatest benefit to mankind in general.* Such means would be, in fact, mere corollaries from the relative investigation mentioned above, provided this last had been made on scientific lines.

Pursuing the same method, anarchism arrives at its own conclusions concerning the different forms of society, especially the State. It could not rest content with current metaphysical assertions like the following:

"The State is the affirmation of the idea of the highest justice in society;" or "The State is the instigation and the instrument of progress;" or, "Without the State, society is impossible." Anarchism has approached the study of the State exactly in the manner the naturalist approaches the study of social life among bees and ants, or among the migratory birds which hatch their young on the shores of subarctic lakes. It would be useless to repeat here the conclusions to which this study has brought us with reference to the history of the different political forms (and to their desirable or probable evolution in the future). If I were to do so, I should have to repeat what has been written by anarchists from the time of Godwin, and what may be found with all necessary explanations, in a whole series of books and pamphlets.

I will say only that the State is a form of social life which has developed in our European civilization, under the influence of a series of causes, only since the end of the sixteenth century. Before the sixteenth century the State, in its Roman form, did not exist—or, more exactly, it existed only in the minds of the historians who trace the genealogy of Russian autocracy to Rurik and that of France to the Merovingian kings.

Furthermore, the State (state-justice, state-church, state-army) and capitalism are, in our opinion, inseparable concepts. In history these institutions developed side by side, mutually supporting and re-enforcing each other. They are bound together, not by a mere coincidence of contemporaneous development, but by the bond of cause and effect, effect and cause. Thus the State appears to us as a society for the mutual insurance of the landlord, the warrior, the judge, and the priest, constituted in order to enable every one of them to assert his respective authority over the people and to exploit the poor.

Such was the origin of the State; such was its history; and such is its present essence.

Consequently, to imagine that capitalism may be abolished while the State is maintained, and with the aid of the State—while the latter was founded for forwarding the development of capitalism and was always growing in power and solidity, in proportion as the power of capitalism grew up—to cherish such an illusion is as unreasonable, in our opinion, as it was to expect the emancipation of labor from the church, or from Cæsarism or imperialism. Certainly, in the first half of the nineteenth century, there have been many socialists who had such dreams; but to live in the same dreamland now that we enter in the twentieth century, is really too childish.

A new form of economic organization will necessarily require a new form of political structure. And, whether the change be accomplished suddenly, by a revolution, or slowly, by the way of a gradual evolution, the two changes, political and economic, must go on abreast, hand in hand.

Each step towards economic freedom, each victory won

over capitalism will be at the same time a step towards political liberty—towards liberation from the yoke of the State by means of free agreement, territorial, professional, and functional. And each step made towards taking from the State any one of its powers and attributes will be helping the masses to win a victory over capitalism.

THE MEANS OF ACTION

It is obvious that, since anarchism differs so widely in its method of investigation and in its fundamental principles, both from the academic sociologists and from its social-democratic fraternity, it must of necessity equally differ from them all in its means of action.

Understanding law, right, and the State as we do, we cannot see any guarantee of progress, still less an approach to the required social changes, in the submission of the individual to the State. We are therefore no longer able to say, as do the superficial interpreters of social phenomena when they require the State management of industries, that modern capitalism has come into being through "the anarchy of exploitation," through "the theory of non-interference," which—we are told—the States have carried out by practicing the formula of "let them do as they like" (*laissez faire, laissez passer*). We know that this is not true. While giving the capitalist any degree of free scope to amass his wealth at the expense of the helpless laborers, the government has *nowhere* and *never* during the whole nineteenth century afforded the laborers the opportunity "to do as they pleased." The terrible revolutionary, that is, Jacobinist, convention treated strikes as a coalition and legislated: "For strikes, for forming a State within the State—death!" In 1813 people were hanged in England for going out on strike, and in 1831 they were deported to Australia for forming the Great Trades' Union (Union of all Trades) of Robert Owen. In the sixties people were still condemned to hard labor for participating in strikes, and even now trade unions are prosecuted for damages for picketing—for having dissuaded laborers from working in times of strike. What is one to say, then, of France, Belgium, Switzerland and especially of Germany and Russia? It is needless also to tell how by means of taxes the State brings laborers to the verge of poverty which puts them body and soul in the power of the factory boss; how the communal lands have been robbed from the people. Or must we remind the reader how even at the present moment, all the States without exception are creating directly all kinds of monopolies—in railroads, tramways, telephones, gasworks, waterworks, electric works, schools, etc. In short, the system of non-interference—*laissez faire*—has never been applied for one single hour by any government.

And therefore if it is permissible for middle-class economists to affirm that the system of "non-interference" is practiced (since they endeavor to prove that poverty is a law of nature), it is simply shameful that socialists should speak thus to the workers. *Freedom to oppose exploitation has so far never and nowhere existed.* Everywhere it had to be taken by force, step by step, at the cost of countless sacrifices. "Non-interference," and more than non-interference,—direct support, help and protection,—existed *only* in the interests of the exploiters. *Nor could it be otherwise.* The mission of the church has been to hold the people in intellectual slavery. The mission of the State was to hold them, half starved, in economic slavery.

The State was established for the precise purpose of imposing the rule of the landowners, the employers of industry, the warrior class, and the clergy upon the peasants on the land and the artisans in the city. And the rich perfectly well know that if the machinery of the State ceased to protect them, their power over the laboring classes would be gone immediately.

Socialism, we have said—whatever form it may take in its evolution towards communism—must find *its own form* of political organization. Serfdom and absolute monarchy have always marched hand-in-hand. The one rendered the other a necessity. The same is true of capitalist rule, whose political form is representative government, either in a republic or in a monarchy. This is why socialism *cannot* utilize representative government as a weapon for liberating labor, just as it cannot utilize the church and its theory of divine right, or imperialism and Cæsarism, with its theory of hierarchy of functionaries, for the same purpose.

A new form of political organization has to be worked out the moment that socialist principles shall enter into our life. And it is self-evident that this new form will have to be *more popular, more decentralized, and nearer to the folk-mote self-government* than representative government can ever be.

Knowing this, we cannot see a guarantee of progress in a still greater submission of all to the State. We seek progress in the fullest emancipation of the individual from the authority of the State; in the greatest development of individual initiative and in the limitation of all the governmental functions, but surely not in their extension. The march forward in political institutions appears to us to consist in abolishing in the first place the State authority which has fixed itself upon society and which now tries to extend its functions more and more; and in the second place, in allowing the broadest possible development for the principle of free agreement, and in acknowledging the independence of all possible associations formed for definite ends, embracing in their federations the whole of society. The life of society itself we understand, not as something complete and rigid, but as something never perfect—something ever striving for new forms, and ever changing these forms in accordance with the needs of the time. This is what *life* is in nature.

Such a conception of human progress and of what we think desirable in the future (what, in our opinion, can increase the sum of happiness) leads us inevitably to our own special tactics in the struggle. It induces us to strive for the greatest possible development of personal initiative in every individual and group, and to secure unity of action, not through discipline, but through the unity of aims and the mutual confidence which never fail to develop when a great number of persons have consciously embraced some common idea.

Then we assert and endeavor to prove that it devolves upon every new economic form of social life to develop *its own* new form of political relations. It has been so in the past, and so it undoubtedly will be in the future. New forms are already germinating all round.

Feudal right and autocracy, or at least the almost unlimited power of a czar or a king, have moved hand in hand in history. They depended on each other in this development. Exactly in the same way the rule of the capitalists has evolved its own characteristic political order—representative government—both in strictly centralized monarchies and in republics.

Socialism, whatever may be the form in which it will appear, and in whatever degree it may approach to its unavoidable goal,—communism,—will also have to choose *its own* form of political structure. Of the old form *it cannot make use*, no more than it could avail itself of the hierarchy of the church or of autocracy. The State bureaucracy and centralization are as irreconcilable with socialism as was autocracy with capitalist rule. One way or another, socialism must become *more popular*, more communalistic, and less dependent upon indirect government through elected representatives. It must become more *self-governing*.

Besides, when we closely observe the modern life of France, Spain, England and the United States, we notice in these countries the evident tendency to form into groups of entirely independent communes, towns and villages, which would combine by means of free federation, in order to satisfy innumerable needs and attain certain immediate ends. In actual life this tendency manifests itself in thousands of attempts at organization outside the State, fully independent of it; as well as in attempts to take hold of various functions which had been previously usurped by the State and which, of course, it has never properly performed. And then as a great social phenomenon of universal import, this tendency found expression in the Paris Commune of 1871 and in a whole series of similar uprisings in France and Spain; while in the domain of thought—of ideas spreading through society—this view has already acquired the force of an extremely important factor of future history. The future revolutions in France and Spain will be *communalist*—not centralist.

On the strength of all this, we are convinced that to work in favor of a centralized state-capitalism and to see in it a *desideratum*, means to work *against* the tendency of progress already manifest. We see in such work as this a gross misunderstanding of the historic mission of socialism itself— a great historical mistake, and we make war upon it. To assure the laborers that they will be able to establish socialism, or even to take the first steps on the road to socialism, by retaining the entire government machinery, and changing only the persons who manage it; not to promote but even to retard the day on which the working people's minds shall be bent upon discovering their own new forms of political life,—this is in our eyes a colossal historical blunder which borders upon crime.

Finally, since we represent a revolutionary party, we try to study the history of the origin and development of past revolutions. We endeavor, first of all, to free the histories of revolutions written up till now from the partisan, and for the most part false, governmental coloring that has been given them. In the histories hitherto written we do not yet see *the people*; nor do we see how revolutions began. The stereotyped phrases about the desperate condition of people previous to revolutions fail to explain whence amid this desperation came the hope of something better—whence came the revolutionary spirit. And therefore after reading these histories, we put them aside, and going back to first sources, try to learn from them what caused the people to rise and what was its true part in revolutions, what advantages it obtained from a revolution, what ideas it launched into circulation, what faults of tactics it committed.

Thus, we understand the Great French Revolution not at all as it is pictured by Louis Blanc, who presents it chiefly as a great political movement directed by the Jacobin Club. We see in it first of all a chaotic *popular* movement, chiefly of the peasant folk ("Every village had its Robespierre," as the Abbé Grégoire, who *knew* the people's revolt, remarked to the historian Schlosser). This movement aimed chiefly at the destruction of every vestige of *feudal rights* and of redemptions that had been imposed for the abolition of some of them, as well as at the recovery of the *lands* which had been seized from the village communes by vultures of various kinds. And in so far the peasant movement was successful.

Then, upon this foundation of revolutionary tumult, of increased pulsation of life and of disorganization of all the powers of the State, we find on the one hand developing among the town laborers a tendency towards a vaguely understood socialist equality and the admirable forms of voluntary popular organization for a variety of functions, economic and political, that they worked out in the "sections" of the great cities and small municipalities; and on the other hand the middle classes working hard and successfully in order to establish their own authority upon the ruins of that of royalty and nobility. To this end the middle classes fought stubbornly and desperately that they might create a powerful, all-inclusive, centralized government, which would preserve and assure to them their right of property (gained partly by plunder before and during the Revolution) and afford them the full opportunity of exploiting the poor without any legal restrictions. We study the development and the struggle of these two powers and try to find out why the latter gained the upper hand over the former. And we see how in the State centralization which was created by the revolutionary Jacobinists, Napoleon found an excellent soil for establishing his empire. From this centralized authority which kills all local life, France is suffering even to this very day, and the first attempt to throw off its yoke—an attempt which opened a new era in history—was made by the proletariat of Paris only in 1871.

Without entering here upon an analysis of other revolutionary movements, it is sufficient to say that we understand the social revolution, not at all as a Jacobinist dictatorship—not at all as a reform of the social institutions by means of laws issued by a convention or a senate or a dictator. Such revolutions have never occurred, and a movement which should take this form would be doomed to inevitable death. We understand the revolution as a widespread popular movement, during which in every town and village within the region of the revolt, the masses will have to take upon themselves the task of rebuilding society—will have to take up themselves *the work of construction upon communistic bases,* without awaiting any orders and directions from above. That is, first of all they will have to organize, one way or another, the means of supplying food to everyone and of providing dwellings for all, and then produce whatever will be found necessary for feeding, clothing, and sheltering everybody.

They may not be—they are sure not to be the *majority* of the nation. But if they are a respectably numerous minority of cities and villages scattered over the country, starting life on their own new socialist lines, they will be able to win the right to pursue their own course. In all probability they will draw towards them a notable portion of the land, as was the case in France in 1793-94.

As to representative government, whether self-appointed or elected—be it "the dictatorship of the proletariat," or an elected "temporary government," or again a Jacobinist "convention,"—we place in it no hopes whatever. We know beforehand that it will be able to do nothing to accomplish the revolution so long as the people themselves do not accomplish the change by working out on the spot the necessary new institutions. We say so, not because we have a personal dislike of governments, but because nowhere and never in history do we find that people carried into government by a revolutionary wave, have proved equal to the occasion.

In the task of reconstructing society on new principles, separate men, however intelligent and devoted they may be, are sure to fail. The collective spirit of the masses is necessary for this purpose. Isolated men can sometimes find the legal expression to sum up the destruction of old social forms —when the destruction is already proceeding. At the utmost, they may widen, perhaps, the sphere of the reconstructive work, extending what is being done in a part of the country, over a larger part of the territory. But to impose the reconstruction by law is absolutely impossible, as was proved, among other examples, by the whole history of the French Revolution. Many thousands of the *laws* passed by the revolutionary convention had not even been put into force when reaction came and flung those laws into the waste-paper basket.

During a revolution new forms of life will always germinate on the ruins of the old forms, but no government will ever be able to find their expression *so long as these forms will not have taken a definite shape during the work itself of reconstruction* which must be going on in thousands of spots at the same time. It is impossible to legislate for *the future*. All we can do is to guess vaguely its essential tendencies and clear the road for it.

Looking upon the problems of the revolution in this light, anarchism obviously cannot take a sympathetic attitude toward the program which aims at "the conquest of power in present society." We know that by peaceful, parliamentary means in the present State such a conquest as this is impossible. The middle class will not give up its power without a struggle. It will resist. And in proportion as the socialists become a power in the present bourgeois society and State, their socialism must die out. Otherwise the middle classes, which are much more powerful both intellectually and numerically than is admitted in the socialist press, will not recognize them as their rulers. And we know also that were a revolution to give France or England or Germany a socialist government, the respective governments would be absolutely powerless without the activity of the people themselves, and that, necessarily, they would soon begin to act fatally as a bridle upon the revolution.

Finally our studies of the preparatory stages of all revolutions bring us to the conclusion that not a single revolution has originated in parliaments or in any other representative assembly. *All began with the people.* And no revolution has appeared in full armor—born, like Minerva out of the head of Jupiter, in a day. They all had their periods of incubation during which the masses were very slowly becoming imbued with the revolutionary spirit, grew bolder, commenced *to hope,* and step by step emerged from their former indifference and resignation. And the awakening of the revolutionary spirit always took place in such a manner that at first single individuals, deeply moved by the existing state of things, protested against it, one by one. Many perished, "uselessly" the arm-chair critic would say. But the indifference of society was shaken by these progenitors. The dullest and most narrow-minded people were compelled to reflect, "Why should men, young, sincere, and full of strength, sacrifice their lives in this way?" It was impossible to remain indifferent; it was necessary to take a stand, for or against: thought was awakening. Then little by little small groups came to be imbued with the same spirit of revolt. They also rebelled—sometimes in the hope of local success—in strikes or in small revolts against some official whom they disliked, or in order to get food for their hungry children, but frequently also without any hope of success: simply because the conditions grew unbearable. Not one, or two, or tens, but *hundreds* of similar revolts have preceded *and must precede* every revolution. Without these no revolution was ever wrought.

Without the menace contained in such revolts not a single concession was ever made by the ruling classes. Even the

famous "peaceful" abolition of serfdom in Russia, of which
Tolstoy often speaks as of a peaceful conquest, was forced
upon the government by a series of peasant uprisings, beginning with the early fifties, spreading from year to year, and
gaining in importance so as to attain proportions hitherto
unknown, until 1857. Alexander Herzen's words, "Better
to abolish serfdom from above than to wait until the abolition
comes from below,"—repeated by Alexander II before the
serf-owners of Moscow—were not mere phrases but expressed
the real state of affairs. This was all the more true as to the
eve of every revolution. Hundreds of partial revolts preceded every one of them. And it may be stated as a general
rule that the character of every revolution is detemined by
the character and the aim of the uprisings by which it is
preceded.

To wait therefore for a *social* revolution to come as a birth-
day present, without a whole series of protests on the part of
the individual conscience, and without hundreds of preliminary revolts by which the very nature of the revolution is
determined, is to say the least, absurd. But to assure the
working people that they will gain all the benefits of a socialist revolution by confining themselves to electoral agitation,
and to attack vehemently every act of individual revolt and
all minor preliminary mass-revolts—means to become as great
an obstacle to the development of the revolutionary spirit and
to all progress as was and is the Christian Church.

CONCLUSION

Without entering into further discussion of the principles
of anarchism and the anarchist program of action, enough
has been said, I think, to show the place of anarchism among
the modern sociological sciences.

Anarchism is an attempt to apply to the study of human
institutions the generalizations gained by means of the natural-scientific inductive method; and an attempt to foresee the

future steps of mankind on the road to liberty, equality, and fraternity, with a view to realizing the greatest sum of happiness for every unit of human society.

It is the inevitable result of that natural-scientific, intellectual movement which began at the close of the eighteenth century, was hampered for half a century by the reaction that set in throughout Europe after the French Revolution, and has been appearing again in full vigor ever since the end of the fifties. Its roots lie in the natural-scientific philosophy of the century mentioned. Its complete scientific basis, however, it could receive only after that awakening of naturalism which brought into being the natural-scientific study of human social institutions.

In anarchism there is no room for those pseudo-scientific laws with which the German metaphysicians of the first thirty years of the nineteenth century had to content themselves. Anarchism does not recognize any method other than the natural-scientific, and it applies this method to all the so-called humanitarian sciences. Availing itself of this method as well as of all researches which have recently been called forth by it, anarchism endeavors to reconstruct all the sciences dealing with man and to revise every current idea of right and justice on the bases which have served for the revision of all natural sciences. Its object is to form a scientific concept of the universe embracing the whole of nature and including man.

This world-concept determines the position anarchism has taken in practical life. In the struggle between the individual and the State, anarchism, like its predecessors of the eighteenth century, takes the side of the individual as against the State, of society as against the authority which oppresses it. And availing itself of the historical data collected by modern science, it has shown that the State—whose sphere of authority there is now a tendency among its admirers to increase, and a tendency to limit in actual life—is in reality a superstructure—as harmful as it is unnecessary, and for us Europeans of a comparatively recent origin. A superstructure in the interests of capitalism—agrarian, industrial, and financial—which in ancient history caused the decay of politically free Rome and Greece, and which caused the death of all other despotic centers of civilization of the east and of Egypt.

The power which was created for the purpose of welding together the interests of the landlord, the judge, the warrior, and the priest, and has been opposed throughout history to every attempt of mankind to create for themselves a more assured and freer mode of life,—this power cannot become an instrument for emancipation, any more than imperialism or the church can become the instrument for a social revolution.

In the economic field anarchism has come to the conclusion that the root of modern evil lies not in the fact that the capitalist appropriates the profits or the surplus-value, but in the very possibility of these profits, which accrue only because millions of people have literally nothing to subsist upon without selling their labor-power at a price which makes profits and the creation of "surplus values" possible.

Anarchism understands therefore that in political economy attention must be directed first of all to so-called "consumption," and that the first concern of the revolution must be to reorganize that so as to provide food, clothing and shelter for all. "Production," on the other hand, must be so adapted as to satisfy this primary, fundamental need of society. Therefore anarchism cannot see in the next coming revolution a mere exchange of monetary symbols for labor-checks, or an exchange of present capitalism for state-capitalism. It sees in it the first step on the road to no-government communism.

Whether or not anarchism is right in its conclusions will be shown by a scientific criticism of its bases and by the practical life of the future. But in one thing it is absolutely right: in that it has included the study of social institutions in the sphere of natural-scientific investigations; has forever parted company with metaphysics; and makes use of the method by which modern natural science and modern materialist philosophy were developed. Owing to this, the very mistakes which anarchism may have made in its researches can be detected the more readily. But its conclusions can be verified only by the same natural-scientific, inductive method by which every science and every scientific concept of the universe is created.

Note for "Law and Authority"

This brilliant little study of the origin of laws and their use in the world today goes to the heart of the anarchist contention that government can be abolished and society still survive. Not only survive, but for the first time grow in freedom. Private capitalism of course must go, too, for it is the root of the inequalities and privileges which governments protect. Weigh the good and evil of laws, and all will agree they do more harm than good.

Kropotkin traces the origin of law, first in primitive superstitions, later in the decrees of conquerors. Our real laws by which most people live are not either of these, but the unwritten customs which antedate them, and which exist even among animals. Side by side with them are the written laws, respected only because they have roots in protection against the caprice of kings. But equality before the law, which is heralded as their basis, is a lie. We now know their class character. They are confused in appearance by embodying two sets of control,—social custom and class advantage; "Do not kill,—and pay your taxes"!

Most laws today have one of two objects,—either to protect private property, which means protecting the unjust appropriation of others' labor, or to keep up the machinery of government by which property is protected. Protection of the person is a very insignificant function of law. Most crimes against the person are for robbery. Repeal all laws protecting the person and crimes of vengeance or passion would not increase. As for the so-called "liberal" laws, examination will show that most of them merely repeal restrictions on a previous liberty.

Abolition of all law through socializing property; social control through custom and education alone,—these are Kropotkin's arguments.

195

LAW AND AUTHORITY

I

"WHEN ignorance reigns in society and disorder in the minds of men, laws are multiplied, legislation is expected to do everything, and each fresh law being a fresh miscalculation, men are continually led to demand from it what can proceed only from themselves, from their own education and their own morality." It is no revolutionist who says this, not even a reformer. It is the jurist, Dalloy, author of the collection of French law known as *Répertoire de la Législation.* And yet, though these lines were written by a man who was himself a maker and admirer of law, they perfectly represent the abnormal condition of our society.

In existing States a fresh law is looked upon as a remedy for evil. Instead of themselves altering what is bad, people begin by demanding a *law* to alter it. If the road between two villages is impassable, the peasant says:—"There should be a law about parish roads." If a park-keeper takes advantage of the want of spirit in those who follow him with servile observance and insults one of them, the insulted man says, "There should be a law to enjoin more politeness upon park-keepers." If there is stagnation in agriculture or commerce, the husbandman, cattle-breeder, or corn speculator argues, "It is protective legislation that we require." Down to the old clothesman there is not one who does not demand a law to protect his own little trade. It the employer lowers wages or increases the hours of labor, the politician in embryo exclaims, "We must have a law to put all that to rights." In short, a law everywhere and for everything! A law about fashions, a law about mad dogs, a law about virtue, a law to put a stop to all the vices and all the evils which result from human indolence and cowardice.

We are so perverted by an education which from infancy seeks to kill in us the spirit of revolt, and to develop that of submission to authority; we are so perverted by this existence under the ferrule of a law, which regulates every event in life —our birth, our education, our development, our love, our friendship—that, if this state of things continues, we shall lose all initative, all habit of thinking for ourselves. Our society seems no longer able to understand that it is possible to exist otherwise than under the reign of law, elaborated by a representative government and administered by a handful of rulers. And even when it has gone so far as to emancipate itself from the thralldom, its first care has been to reconstitute it immediately. "The Year I of Liberty" has never lasted more than a day, for after proclaiming it men put themselves the very next morning under the yoke of law and authority.

Indeed, for some thousands of years, those who govern us have done nothing but ring the changes upon "Respect for law, obedience to authority." This is the moral atmosphere in which parents bring up their children, and school only serves to confirm the impression. Cleverly assorted scraps of spurious science are inculcated upon the children to prove necessity of law; obedience to the law is made a religion; moral goodness and the law of the masters are fused into one and the same divinity. The historical hero of the schoolroom is the man who obeys the law, and defends it against rebels.

Later when we enter upon public life, society and literature, impressing us day by day and hour by hour as the water-drop hollows the stone, continue to inculcate the same prejudice. Books of history, of political science, of social economy, are stuffed with this respect for law. Even the physical sciences have been pressed into the service by introducing artificial modes of expression, borrowed from theology and arbitrary power, into knowledge which is purely the result of observation. Thus our intelligence is successfully befogged, and always to maintain our respect for law. The same work is done by newspapers. They have not an article which does not preach respect for law, even where the third page proves every day the imbecility of that law, and shows how it is dragged through every variety of mud and filth by those charged with its administration. Servility before the law has become a virtue, and I doubt if there was ever even a revolutionist who did not begin in his youth as the defender of law against what are generally called "abuses," although these last are inevitable consequences of the law itself.

Art pipes in unison with would-be science. The hero of the sculptor, the painter, the musician, shields Law beneath his buckler, and with flashing eyes and distended nostrils stands ever ready to strike down the man who would lay hands upon her. Temples are raised to her; revolutionists themselves hesitate to touch the high priests consecrated to her service, and when revolution is about to sweep away some ancient institution, it is still by law that it endeavors to sanctify the deed.

The confused mass of rules of conduct called law, which has been bequeathed to us by slavery, serfdom, feudalism, and royalty, has taken the place of those stone monsters, before whom human victims used to be immolated, and whom slavish savages dared not even touch lest they should be slain by the thunderbolts of heaven.

This new worship has been established with especial success since the rise to supreme power of the middle class—since the great French Revolution. Under the ancient régime, men spoke little of laws; unless, indeed, it were, with Montesquieu, Rousseau and Voltaire, to oppose them to royal caprice. Obedience to the good pleasure of the king and his lackeys was compulsory on pain of hanging or imprisonment. But during and after the revolutions, when the lawyers rose to power, they did their best to strengthen the principle upon which their ascendancy depended. The middle class at once accepted it as a dyke to dam up the popular torrent. The priestly crew hastened to sanctify it, to save their bark from foundering amid the breakers. Finally the people received it

as an improvement upon the arbitrary authority and violence
of the past.

To understand this, we must transport ourselves in imagination into the eighteenth century. Our hearts must have
ached at the story of the atrocities committed by the all-
powerful nobles of that time upon the men and women of
the people before we can understand what must have been
the magic influence upon the peasant's mind of the words,
"Equality before the law, obedience to the law without distinction of birth or fortune." He who until then had been
treated more cruelly than a beast, he who had never had any
rights, he who had never obtained justice against the most
revolting actions on the part of a noble, unless in revenge he
killed him and was hanged—he saw himself recognized by
this maxim, at least in theory, at least with regard to his
personal rights, as the equal of his lord. Whatever this law
might be, it promised to affect lord and peasant alike; it
proclaimed the equality of rich and poor before the judge.
The promise was a lie, and to-day we know it; but at that
period it was an advance, a homage to justice, as hypocrisy
is a homage rendered to truth. This is the reason that when
the saviors of the menaced middle class (the Robespierres
and the Dantons) took their stand upon the writings of the
Rousseaus and the Voltaires, and proclaimed "respect for
law, the same for every man," the people accepted the compromise; for their revolutionary impetus had already spent
its force in the contest with a foe whose ranks drew closer
day by day; they bowed their neck beneath the yoke of law
to save themselves from the arbitrary power of their lords.

The middle class has ever since continued to make the
most of this maxim, which with another principle, that of
representative government, sums up the whole philosophy
of the bourgeois age, the nineteenth century. It has preached
this doctrine in its schools, it has propagated it in its writings,
it has moulded its art and science to the same purpose, it has
thrust its beliefs into every hole and corner—like a pious Eng-
lishwoman, who slips tracts under the door—and it has done

all this so successfully that today we behold the issue in the detestable fact that men who long for freedom begin the attempt to obtain it by entreating their masters to be kind enough to protect them by modifying the laws which these masters themselves have created!

But times and tempers are changed. Rebels are everywhere to be found who no longer wish to obey the law without knowing whence it comes, what are its uses, and whither arises the obligation to submit to it, and the reverence with which it is encompassed. The rebels of our day are criticizing the very foundations of society which have hitherto been held sacred, and first and foremost amongst them that fetish, law.

The critics analyze the sources of law, and find there either a god, product of the terrors of the savage, and stupid, paltry and malicious as the priests who vouch for its supernatural origin, or else, bloodshed, conquest by fire and sword. They study the characteristics of law, and instead of perpetual growth corresponding to that of the human race, they find its distinctive trait to be immobility, a tendency to crystallize what should be modified and developed day by day. They ask how law has been maintained, and in its service they see the atrocities of Byzantinism, the cruelties of the Inquisition, the tortures of the middle ages, living flesh torn by the lash of the executioner, chains, clubs, axes, the gloomy dungeons of prisons, agony, curses and tears. In our own days they see, as before, the axe, the cord, the rifle, the prison; on the one hand, the brutalized prisoner, reduced to the condition of a caged beast by the debasement of his whole moral being, and on the other, the judge, stripped of every feeling which does honor to human nature, living like a visionary in a world of legal fictions, revelling in the infliction of imprisonment and death, without even suspecting, in the cold malignity of his madness, the abyss of degradation into which he has himself fallen before the eyes of those whom he condemns.

They see a race of law-makers legislating without knowing

what their laws are about; today voting a law on the sanitation of towns, without the faintest notion of hygiene, tomorrow making regulations for the armament of troops, without so much as understanding a gun; making laws about teaching and education without ever having given a lesson of any sort, or even an honest education to their own children; legislating at random in all directions, but never forgetting the penalties to be meted out to ragamuffins, the prison and the galleys, which are to be the portion of men a thousand times less immoral than these legislators themselves.

Finally, they see the jailer on the way to lose all human feeling, the detective trained as a blood-hound, the police spy despising himself; "informing," metamorphosed into a virtue; corruption, erected into a system; all the vices, all the evil qualities of mankind countenanced and cultivated to insure the triumph of law.

All this we see, and, therefore, instead of inanely repeating the old formula, "Respect the law," we say, "Despise law and all its attributes!" In place of the cowardly phrase, "Obey the law," our cry is "Revolt against all laws!"

Only compare the misdeeds accomplished in the name of each law with the good it has been able to effect, and weigh carefully both good and evil, and you will see if we are right.

II

Relatively speaking, law is a product of modern times. For ages and ages mankind lived without any written law, even that graved in symbols upon the entrance stones of a temple. During that period, human relations were simply regulated by customs, habits and usages, made sacred by constant repetition, and acquired by each person in childhood, exactly as he learned how to obtain his food by hunting, cattle-rearing, or agriculture.

All human societies have passed through this primitive phase, and to this day a large proportion of mankind have no written law. Every tribe has its own manners and customs; customary law, as the jurists say. It has social habits, and that suffices to maintain cordial relations between the inhabitants of the village, the members of the tribe or community. Even amongst ourselves—the "civilized" nations—when we leave large towns, and go into the country, we see that there the mutual relations of the inhabitants are still regulated according to ancient and generally accepted customs, and not according to the written law of the legislators. The peasants of Russia, Italy and Spain, and even of a large part of France and England, have no conception of written law. It only meddles with their lives to regulate their relations with the State. As to relations between themselves, though these are sometimes very complex, they are simply regulated according to ancient custom. Formerly, this was the case with mankind in general.

Two distinctly marked currents of custom are revealed by analysis of the usages of primitive people.

As man does not live in a solitary state, habits and feelings develop within him which are useful for the preservation of society and the propagation of the race. Without social feelings and usages, life in common would have been absolutely impossible. It is not law which has established them; they are anterior to all law. Neither is it religion which has ordained them; they are anterior to all religions. They are found amongst all animals living in society. They are spontaneously developed by the very nature of things, like those habits in animals which men call instinct. They spring from a process of evolution, which is useful, and, indeed, necessary, to keep society together in the struggle it is forced to maintain for existence. Savages end by no longer eating one another because they find it in the long run more advantageous to devote themselves to some sort of cultivation than to enjoy the pleasure of feasting upon the flesh of an aged relative once a year. Many travelers have depicted the manners of absolutely independent tribes, where laws and chiefs are unknown, but where the members of the tribe have given up stabbing one another in every dispute, because the habit of living in society has ended by developing certain feelings of fraternity and oneness of interest, and they prefer appealing to a third person to settle their differences. The hospitality of primitive peoples, respect for human life, the sense of reciprocal obligation, compassion for the weak, courage, extending even to the sacrifice of self for others which is first learnt for the sake of children and friends, and later for that of members of the same community—all these qualities are developed in man anterior to all law, independently of all religion, as in the case of the social animals. Such feelings and practices are the inevitable results of social life. Without being, as say priests and metaphysicians, inherent in man, such qualities are the consequence of life in common.

But side by side with these customs, necessary to the life of societies and the preservation of the race, other desires, other passions, and therefore other habits and customs, are evolved in human association. The desire to dominate others and impose one's own will upon them; the desire to seize upon the products of the labor of a neighboring tribe; the desire to surround oneself with comforts without producing anything, while slaves provide their master with the means of procuring every sort of pleasure and luxury—these selfish, personal desires give rise to another current of habits and customs. The priest and the warrior, the charlatan who makes a profit out of superstition, and after freeing himself from the fear of the devil cultivates it in others; and the bully, who procures the invasion and pillage of his neighbors that he may return laden with booty and followed by slaves. These two, hand in hand, have succeeded in imposing upon primitive society customs advantageous to both of them, but tending to perpetuate their domination of the masses. Profiting by the indolence, the fears, the inertia of the crowd, and thanks to the continual repetition of the same acts, they have permanently established customs which have become a solid basis for their own domination.

For this purpose, they would have made use, in the first

place, of that tendency to run in a groove, so highly developed in mankind. In children and all savages it attains striking proportions, and it may also be observed in animals. Man, when he is at all superstitious, is always afraid to introduce any sort of change into existing conditions; he generally venerates what is ancient. "Our fathers did so and so; they got on pretty well; they brought you up; they were not unhappy; do the same!" the old say to the young every time the latter wish to alter things. The unknown frightens them, they prefer to cling to the past even when that past represents poverty, oppression and slavery.

It may even be said that the more miserable a man is, the more he dreads every sort of change, lest it may make him more wretched still. Some ray of hope, a few scraps of comfort, must penetrate his gloomy abode before he can begin to desire better things, to criticize the old ways of living, and prepare to imperil them for the sake of bringing about a change. So long as he is not imbued with hope, so long as he is not freed from the tutelage of those who utilize his superstition and his fears, he prefers remaining in his former position. If the young desire any change, the old raise a cry of alarm against the innovators. Some savages would rather die than transgress the customs of their country because they have been told from childhood that the least infraction of established routine would bring ill-luck and ruin the whole tribe. Even in the present day, what numbers of politicians, economists, and would-be revolutionists act under the same impression, and cling to a vanishing past. How many care only to seek for precedents. How many fiery innovators are mere copyists of bygone revolutions.

The spirit of routine, originating in superstition, indolence, and cowardice, has in all times been the mainstay of oppression. In primitive human societies it was cleverly turned to account by priests and military chiefs. They perpetuated customs useful only to themselves, and succeeded in imposing them on the whole tribe. So long as this conservative spirit could be exploited so as to assure the chief in his encroachments upon individual liberty, so long as the only inequalities between men were the work of nature, and these were not increased a hundred-fold by the concentration of power and wealth, there was no need for law and the formidable paraphernalia of tribunals and ever-augmenting penalties to enforce it.

But as society became more and more divided into two hostile classes, one seeking to establish its domination, the other struggling to escape, the strife began. Now the conqueror was in a hurry to secure the results of his actions in a permanent form, he tried to place them beyond question, to make them holy and venerable by every means in his power. Law made its appearance under the sanction of the priest, and the warrior's club was placed at its service. Its office was to render immutable such customs as were to the advantage of the dominant minority. Military authority undertook to ensure obedience. This new function was a fresh guarantee to the power of the warrior; now he had not only mere brute force at his service; he was the defender of law.

If law, however, presented nothing but a collection of prescriptions serviceable to rulers, it would find some difficulty in insuring acceptance and obedience. Well, the legislators confounded in one code the two currents of custom of which we have just been speaking, the maxims which represent principles of morality and social union wrought out as a result of life in common, and the mandates which are meant to ensure external existence to inequality. Customs, absolutely essential to the very being of society, are, in the code, cleverly intermingled with usages imposed by the ruling caste, and both claim equal respect from the crowd. "Do not kill," says the code, and hastens to add, "And pay tithes to the priest." "Do not steal," says the code, and immediately after, "He who refuses to pay taxes, shall have his hand struck off."

Such was law; and it has maintained its two-fold character to this day. Its origin is the desire of the ruling class to give permanence to customs imposed by themselves for their own advantage. Its character is the skilful commingling of customs useful to society, customs which have no need of law to insure respect, with other customs useful only to rulers, injurious to the mass of the people, and maintained only by the fear of punishment.

Like individual capital, which was born of fraud and violence, and developed under the auspices of authority, law has no title to the respect of men. Born of violence and superstition, and established in the interests of consumer, priest and rich exploiter, it must be utterly destroyed on the day when the people desire to break their chains.

We shall be still better convinced of this when, later, we shall have analyzed the ulterior development of laws under the auspices of religion, authority and the existing parliamentary system.

III

We have seen how law originated in established usage and custom, and how from the beginning it has represented a skilful mixture of social habits, necessary to the preservation of the human race, with other customs imposed by those who used popular superstition as well as the right of the strongest for their own advantage. This double character of law has determined its own later development during the growth of political organization. While in the course of ages the nucleus of social custom inscribed in law has been subjected to but slight and gradual modifications, the other portion has been largely developed in directions indicated by the interests of the dominant classes, and to the injury of the classes they oppress.

From time to time these dominant classes have allowed a law to be extorted from them which presented, or appeared to present, some guarantee for the disinherited. But then such laws have but repealed a previous law, made for the advantage of the ruling caste. "The best laws," says Buckle, "were those which repealed the preceding ones." But what terrible efforts have been needed, what rivers of blood have been spilt, every time there has been a question of the repeal of one of these fundamental enactments serving to hold the people in fetters. Before she could abolish the last vestiges of serfdom and feudal rights, and break up the power of the royal court, France was forced to pass through four years of revolution and twenty years of war. Decades of conflict are needful to repeal the least of the iniquitous laws, bequeathed us by the past, and even then they scarcely disappear except in periods of revolution.

The history of the genesis of capital has already been told by socialists many times. They have described how it was born of war and pillage, of slavery and serfdom, of modern fraud and exploitation. They have shown how it is nourished by the blood of the worker, and how little by little it has conquered the whole world. The same story, concerning the genesis and development of law has yet to be told. As usual, the popular intelligence has stolen a march upon men of books. It has already put together the philosophy of this history, and is busy laying down its essential landmarks.

Law, in its quality of guarantee of the results of pillage, slavery and exploitation, has followed the same phases of development as capital. Twin brother and sister, they have advanced hand in hand, sustaining one another with the suffering of mankind. In every country in Europe their history is approximately the same. It has differed only in detail; the main facts are alike; and to glance at the development of law in France or Germany is to know its essential traits and its phases of development in most of the European nations.

In the first instance, law was a national pact or contract. It is true that this contract was not always freely accepted. Even in the early days the rich and strong were imposing their will upon the rest. But at all events they encountered an obstacle to their encroachments in the mass of the people, who often made them feel their power in return.

But as the church on one side and the nobles on the other succeeded in enthralling the people, the right of law-making escaped from the hands of the nation and passed into those of the privileged orders. Fortified by the wealth accumulating in her coffers, the church extended her authority. She tampered more and more with private life, and under pretext of saving souls, seized upon the labor of her serfs, she gathered taxes from every class, she increased her jurisdiction, she multiplied penalties, and enriched herself in proportion to the number of offenses committed, for the produce of every fine poured into her coffers. Laws had no longer any connection with the interest of the nation. "They might have been supposed to emanate rather from a council of religious fanatics than from legislators," observes an historian of French Law.

At the same time, as the baron likewise extended his authority over laborers in the fields and artisans in the towns, he, too, became legislator and judge. The few relics of national law dating from the tenth century are merely agreements regulating service, statute-labor, and tribute due from serfs and vassals to their lord. The legislators of that period were a handful of brigands organized for the plunder of a people daily becoming more peaceful as they applied themselves to agricultural pursuits. These robbers exploited the feelings for justice inherent in the people, they posed as the administrators of that justice, made a source of revenue for themselves out of its fundamental principles and concocted laws to maintain their own domination.

Later on, these laws collected and classified by jurists formed the foundation of our modern codes. And are we to talk about respecting these codes, the legacy of baron and priest?

The first revolution, the revolt of the townships, was successful in abolishing only a portion of these laws; the charters of enfranchised towns are, for the most part, a mere compromise between baronial and episcopal legislation, and the new relations created within the free borough itself. Yet what a difference between these laws and the laws we have now! The town did not take upon itself to imprison and execute citizens for reasons of State: it was content to expel anyone who plotted with the enemies of the city, and to raze his house to the ground. It confined itself to imposing fines for so-called "crimes and misdemeanors" and in the townships of the twelfth century may even be discerned the just principle today forgotten which holds the whole community responsible for the misdoing of each of its members. The societies of that time looked upon crime as an accident or misfortune; a conception common among the Russian peasantry at this moment. Therefore they did not admit of the principle of personal vengeance as preached by the Bible, but considered that the blame for each misdeed reverted to the whole society. It needed all the influence of the Byzantine church, which imported into the West the refined cruelties of Eastern despotism, to introduce into the manners of Gauls and Germans the penalty of death, and the horrible tortures afterwards inflicted on those regarded as criminals. Just in the same way, it needed all the influence of the Roman code, the product of the corruption of imperial Rome, to introduce the notions as to absolute property in land, which have overthrown the communistic customs of primitive people.

As we know, the free townships were not able to hold their own. Torn by internal dissensions between rich and poor, burgher and serf, they fell an easy prey to royalty. And as royalty acquired fresh strength, the right of legislation passed more and more into the hands of a clique of courtiers. Appeal to the nation was made only to sanction the taxes demanded by the king. Parliament summoned at intervals of two centuries, according to the good pleasure or caprice of the court, "Councils Extraordinary," assemblies of notables, ministers, scarce heeding the "grievances of the king's subjects"—these are the legislators of France. Later still, when all power is concentrated in a single man, who can say "I am the State," edicts are concocted in the "secret counsels of the prince," according to the whim of a minister, or of an imbecile king; and subjects must obey on pain of death. All judicial guarantees are abolished; the nation is the serf of royalty, and of a handful of courtiers. And at this period the most horrible penalties startle our gaze—the wheel, the stake, flaying alive, tortures of every description, invented by the sick fancy of monks and madmen, seeking delight in the sufferings of executed criminals.

The great Revolution began the demolition of this framework of law, bequeathed to us by feudalism and royalty. But after having demolished some portions of the ancient edifice, the Revolution delivered over the power of law-making to the bourgeoisie, who, in their turn, began to raise a fresh framework of laws intended to maintain and perpetuate middle-class domination among the masses. Their parliament makes laws right and left, and mountains of law accumulate with frightful rapidity. But what *are* all these laws at bottom?

The major portion have but one object—to protect private property, i. e., wealth acquired by the exploitation of man by man. Their aim is to open out to capital fresh fields for exploitation, and to sanction the new forms which that exploitation continually assumes, as capital swallows up another branch of human activity, railways, telegraphs, electric light, chemical industries, the expression of man's thought in literature and science, etc. The object of the rest of these laws is fundamentally the same. They exist to keep up the machinery of government which serves to secure to capital the exploitation and monopoly of the wealth produced. Magistrature, police, army, public instruction, finance, all serve one God—capital; all have but one object—to facilitate the exploitation of the worker by the capitalist. Analyze all the laws passed and you will find nothing but this.

The protection of the person, which is put forward as the true mission of law, occupies an imperceptible space among them, for, in existing society, assaults upon the person directly dictated by hatred and brutality tend to disappear. Nowadays, if anyone is murdered, it is generally for the sake of robbing him; rarely because of personal vengeance. But if this class of crimes and misdemeanors is continually diminishing, we certainly do not owe the change to legislation. It is due to the growth of humanitarianism in our societies, to our increasingly social habits rather than to the prescriptions of our laws. Repeal tomorrow every law dealing with the protection of the person, and tomorrow stop all proceedings for assault, and the number of attempts dictated by personal vengeance and by brutality would not be augmented by one single instance.

It will perhaps be objected that during the last fifty years, a good many liberal laws have been enacted. But, if these laws are analyzed, it will be discovered that this liberal legislation consists in the repeal of the laws bequeathed to us by the barbarism of preceding centuries. Every liberal law, every radical program, may be summed up in these words,— abolition of laws grown irksome to the middle-class itself, and return and extension to all citizens of liberties enjoyed by the townships of the twelfth century. The abolition of capital punishment, trial by jury for all "crimes" (there was a more liberal jury in the twelfth century), the election of magistrates, the right of bringing public officials to trial, the abolition of standing armies, free instruction, etc., everything that is pointed out as an invention of modern liberalism, is but a return to the freedom which existed before church and king had laid hands upon every manifestation of human life.

Thus the protection of exploitation directly by laws on property, and indirectly by the maintenance of the State is both the spirit and the substance of our modern codes, and the one function of our costly legislative machinery. But it is time we gave up being satisfied with mere phrases, and learned to appreciate their real significance. The law, which on its first appearance presented itself as a compendium of customs useful for the preservation of society, is now perceived to be nothing but an instrument for the maintenance of exploitation and the domination of the toiling masses by rich idlers. At the present day its civilizing mission is *nil;* it has but one object,—to bolster up exploitation.

This is what is told us by history as to the development of law. Is it in virtue of this history that we are called upon to respect it? Certainly not. It has no more title to respect than capital, the fruit of pillage. And the first duty of the revolution will be to make a bonfire of all existing laws as it will of all titles to property.

IV

The millions of laws which exist for the regulation of humanity appear upon investigation to be divided into three principal categories: protection of property, protection of persons, protection of government. And by analyzing each of these three categories, we arrive at the same logical and necessary conclusion: *the uselessness and hurtfulness of law.*

Socialists know what is meant by protection of property. Laws on property are not made to guarantee either to the individual or to society the enjoyment of the produce of their own labor. On the contrary, they are made to rob the producer of a part of what he has created, and to secure to certain other people that portion of the produce which they have stolen either from the producer or from society as a whole. When, for example, the law establishes Mr. So-and-So's right to a house, it is not establishing his right to a cottage he has built for himself, or to a house he has erected with the help of some of his friends. In that case no one would have disputed his right. On the contrary, the law is establishing his right to a house which is *not* the product of his labor; first of all because he has had it built for him by others to whom he has not paid the full value of their work, and next because that house represents a social value which he could not have produced for himself. The law is establishing his right to what belongs to everybody in general and to nobody in particular. The same house built in the midst of Siberia would not have the value it possesses in a large town, and, as we know, that value arises from the labor of something like fifty generations of men who have built the town, beautified it, supplied it with water and gas, fine promenades, colleges, theatres, shops, railways and roads leading in all directions. Thus, by recognizing the right of Mr. So-and-So to a particular house in Paris, London or Rouen, the law is unjustly appropriating to him a certain portion of the produce of the labor of mankind in general. And it is precisely because this appropriation and all other forms of property bearing the same character are a crying injustice, that a whole arsenal of laws and a whole army of soldiers, policemen and judges are needed to maintain it against the good sense and just feeling inherent in humanity.

Half our laws,—the civil code in each country,—serves no other purpose than to maintain this appropriation, this monopoly for the benefit of certain individuals against the whole of mankind. Three-fourths of the causes decided by the tribunals are nothing but quarrels between monopolists— two robbers disputing over their booty. And a great many of our criminal laws have the same object in view, their end being to keep the workman in a subordinate position towards his employer, and thus afford security for exploitation.

As for guaranteeing the product of his labor to the producer, there are no laws which even attempt such a thing. It is so simple and natural, so much a part of the manners and customs of mankind, that law has not given it so much as a thought. Open brigandage, sword in hand, is no feature of our age. Neither does one workman ever come and dispute the produce of his labor with another. If they have a misunderstanding they settle it by calling in a third person, without having recourse to law. The only person who exacts from another what that other has produced, is the proprietor, who comes in and deducts the lion's share. As for humanity in general, it everywhere respects the right of each to what he has created, without the interposition of any special laws.

As all the laws about property which make up thick volumes of codes and are the delight of our lawyers have no other object than to protect the unjust appropriation of human labor by certain monopolists, there is no reason for their existence, and, on the day of the revolution, social revolutionists are thoroughly determined to put an end to them. Indeed, a bonfire might be made with perfect justice of all laws bearing upon the so-called "rights of property," all title-deeds, all registers, in a word, of all that is in any way connected with an institution which will soon be looked upon as a blot in the history of humanity, as humiliating as the slavery and serfdom of past ages.

The remarks just made upon laws concerning property are quite as applicable to the second category of laws; those for the maintenance of government, i. e., constitutional law.

It again is a complete arsenal of laws, decrees, ordinances, orders in council, and what not, all serving to protect the diverse forms of representative government, delegated or usurped, beneath which humanity is writhing. We know very well—anarchists have often enough pointed out in their perpetual criticism of the various forms of government— that the mission of all governments, monarchical, constitutional, or republican, is to protect and maintain by force the privileges of the classes in possession, the aristocracy, clergy and traders. A good third of our laws—and each country possesses some tens of thousands of them—the fundamental laws on taxes, excise duties, the organization of ministerial departments and their offices, of the army, the police, the church, etc., have no other end than to maintain, patch up, and develop the administrative machine. And this machine in its turn serves almost entirely to protect the privileges of the possessing classes. Analyze all these laws, observe them in action day by day, and you will discover that not one is worth preserving.

About such laws there can be no two opinions. Not only anarchists, but more or less revolutionary radicals also, are agreed that the only use to be made of laws concerning the organization of government is to fling them into the fire.

The third category of law still remains to be considered; that relating to the protection of the person and the detection and prevention of "crime." This is the most important because most prejudices attach to it; because, if law enjoys a certain amount of consideration, it is in consequence of the belief that this species of law is absolutely indispensable to the maintenance of security in our societies. These are laws developed from the nucleus of customs useful to human communities, which have been turned to account by rulers to sanctify their own domination. The authority of the chiefs of tribes, of rich families in towns, and of the king, depended upon their judicial functions, and even down to the present day, whenever the necessity of government is spoken of, its function as supreme judge is the thing implied. "Without a government men would tear one another to pieces," argues the village orator. "The ultimate end of all government is to secure twelve honest jurymen to every accused person," said Burke.

Well, in spite of all the prejudices existing on this subject, it is quite time that anarchists should boldly declare this category of laws as useless and injurious as the preceding ones.

First of all, as to so-called "crimes"—assaults upon persons—it is well known that two-thirds, and often as many as three-fourths, of such "crimes" are instigated by the desire to obtain possession of someone's wealth. This immense class of so-called "crimes and misdemeanors" will disappear on the day on which private property ceases to exist. "But," it will be said, "there will always be brutes who will attempt the lives of their fellow citizens, who will lay their hands to a knife in every quarrel, and revenge the slightest offense by murder, if there are no laws to restrain and punishments to withhold them." This refrain is repeated every time the right of society *to punish* is called in question.

Yet there is one fact concerning this head which at the present time is thoroughly established; the severity of punishment does not diminish the amount of crime. Hang, and, if you like, quarter murderers, and the number of murders will not decrease by one. On the other hand, abolish the penalty of death, and there will not be one murder more; there will be fewer. Statistics prove it. But if the harvest is good, and bread cheap, and the weather fine, the number of murders immediately decreases. This again is proved by statistics. The amount of crime always augments and diminishes in proportion to the price of provisions and the state of the weather. Not that all murderers are actuated by hunger. That is not the case. But when the harvest is good, and provisions are at an obtainable price, and when the sun shines, men, lighter-hearted and less miserable than usual, do not give way to gloomy passions, do not from trivial motives plunge a knife into the bosom of a fellow creature.

Moreover, it is also a well known fact that the fear of punishment has never stopped a single murderer. He who kills his neighbor from revenge or misery does not reason much about consequences; and there have been few murderers who were not firmly convinced that they should escape prosecution.

Without speaking of a society in which a man will receive a better education, in which the development of all his faculties, and the possibility of exercising them, will procure him so many enjoyments that he will not seek to poison them by remorse—even in our society, even with those sad products of misery whom we see today in the public houses of great cities—on the day when no punishment is inflicted upon murderers, the number of murders will not be augmented by a single case. And it is extremely probable that it will be, on the contrary, diminished by all those cases which are due at present to habitual criminals, who have been brutalized in prisons.

We are continually being told of the benefits conferred by law, and the beneficial effect of penalties, but have the speakers ever attempted to strike a balance between the benefits attributed to laws and penalties, and the degrading effect of these penalties upon humanity? Only calculate all the evil passions awakened in mankind by the atrocious punishments formerly inflicted in our streets! Man is the cruelest animal upon earth. And who has pampered and developed the cruel instincts unknown, even among monkeys, if it is not the king, the judge, and the priests, armed with law, who caused flesh to be torn off in strips, boiling pitch to be poured into wounds, limbs to be dislocated, bones to be crushed, men to

be sawn asunder to maintain their authority? Only estimate
the torrent of depravity let loose in human society by the
"informing" which is countenanced by judges, and paid in
hard cash by governments, under pretext of assisting in the
discovery of "crime." Only go into the jails and study what
man becomes when he is deprived of freedom and shut up
with other depraved beings, steeped in the vice and corruption which oozes from the very walls of our existing prisons.
Only remember that the more these prisons are reformed,
the more detestable they become. Our model modern peni-
tentiaries are a hundred-fold more abominable than the dungeons of the middle ages. Finally, consider what corruption,
what depravity of mind is kept up among men by the idea
of obedience, the very essence of law; of chastisement; of
authority having the right to punish, to judge irrespective
of our conscience and the esteem of our friends; of the necessity for executioners, jailers, and informers—in a word, by
all the attributes of law and authority. Consider all this,
and you will assuredly agree with us in saying that a law
inflicting penalties is an abomination which should cease to
exist.

Peoples without political organization, and therefore less
depraved than ourselves, have perfectly understood that the
man who is called "criminal" is simply unfortunate; that the
remedy is not to flog him, to chain him up, or to kill him on
the scaffold or in prison, but to help him by the most broth-
erly care, by treatment based on equality, by the usages of
life among honest men. In the next revolution we hope
that this cry will go forth:

"Burn the guillotines; demolish the prisons; drive away the
judges, policemen and informers—the impurest race upon the
face of the earth; treat as a brother the man who has been
led by passion to do ill to his fellow; above all, take from
the ignoble products of middle-class idleness the possibility of
displaying their vices in attractive colors; and be sure that
but few crimes will mar our society."

The main supports of crime are idleness, law and authority;

laws about property, laws about government, laws about penalties and misdemeanors; and authority, which takes upon itself to manufacture these laws and to apply them.

No more laws! No more judges! Liberty, equality, and practical human sympathy are the only effectual barriers we can oppose to the anti-social instincts of certain among us.

NOTE FOR "PRISONS AND THEIR MORAL INFLUENCE
ON PRISONERS"

This is the edited text of a speech delivered in Paris before
a large audience of workingmen and women on December
20, 1877. It was published in France in pamphlet form and
widely distributed. This is its first appearance in English.
While Kropotkin often voiced his views of the iniquity of
prisons and the need of a right-about-face method of dealing with offenders, he nowhere so clearly described the evils
of the prison system. It has not been done better by any
writer in so brief a compass. It does not require an anarchist philosopher to point them out, and save in discussing
the remedy he makes no contributions peculiar to anarchist
thought.

But his remedy is revolutionary, and his indictment is necessary to give it point. Abolish the prisons and treat all offenders as brothers, applying to them where necessary all that
medical science and modern psychology offer to cure anti-
social conduct. And with his naive faith in an approaching
general revolution he foresaw the abolition of all prisons as
one of its first tasks, followed by such a régime of mutual
aid and opportunity through cooperation that anti-social
conduct would be unknown. Until that was achieved he
saw the community spontaneously protecting itself against
offenders,—though he passed lightly over that difficulty.

The treatment is stimulating, thoroughly modern in its
analysis of crime, and significant of that direction alone in
which progress can be made.

PRISONS AND THEIR MORAL INFLUENCE ON PRISONERS

AFTER the economic problem and after the problem of the State, perhaps the most important of all is that concerning the control of anti-social acts. The meting out of justice was always the principal instrument for creating rights and privilege, since it was based on solid foundations of constituted rights; the problem of what is to be done with those who commit anti-social acts therefore contains within itself the great problem of government and the State.

It is time to ask if condemnation to death or to prison is just. Does it attain the dual end it has as its goal—that of preventing the repetition of the anti-social deed, and (as regards prisons) that of reforming the offender?

They are grave questions. On their answers depend not only the happiness of thousands of prisoners, not only the fate of miserable women and children, whose husbands and fathers are helpless to aid them from behind their bars, but also the happiness of humanity. Every injustice committed against one individual is, in the end, experienced by humanity as a whole.

Having had occasion to become acquainted with two prisons in France and several in Russia, having been led by various circumstances in my life to return to the study of penal questions, I think it is my duty to state openly what prisons are,—to relate my observations and my beliefs as a result of these observations.

THE PRISON AS A SCHOOL OF CRIME

Once a man has been in prison, he will return. It is inevitable, and statistics prove it. The annual reports of the administration of criminal justice in France show that one-half of all those tried by juries and two-fifths of all those who yearly get into the police courts for minor offenses received their education in prisons. Nearly half of all those tried for murder and three-fourths of those tried for burglary are repeaters. As for the central prisons, more than one-third of the prisoners released from these supposedly correctional institutions are reimprisoned in the course of twelve months after their liberation.

Another significant angle is that the offense for which a man returns to prison is always more serious than his first. If, before, it was petty thieving, he returns now for some daring burglary, if he was imprisoned for the first time for some act of violence, often he will return as a murderer. All writers on criminology are in accord with this observation. Former offenders have become a great problem in Europe. And you know how France has solved it; she ordains their wholesale destruction by the fevers of Cayenne, an extermination which begins on the voyage.

THE FUTILITY OF PRISONS

In spite of all the reforms made up to the present,—in spite of all the experiments of different prison systems, the results are always the same. On the one hand, the number of offenses against existing laws neither increases nor diminishes, *no matter what the system of punishments is*—the knout has been abolished in Russia and the death penalty in Italy, and the number of murders there has remained the same. The cruelty of the judges grows or lessens, the cruelty of the Jesuitical penal system changes, but the number of acts designated as crimes remains constant. It is affected only by other causes which I shall shortly mention. On the other hand, no matter what changes are introduced in the prison régime, the problem of second offenders does not decrease. That is inevitable;—*it must be so;*—the prison kills all the qualities in a man which make him best adapted to community life. It makes him the kind of a person who will inevitably return to prison to end his days in one of those stone tombs over which is engraved—"House of Detention and Correction." There is only one answer to the question: "What can be done to better this penal system?" Nothing. A prison cannot be improved. With the exception of a few unimportant little improvements, there is absolutely nothing to do but demolish it.

I might propose that a Pestalozzi be placed at the head of each prison. I refer to the great Swiss pedagogue who used to take in abandoned children and make good citizens of them. I might also propose that in the place of the present guards, ex-soldiers and ex-policemen, sixty Pestalozzis be substituted. But, you will ask, "Where are we to find them?"—a pertinent question. The great Swiss teacher would certainly refuse to be a prison guard, for, basically, the principle of all prisons is wrong because it deprives man of liberty. So long as you deprive a man of his liberty, you will not make him better. You will cultivate habitual criminals: that is what I shall now prove.

THE CRIMINALS IN PRISON AND OUTSIDE

To begin with, there is the fact that none of the prisoners recognize the justice of the punishment inflicted on them. This is in itself a condemnation of our whole judicial system. Speak to an imprisoned man or to some great swindler. He will say: "The little swindlers are here but the big ones are free and enjoy public respect." What can you answer, knowing the existence of great financial companies expressly designed to take the last pennies of the savings of the poor, with the founders retiring in time to make good legal hauls out of these small fortunes? We all know these great stock-issuing companies with their lying circulars and their huge swindles. What can we answer the prisoner except that he is right?

Or this man, imprisoned for robbing a till, will tell you:

"I simply wasn't clever enough; that's all." And what can you answer, knowing what goes on in important places, and how, following terrible scandals, the verdict "not guilty" is handed out to these great robbers? How many times have you heard prisoners say: "It's the big thieves who are holding us here; we are the little ones." Who can dispute this when he knows the incredible swindles perpetrated in the realm of high finance and commerce; when he knows that the thirst for riches, acquired by every possible means, is the very essence of bourgeois society. When he has examined this immense quantity of suspicious transactions divided between the honest man (according to bourgeois standards) and the criminal, when he has seen all this, he must be convinced that jails are made for the unskillful, not for criminals. This is the standard on the outside. As for the standard in the prison itself, it is needless to dwell on it long. We know well enough what it is. Whether in regard to food or the distribution of favors, in the words of the prisoners, from San Francisco to Kamtchatka: "The biggest thieves are those who hold us here, not ourselves."

PRISON LABOR

Everyone knows the evil influence of laziness. Work relieves a man. But there is work and work. There is the work of the free individual which makes him feel a part of the immense whole. And there is that of the slave which degrades. Convict labor is unwillingly done, done only through fear of worse punishment. The work, which has no attraction in itself because it does not exercise any of the mental faculties of the worker, is so badly paid that it is looked upon as a punishment.

When my anarchist friends at Clairvaux made corsets or mother of pearl buttons and received twelve cents for ten hours' labor, of which four cents were retained by the State, we can understand very well the disgust which this work aroused in a man condemned to it. When he receives thirty-six cents at the end of a week, he is right to say: "Those who keep us here are thieves, not we."

THE EFFECT OF CUTTING OFF SOCIAL CONTACTS

And what inspiration can a prisoner get to work for the common good, deprived as he is of all connections with life outside? By a refinement of cruelty, those who planned our prisons did everything they could to break all relationships of the prisoner with society. In England the prisoner's wife and children can see him only once every three months, and the letters he is allowed to write are really preposterous. The philanthropists have even at times carried defiance of human nature so far as to restrict a prisoner from writing anything but his signature on a printed circular. The best influence to which a prisoner could be subjected, the only one which could bring him a ray of light, a softer element in his life,—the relationship with his kin,—is systematically prevented.

In the sombre life of the prisoner which flows by without passion or emotion, all the finer sentiments rapidly become atrophied. The skilled workers who loved their trade lose their taste for work. Bodily energy slowly disappears. The mind no longer has the energy for sustained attention; thought is less rapid, and in any case less persistent. It loses depth. It seems to me that the lowering of nervous energy in prisons is due, above all, to the lack of varied impressions. In ordinary life a thousand sounds and colors strike our senses daily, a thousand little facts come to our consciousness and stimulate the activity of our brains. No such things strike the prisoners' senses. Their impressions are few and always the same.

THE THEORY OF WILL POWER

There is another important cause of demoralization in prisons. All transgressions of accepted moral standards may be ascribed to lack of a strong will. The majority of the inmates of prisons are people who did not have sufficient strength to resist the temptations surrounding them or to control a passion which momentarily carried them away. In prisons as in monasteries, everything is done to kill a man's will. He generally has no choice between one of two acts. The rare occasions on which he can exercise his will are very brief. His whole life is regulated and ordered in advance. He has only to swim with the current, to obey under pain of severe punishment.

Under these conditions all the will power that he may have had on entering disappears. And where will he find the strength with which to resist the temptations which will arise before him, as if by magic, when he is free of the prison walls? Where will he find the strength to resist the first impulse to a passionate outbreak, if during several years everything was done to kill this inner strength, to make him a docile tool in the hands of those who control him? This fact is, according to my mind, *the most terrible condemnation of the whole penal system based on the deprivation of individual liberty.*

The origin of this suppression of individual will, which is the essence of all prisons, is easy to see. It springs from the desire of guarding the greatest number of prisoners with the fewest possible guards. The ideal of prison officials would be thousands of automatons, arising, working, eating and going to sleep by means of electric currents switched on by one of the guards. Economies might then be made in the budget, but no astonishment should be expressed that men, reduced to machines, are not, on their release, the type which society wants. As soon as a prisoner is released, his old companions await him. He is fraternally received and once again engulfed by the current which once swept him to prison. Protective organizations can do nothing. All that they can do to combat the evil influence of the prison is to counterbalance some of those results in the liberated men.

And what a contrast between the reception by his old companions and that of the people in philanthropic work for released prisoners! Who of them will invite him to his home and say to him simply, "Here is a room, here is work, sit down at this table and become part of the family"? The released man is only looking for the outstretched hand of warm friendship. But society, after having done everything it could to make an enemy of him, having inoculated him with the vices of the prison, rejects him. He is condemned to become a "repeater."

THE EFFECT OF PRISON CLOTHES AND DISCIPLINE

Everyone knows the influence of decent clothing. Even an animal is ashamed to appear before his fellow creatures if something makes him look ridiculous. A cat whom somebody has painted black and yellow will not dare mingle with other cats. But men begin by giving the clothes of a lunatic to those whom they profess to want to reform.

During all his prison life the prisoner is subjected to treatment which shows the greatest contempt of his feelings. A prisoner is not accorded the single respect due a human being. He is a thing, a number, and he is treated like a numbered thing. If he yields to the most human of all desires, that of communicating with a comrade, he is guilty of a breach of discipline. Before entering prison he may not have lied or deceived, but in prison he will learn to lie and deceive so that it will become second nature to him.

And it goes hard with those who do not submit. If being searched is humiliating, if a man finds the food distasteful, if he shows disgust in the keeper's trafficking in tobacco, if he divides his bread with his neighbor, if he still has enough dignity to be irritated by an insult, if he is honest enough to be revolted by the petty intrigues, prison will be a hell for him. He will be overburdened with work unless he is sent to rot in solitary confinement. The slightest infraction of discipline will bring down the severest punishment. And each punishment will lead to another. He will be driven to madness through persecution. He can consider himself lucky to leave prison otherwise than in a coffin.

PRISON GUARDS

It is easy to write in the newspapers that the guards must be carefully watched, that the wardens must be chosen from good men. Nothing is easier than to build administrative utopias. But man will remain man—guard as well as prisoner. And when these guards are condemned to spend the rest of their lives in these false positions, they suffer the consequences. They become fussy. Nowhere, save in monasteries or convents, does such a spirit of petty intrigue reign. Nowhere are scandal and tale-bearing so well developed as among prison guards.

You cannot give an individual any authority without corrupting him. He will abuse it. He will be less scrupulous and feel his authority even more when his sphere of action is limited. Forced to live in any enemy's camp, the guards cannot become models of kindness. To the league of prisoners there is opposed the league of jailers. It is the institution which makes them what they are—petty, mean persecutors. Put a Pestalozzi in their place and he will soon become a prison guard.

Quickly rancor against society gets into the prisoner's heart. He becomes accustomed to detesting those who oppress him. He divides the world into two parts,—one in which he and his comrades belong, the other, the external world, represented by the guards and their superiors. A league is formed by the prisoners against all those who do not wear prison garb. These are their enemies and everything that can be done to deceive them is right.

As soon as he is freed, the prisoner puts this code into practice. Before going to prison he could commit his offenses unthinkingly. Now he has a philosophy, which can be summed up in the words of Zola, "What rascals these honest men are."

If we take into consideration all the different influences of the prison on the prisoner, we will be convinced that they make a man less and less fitted for life in society. On the other hand, none of these influences raises the intellectual and moral faculties of the prisoner, or leads him to a higher conception of life. Prison does not improve the prisoner. And furthermore, we have seen that it does not prevent him from committing other crimes. It does not then achieve any of the ends which it has set itself.

HOW SHALL WE DEAL WITH OFFENDERS?

That is why the question must be asked: "What should be done with those who break the laws?" I do not mean the written laws—they are a sad heritage of a sad past—but the principles of morality which are engraved on the hearts of each one of us.

There was a time when medicine was the art of administering some drugs, gropingly discovered through experiment. But our times have attacked the medical problem from a new angle. Instead of curing diseases medicine now seeks primarily to prevent them. Hygiene is the best of all medicines.

We have yet to do the same thing for this great social phenomenon which we still call "crime" but which our children will call a "social disease." To prevent this illness will be the best of cures. And this conclusion has already become the watchword of a whole school of modern thinkers concerned with "crime." In the works published by these innovators we have all the elements necessary for taking a new stand towards those whom society, until now, has in cowardly fashion decapitated, hanged or imprisoned.

CAUSES OF CRIME

Three great categories of causes produce these anti-social acts called crimes. They are social, physiological, and physical. I shall begin with the last-named causes. They are less well known, but their influence is indisputable.

Physical Causes

When one sees a friend mail a letter which he has forgotten to address, one says this is an accident—it is unforeseen. These accidents, these unexpected events, occur in human societies with the same regularity as those which can be foreseen. The number of unaddressed letters which will be mailed continues from year to year with astounding regularity. Their number may vary slightly each year, but only slightly. Here we have so capricious a factor as absentmindedness. However, this factor is subject to laws that are just as rigorous as those governing the movements of the planets.

The same is true for the number of murders committed from year to year. With the statistics for previous years in hand, anyone can predict in advance, with striking exactitude, the approximate number of murders that will be committed in the course of the year in every country of Europe.

The influence of physical causes on our actions is still far from being completely analyzed. It is, however, known that acts of violence predominate in summer whereas in winter acts against property take the lead. When one examines the curves traced by Prof. Enrico Ferri and when one observes the curve for acts of violence rise and fall with the curve for temperature, one is vividly impressed by the similarity of the two curves and one understands how much of a machine man is. Man who boasts of his free will is as dependent on the temperature, the winds and the rain as any other organism. Who will doubt these influences? When the weather is fine and the harvest good, and when the villagers feel at their ease, certainly they will be less likely to end their petty squabbles with knife thrusts. When the weather is bad and the harvest poor the villagers become morose and their quarrels will take on a more violent character.

Physiological Causes

The physiological causes, those which depend on the brain structure, the digestive organs and the nervous system, are certainly more important than the physical causes. The influence of inherited capacities as well as of physical organization on our acts has been the object of such searching investigation that we can form a fairly correct idea of its importance.

When Cesare Lombroso maintains that the majority of our prison inmates have some defect of their brain structure, we can accept this declaration on condition that we compare the brains of those who died in prison with those who died outside under generally bad living conditions. When he demonstrates that the most brutal murders are perpetrated by individuals who have some serious mental defect, we agree because this statement has been confirmed by observation. But when Lombroso declares that society has the right to take measures against the defectives we refuse to follow him. Society has no right to exterminate those who have diseased brains. We admit that many of those who commit these atrocious acts are almost idiots. But not all idiots become murderers.

In many families, in palaces as well as insane asylums, idiots were found with the same traits which Lombroso considers characteristic of "criminal insanity." The only difference between them and those sent to the gallows is the environment in which they lived. Cerebral diseases can certainly stimulate the development of an inclination to murder, but it is not inevitable. Everything depends on the circumstances in which the individual suffering from a mental disease is placed.

Every intelligent person can see from the accumulated facts that the majority of those now treated as criminals are people suffering from some malady, and that, consequently, it is necessary to cure him by the best of care instead of sending them to prison where the disease will only be aggravated.

If each one of us subjects himself to a severe analysis, he will see that at times there pass through his mind the germs of ideas, quick as a flash, which constitute the foundations for evil deeds. We repudiated these ideas, but if they had found a favorable response in our circumstances, or, if other sentiments, such as love, pity and the sense of brotherhood, had not counteracted these flashes of egoistic and brutal thoughts, they would have ended by leading to an evil act. In brief, the physiological causes play an important part in leading men to prison, but they are not the causes of "criminality" properly speaking. These affections of the mind, the cerebro-spinal system, etc., might be found in their incipience among us all. The great majority of us have some one of these maladies. But they do not lead a person to commit an anti-social act unless external circumstances give them a morbid turn.

The Social Causes

But if physical causes have so strong an influence on our actions, if our physiology so often becomes the cause of the anti-social deeds we commit, how much more potent are the social causes. The most forward-looking and intelligent minds of our time proclaim that society as a whole is responsible for every anti-social act committed. We have our part in the glory of our heroes and geniuses; we also share in the acts of our assassins. It is we who have made them what they are,—the one as well as the other.

Year in and year out thousands of children grow up in the midst of the moral and material filth of our great cities, in the midst of a population demoralized by hand to mouth living. These children do not know a real home. Their home is a wretched lodging today, the streets tomorrow. They grow up without any decent outlets for their young energies. When we see the child population of large cities grow up in this fashion, we can only be astonished that so few of them become highwaymen and murderers. What surprises me is the depth of the social sentiments among humanity, the warm friendliness of even the worst neighborhoods. Without it, the number of these that would declare open warfare on society would be even greater. Without this friendliness, this aversion to violence, not a stone would be left of our sumptuous city palaces.

And at the other end of the ladder, what does the child growing up on the streets see? Luxury, stupid and insensate, smart shops, reading matter devoted to exhibiting wealth, a money-worshipping cult developing a thirst for riches, a passion for living at the expense of others. The watchword is: "Get rich. Destroy everything that stands in your way, and do it by any means save those that will land you in jail." Manual labor is despised to a point where our ruling classes prefer to indulge in gymnastics than handle a spade or a saw. A calloused hand is considered a sign of inferiority and a silk dress of superiority.

Society itself daily creates these people incapable of leading a life of honest labor, and filled with anti-social desires. She glorifies them when their crimes are crowned with financial success. She sends them to prison when they have not "succeeded." We will no longer have any use for prisons, executioners or judges when the social revolution will have wholly changed the relations between capital and labor, when there are no more idlers, when each can work according to his inclination for the common good, when every child will be taught to work with his hands at the same time that his mind and soul get normal development.

Man is the result of the environment in which he grows up and spends his life. If he is accustomed to work from childhood, to being considered as a part of society as a whole, to understanding that he cannot injure anyone without finally feeling the effects himself, then there will be found few cases of violation of moral laws.

Two-thirds of the acts condemned as crimes today are acts against property. They will disappear along with private property. As for acts of violence against people, they already decrease in proportion to the growth of the social sense and they will disappear when we attack the causes instead of the effects.

HOW SHALL OFFENDERS BE CURED?

Until now, penal institutions, so dear to the lawyers, were a compromise between the Biblical idea of vengeance, the belief of the middle ages in the devil, the modern lawyers' idea of terrorization, and the idea of the prevention of crime by punishment.

It is not insane asylums that must be built instead of prisons. Such an execrable idea is far from my mind. The insane asylum is always a prison. Far from my mind also is the idea, launched from time to time by the philanthropists, that the prison be kept but entrusted to physicians and teachers. What prisoners have not found today in society is a helping hand, simple and friendly, which would aid them from childhood to develop the higher faculties of their minds and souls;—faculties whose natural development has been impeded either by an organic defect or by the evil social conditions which society itself creates for millions of people. But these superior faculties of the mind and heart cannot be exercised by a person deprived of his liberty, if he never has choice of action. The physicians' prison, the insane asylum, would be much worse than our present jails. Human fraternity and liberty are the only correctives to apply to those diseases of the human organism which lead to so-called crime.

Of course in every society, no matter how well organized, people will be found with easily aroused passions, who may, from time to time, commit anti-social deeds. But what is necessary to prevent this is to give their passions a healthy direction, another outlet.

Today we live too isolated. Private property has led us to an egoistic individualism in all our mutual relations. We know one another only slightly; our points of contact are too rare. But we have seen in history examples of a communal life which is more intimately bound together,—the "composite family" in China, the agrarian communes, for example. These people really know one another. By force of circumstances they must aid one another materially and morally.

Family life, based on the original community, has disappeared. A new family, based on community of aspirations, will take its place. In this family people will be obliged to know one another, to aid one another and to lean on one another for moral support on every occasion. And this mutual prop will prevent the great number of anti-social acts which we see today.

It will be said, however, there will always remain some people, the sick, if you wish to call them that, who constitute a danger to society. Will it not be necessary somehow to rid ourselves of them, or at least prevent their harming others?

No society, no matter how little intelligent, will need such an absurd solution, and this is why. Formerly the insane were looked upon as possessed by demons and were treated accordingly. They were kept in chains in places like stables, riveted to the walls like wild beasts. But along came Pinel, a man of the Great Revolution, who dared to remove their chains and tried treating them as brothers. "You will be devoured by them," cried the keepers. But Pinel dared. Those who were believed to be wild beasts gathered around Pinel and proved by their attitude that he was right in believing in the better side of human nature even when the intelligence is clouded by disease. Then the cause was won. They stopped chaining the insane.

Then the peasants of the little Belgian village, Gheel, found something better. They said: "Send us your insane. We will give them absolute freedom." They adopted them into their families, they gave them places at their tables, chance alongside them to cultivate their fields and a place among their young people at their country balls. "Eat, drink, and dance with us. Work, run about the fields and be free." That was the system, that was all the science the Belgian peasant had. (I am speaking of the early days. Today the treatment of the insane at Gheel has become a profession and where it is a profession for profit, what significance can there be in it?) And liberty worked a miracle. The insane became cured. Even those who had incurable, organic lesions became sweet, tractable members of the family like the rest. The diseased mind would always work in an abnormal fashion but the heart was in the right place. They cried that it was a miracle. The cures were attributed to a saint and a virgin. But this virgin was liberty and the saint was work in the fields and fraternal treatment. At one of the extremes of the immense "space between mental disease and crime" of which Maudsley speaks, liberty and fraternal treatment have worked their miracle. They will do the same at the other extreme.

TO SUM UP

The prison does not prevent anti-social acts from taking place. It increases their numbers. It does not improve those who enter its walls. However it is reformed it will always remain a place of restraint, an artificial environment, like a monastery, which will make the prisoner less and less fit for life in the community. It does not achieve its end. It degrades society. It must disappear. It is a survival of barbarism mixed with Jesuitical philanthropy.

The first duty of the revolution will be to abolish prisons, —those monuments of human hyprocrisy and cowardice. Anti-social acts need not be feared in a society of equals, in the midst of a free people, all of whom have acquired a healthy education and the habit of mutually aiding one another. The greater number of these acts will no longer have any *raison d'être*. The others will be nipped in the bud.

As for those individuals with evil tendencies whom existing society will pass on to us after the revolution, it will be our task to prevent their exercising these tendencies. This is already accomplished quite efficiently by the solidarity of all the members of the community against such aggressors. If we do not succeed in all cases, the only practical corrective still will be fraternal treatment and moral support.

This is not Utopia. It is already done by isolated individuals and it will become the general practice. And such means will be far more powerful to protect society from anti-social acts than the existing system of punishment which is an ever-fertile source of new crimes.

Note for "Revolutionary Government"

This pamphlet was made up from articles in *Le Révolté*, written about 1880, when Kropotkin was hitting hard at the two chief means advocated by socialists for achieving a revolutionary change,—the ballot and dictatorship by force. Parliamentary forms of government, advocated by the socialist political movement, are as futile in achieving revolutionary aims, according to his view, as a dictatorship based on armed force, now championed by the communists.

This brief exposition endeavors to show by historical examples the impossibility of creating any government that will act in the interest of revolutionary principles,—that is, to transfer power and property to the masses. Only the collective work of the masses of the people in their own free associations, he says, can achieve and maintain a real revolution.

REVOLUTIONARY GOVERNMENT

PARLIAMENT

THAT the governments existing at present ought to be abolished, so that liberty, equality, and fraternity should no longer be empty words but become living realities, and that all forms of government as yet tried have only been so many forms of oppression and ought to be replaced by a new form of grouping, will be agreed by all who have a brain and temperament ever so little revolutionary. One does not need to be much of an innovator to arrive at this conclusion. The vices of the governments of today and the impossibility of reforming them are too evident to be hidden from the eyes of any reasonable observer. And as for overturning governments, it is well known that at certain epochs that can be done without much difficulty. There are times when governments crumble to pieces almost of themselves like houses of cards, before the breath of the people in revolt.

To overturn a government—is for a revolutionary middle-class man everything; for us it is only the beginning of the social revolution. The machine of the State once out of gear, the hierarchy of functionaries disorganized and not knowing in what direction to take a step, the soldiers having lost confidence in their officers—in a word, the whole army of defenders of capital once routed—then it is that the grand work of destruction of all the institutions which serve to perpetuate economic and political slavery will become ours. The possibility of acting freely being attained, what will revolutionists do next?

To this question the anarchists alone give the proper answer: "No Government!" All the others say "A Revolu-

237

tionary Government!" and they differ only as to the form to be given to that government. Some decide for a government elected by universal suffrage in the State or in the commune; others decide on a revolutionary dictatorship.

A revolutionary government! These are two words which sound very strange in the ears of those who really understand what the social revolution means, and what a government means. The words contradict each other, destroy each other. We have seen, of course, many despotic governments,—it is the essence of all government to take the side of the reaction against revolution, and to have a tendency towards despotism. But such a thing as a revolutionary government has never been seen, and the reason is that the revolution—meaning the demolition by violence of the established forms of property, the destruction of castes, the rapid transformation of received ideas about morality, is precisely the opposite, the very negation of government, this being the synonym of "established order," of conservatism, of the maintenance of existing institutions, the negation of free initiative and individual action. And yet we continually hear this white blackbird spoken of as if a "revolutionary government" were the simplest thing in the world, as common and as well known to all as royalty, the empire, and the papacy!

That the so-called revolutionists of the middle class should preach this idea is nothing strange. We know well what they understand by revolution. They understand by it a bolstering up of their republic, the taking possession by the so-called republicans of the lucrative employments reserved today for the royalists. It means at the most the divorce of church and state, replaced by the concubinage of the two, the sequestration of the goods of the clergy for benefit of the State, and above all for that of the future administrators of these goods. Perhaps it may mean the referendum, or some other political machinery. But that revolutionary socialists should make themselves the apostles of such an idea can only be explained by supposing one of two things. Either they are imbued with prejudices which they have imbibed without knowing it from literature, and above all from history written to suit middle-class ideas; or else they do not really desire this revolution which they have always on their lips. They would be content with a simple plastering up of present institutions, provided that they would secure power for themselves, leaving to the future to decide what they should do to satisfy "the beast" called "the people." They only go against the governors of the present time in order to take their places. With these people we care not to argue. We will therefore only speak to those who honestly deceive themselves.

Let us begin with the first of the forms of "revolutionary government" which is advocated,—the elected government.

The power of the royalty we will suppose has just been overturned, the army of the defenders of capital is routed; everywhere there is fermentation, discussion of public affairs, everywhere a desire to march onward. New ideas arise, the necessity of important changes is perceived. It is necessary to act, it is necessary to begin without pity the work of demolition in order to prepare the ground for the new life. But what do they propose to us to do? To convoke the people to elections, to elect at once a government and confide to it the work which we all of us, and each of us, should undertake of our own initiative.

This is what Paris did after the 18th of March, 1871. "I will never forget," said a friend to us, "those delightful moments of deliverance. I came down from my upper chamber in the Latin Quarter to join that immense open-air club which filled the boulevards from one end of Paris to the other. Everyone talked about public affairs; all mere personal preoccupations were forgotten; no more was thought of buying or selling; all felt ready, body and soul, to advance towards the future. Men of the middle-class even, carried away by the general enthusiasm, saw with joy a new world opened up. 'If it is necessary to make a social revolution,' they said, 'make it then. Put all things in common; we are ready for it.' All the elements of the revolution were there, it was only necessary to set them to work. When I returned to my lodging at night I said to myself, 'How fine is humanity after all, but no one knew it; it has always been calumniated.' Then came the elections, the members of the commune were named—and then little by little the ardor of devotion and the desire for action were extinguished. Everyone returned to his usual task, saying to himself, 'Now we have an honest government, let it act for us.' " What followed everyone knows.

Instead of acting for themselves, instead of marching forward, instead of advancing in the direction of a new order of things, the people, confiding in their governors, entrusted to them the charge of taking the initiative. This was the first consequence of the inevitable result of elections. Let us see now what these governors did who were invested with the confidence of all.

Never were elections more free than those of March, 1871. The opponents of the commune admit it themselves. Never was the great mass of electors more influenced with the desire to place in power the best men, men of the future, true revolutionists. And so they did. All well-known revolutionists were elected by immense majorities; Jacobins, Blanquists, Internationalists, all three revolutionary divisions were represented in the Council of the Commune. No election could give a better government.

But what was the result of it? Shut up in the City Hall, charged to proceed after the forms established by preceding governments, these ardent revolutionists, these reformers found themselves smitten with incapacity and sterility. With all their good will and their courage they did not even know how to organize the defense of Paris. Of course people now blame the men, the individuals for this; but it was not the men who were the cause of this failure—it was the system.

In fact, universal suffrage, when it is quite free, can only produce, at best, an assembly which represents the average of the opinions which at the time are held by the mass of the people. And this average at the outbreak of the revolution has only a vague idea of the work to be accomplished, without understanding at all how they ought to undertake it. Ah, if the bulk of the nation, of the commune, could only understand before the movement what is necessary to be done as soon as the government is overturned! If this dream of the utopians of the chair could be realized, we never would have had bloody revolutions. The will of the bulk of the nation once expressed, the rest would submit to it with a good grace. But this is not how things are done. The revolution bursts out long before a general understanding has come, and those who have a clear idea of what should be done the next day are only a very small minority. The great mass of the people have as yet only a general idea of the end which they wish realized, without knowing much how to advance towards that end, and without having much confidence in the direction to follow. The practical solution will not be found, will not be made clear until the change will have already begun. It will be the product of the revolution itself, of the people in action,—or else it will be nothing, the brain of a few individuals being absolutely incapable of finding solutions which can only spring from the life of the people.

This is the situation which is reflected in the body elected by universal suffrage, even if it had not the vices inherent in representative governments in general. The few men who represent the revolutionary idea of the epoch find themselves swamped among the representatives of the revolutionary schools of the past, and the existing order of things. These men who would be so necessary among the people, particularly in the days of revolution, to sow broadcast their ideas, to put the mass in movement, to demolish the institutions of the past, find themselves shut up in a hall, vainly discussing how to wrest concessions from the moderates, and how to convert their enemies, while there is really only one way of inducing them to accept the new idea—namely, to put it into execution. The government becomes a parliament with all the vices of a middle-class parliament. Far from being a "revolutionary" government it becomes the greatest obstacle to the revolution, and at last the people find themselves compelled to put it out of the way, to dismiss those that but yesterday they acclaimed as their chosen.

But it is not so easy to do so. The new government which has hastened to organize a new administration in order to extend its domination and make itself obeyed does not understand giving up so easily. Jealous of maintaining its power, it clings to it with all the energy of an institution which has not yet had time to fall into senile decay. It decides to oppose force with force, and there is only one means then to dislodge it, namely, to take up arms, to make another revolution in order to dismiss those in whom the people had placed all their hopes.

There you see the revolution divided against itself! After losing precious time in delays, it now loses its strength in internecine divisions between the friends of the new government and those who see the necessity of dissolving it. And all this happens because it has not been understood that a new life requires new forms; that it is not by clinging to ancient forms that a revolution can be carried out! All this for not having understood the incompatibility of revolution and government, for not having seen that the one is, under whatever form it presents itself, the negation of the other, and that outside of anarchism there is no such thing as revolution.

It is just the same with regard to that other form of "revolutionary government" so often extolled,—a revolutionary dictatorship.

DICTATORSHIP

The dangers to whch the revolution is exposed when it allows itself to be controlled by an elected government are so evident that a whole school of revolutionists entirely renounces the idea of it. They understand that it is impossible for a people in insurrection to give themselves, by means of elections, any government but one that represents the past, and which must be like leaden shoes on the feet of the people, above all when it is necessary to accomplish that imense regeneration, economic, political, and moral, which we understand by the social revolution. They renounce then the idea of "legal" government at least during that period which is a revolt against legality, and they advocate a "revolutionary dictatorship."

"The party," say they, "which will have overturned the government will take the place of it, of course. It will seize upon power and proceed in a revolutionary manner. It will take the measures necessary to secure the success of the insurrection. It will demolish the old institutions; it will organize the defense of the country. As for those who will not recognize its authority, why the guillotine will settle them, whether they belong to the people or the middle class, if they refuse to obey the orders necessary for the advance of the revolution." The guillotine still in action? See how these budding Robespierres argue, who know nothing of the grand epic of the century but its period of decline, men who have never learned anything about it except from speeches of the hangers-on of the Republic.

For us anarchists the dictatorship of an individual or of a party (at bottom the very same thing) has been finally condemned. We know that revolution and government are incompatible. One must destroy the other no matter what name is given to government, whether dictatorship, royalty, or parliament. We know that what makes the strength and the truth of our party is contained in this formula—"Nothing good or durable can be done except by the free initiative of the people, and every government tends to destroy it." And so the very best among us, if they should become masters of that formidable machine, the government, would become, in a week, fit only for the gallows, if their ideas had not to pass through the crucible of the popular mind before being put into execution. We know whither every dictatorship leads, even the best intentioned,—namely, to the death of all revolutionary movement. We know also, that this idea of dictatorship is never anything more than a sickly product of governmental fetish-worship, which, like religious fetish-worship, has always served to perpetuate slavery.

But we do not now address ourselves to anarchists. We speak to those governmental revolutionists who, led astray by the prejudices of their education, honestly deceive themselves, and ask nothing better than to discuss the question. We therefore speak to them from their own point-of-view.

To begin with one general observation: those who preach dictatorship do not in general perceive that in sustaining this prejudice they only prepare the way for those who later on will cut their throats. There is, however, one word of Robespierre's which his admirers would do well to remember. He did not deny the dictatorship in principle; but "have good care about it," he answered abruptly to Mandar when he spoke to him of it, "Brissot would be the Dictator!" Yes, Brissot, the crafty Girondin, deadly enemy of the levelling tendencies of the people, furious defender of property (though he once called it theft), Brissot, who would cooly have consigned to the Abbaye Prison, Hébert, Marat, and all the moderate Jacobins!

Now this was said in 1792! At that time France had already been three years in revolution! In fact, royalty no longer existed; it only awaited its death stroke. The feudal régime was actually abolished. And yet even at this time when the revolution rolled its waves untrammelled, it was still the counter-revolutionist Brissot who had the best chance to be made dictator! And who would it have been previously, in 1789? Mirabeau is the man who would have been acknowledged as the head of the government! The man who made a bargain with the king to sell him his eloquence,—this is the man who would have been thrust into power at this time, if the insurgent people had not imposed its sovereignty, sustained by its pikes, and if it had not proceeded by the accomplished facts of the Jacquerie, in making illusory every government constituted at Paris or in the departments.

But governmental prejudice so thoroughly blinds those who speak of dictatorship, that they prefer the dictatorship of a new Brissot or a Napoleon to abandoning the idea of giving another master to men who are breaking the chains of their slavery!

The secret societies of the time of the Restoration and of Louis-Philippe contributed powerfully to maintain this prejudice of dictatorship. The middle-class republicans of the time, aided by the workers, made a long series of conspiracies, with the object of overturning royalty and proclaiming the Republic. Not understanding the profound change that would have to be effected in France before even a republican régime could be established, they imagined that by means of a vast conspiracy they would some day overturn royalty, take possession of power and proclaim the Republic. For more than thirty years those secret societies never ceased to work with an unlimited devotion and heroic courage and perseverance. If the Republic resulted from the insurrection of 1848, it was thanks to these societies, and thanks to the propaganda by deed made by them for thirty years. Without their noble efforts the Republic would have been impossible.

The end they had in view was to get possession of power themselves and to instal a republican dictatorship. But of course they never succeeded. As ever, from the very nature of things, a conspiracy could not overturn royalty. The conspirators had indeed prepared the way for its fall. They had spread widely the republican idea; their martyrs had made it the ideal of the people. But the final effort which definitely overturned the king of the bourgeoisie was much greater and stronger than any that could come from a secret society; it came from the mass of the people.

The result is known. The party which had prepared the way for the fall of royalty found itself thrust aside from the steps of the Government House. Others, too prudent to run the risk of conspiracy, but better known, more moderate also, lying in wait for the opportunity of grasping power, took the place which the conspirators hoped to conquer at the point of the bayonet. Journalists, lawyers, good talkers who worked hard to make a name for themselves while the true republicans forged weapons or expired in jail, took possession of power. Some of them, already well known, were acclaimed by the people; others pushed themselves forward and were accepted because their name represented nothing more than a program of agreement with everybody.

It is useless to tell us that this happened because of a want of practical spirit in the party of action, and that others will be able to do better in future. No, a thousand times no! It is a law as immutable as that which governs the movement of the stars, that the party of action must be thrown aside, and the intriguers and talkers seize upon power. They are always better known to the great mass that makes the final effort. They get more votes, because with or without voting papers, by acclamation or by the ballot-box, at the bottom it is always a kind of tacit election which is made in such cases by acclamation. They are acclaimed by everybody and above all by the enemies of the revolution, who prefer to put forward nobodies, and thus by acclamation those men are accepted as rulers who are really either enemies of the movement or indifferent toward it.

The man who more than any other was the incarnation of this system of conspiracy, the man who by a life spent in prison paid for his devotion to this system, on the eve of his death uttered these words, which of themselves make an entire program—"Neither God nor Master!"

THE IMPOTENCE OF REVOLUTIONARY GOVERNMENTS

To imagine that a government can be overturned by a secret society, and that that secret society can take its place, is an error into which have fallen all the revolutionary organizations which sprang to life in the bosom of the republican middle class since 1820. And yet facts abound which prove what an error it is. What devotion, what abnegation, what perseverance was not displayed by the republican secret societies of the Young Italy Party! And yet all this immense work, all these sacrifices made by the youth of Italy, before which even those of the Russian revolutionary youth pale, all the corpses piled up in the casemates of Austrian fortresses, and under the knife and bullets of the executioner—all this only brought into power the crafty, robbing middle class and royalty!

It is inevitable, it cannot be otherwise. For it is not secret societies nor even revolutionary organizations that can give the finishing blow to governments. Their function, their historic mission is to prepare men's minds for the revolution, and then when men's minds are prepared and external circumstances are favorable, the final rush is made, not by the group that initiated the movement, but by the mass of the people altogether outside of the society. On the 31st of August Paris was deaf to the appeals of Blanqui. Four days later he proclaimed the fall of the government; but then the Blanquists were no longer the initiators of the movement. It was the people, the millions who dethroned the man of December and proclaimed the humbugs whose names for two years had resounded in their ears. When a revolution is ready to burst out, when the movement is felt in the air, when its success is already certain, then a thousand new men, on whom the organization has never exercised any direct influence, come and join the movement like birds of prey coming to the field of battle to feed on the victims. These help to make the final effort, but it is not in the ranks of the sincere and irreconcilable conspirators, it is among the men on the fence that they look for their leaders. The conspirators who still are possessed with the prejudice of a dictatorship then unconsciously work to put into power their own enemies.

But if all this that we have just said is true with regard to political revolutions or rather outbreaks, it is much more true with regard to the revolution we desire—the social revolution. To allow any government to be established, a strong and recognized power, is to paralyze the work of the revolution at once. The good that this government would do is nil, and the evil immense.

What do we understand by revolution? It is not a simple

change of governors. It is the taking possession by the people of all social wealth. It is the abolition of all the forces which have so long hampered the development of humanity. But is it by decrees emanating from a government that this immense economic revolution can be accomplished? We have seen in the past century the Polish revolutionary dictator Kosciusko decree the abolition of personal servitude, yet the servitude continued to exist for eighty years after this decree. We have seen the Convention, the omnipotent Convention, the terrible Convention as its admirers call it, decree the equal division per head of all the communal lands taken back from the nobles. Like so many others, this decree remained a dead letter because in order to carry it out it was necessary that the proletarians of the rural districts should make an entirely new revolution, and revolutions are not made by the force of decrees. In order that the taking possession of social wealth should become an accomplished fact it is necessary that the people should have their hands free, that they should shake off the slavery to which they are too much habituated, that they act according to their own will, and march forward without waiting for orders from anyone. And it is this very thing which a dictatorship would prevent however well intentioned it might be, while it would be incapable of advancing in the slightest degree the march of the revolution.

But if government, were it even an ideal revolutionary government, creates no new force and is of no use whatever in the work of demolition which we have to accomplish, still less can we count on it for the work of reorganization which must follow that of demolition. The economic change which will result from the social revolution will be so immense and so profound, it must so change all the relations based today on property and exchange, that it is impossible for one or any individual to elaborate the different social forms which must spring up in the society of the future. This elaboration of new social forms can only be made by the collective work of the masses. To satisfy the immense variety of conditions and needs which will spring up as soon as private property shall be abolished, it is necessary to have the collective suppleness of mind of the whole people. Any authority external to it will only be an obstacle, and beside that a source of discord and hatred.

But it is full time to give up this illusion, so often proved false and so often dearly paid for, of a revolutionary government. It is time to admit, once for all, this political axiom that a government cannot be revolutionary. People talk of the Convention, but let us not forget that the few measures taken by the Convention, little revolutionary though they were, were only the sanction of action accomplished by the people who at the time trampled under foot all governments. As Victor Hugo had said, Danton pushed forward Robespierre, Marat watched and pushed on Danton, and Marat himself was pushed on by Cimourdain—this personification of the clubs of wild enthusiasts and rebels. Like all the governments that preceded it and followed it, the Convention was only a drag on the action of the people.

The facts which history teach us are so conclusive in this respect, the impossibility of a revolutionary government and the injurious effect of that which is called by the name are so evident, that it would seem difficult to explain the determination with which a certain school calling itself socialist maintains the idea of a government. But the explanation is very simple. It is that socialists, though they say they are the followers of this school, have an entirely different conception from ours of the revolution which we have to accomplish. For them, as for all the middle-class radicals, the social revolution is rather an affair of the future about which we have not to think much at present. What they dream of in their inmost thoughts, though they don't dare to confess it, is something entirely different. It is the installation of a government like that of Switzerland or the United States, making some attempts at expropriation, in favor of the State, of what they call "public services." It is something after the ideal of

Bismarck. It is a compromise made in advance between the socialistic aspirations of the masses and the desires of the middle class. They would, indeed, wish the expropriation to be complete, but they have not the courage to attempt it; so they put it off to the next century, and before the battle they enter into negotiation with the enemy.

NOTE FOR "THE RUSSIAN REVOLUTION AND THE SOVIET GOVERNMENT"

Kropotkin's attitude to the Soviet Government in relation to the Russian revolution was voiced only in letters to friends and in two public statements, which are printed here, with slight omissions of unimportant parts. The *Letter to the Workers of Western Europe*, written early in 1919, and sent to Georg Brandes, the great Danish critic, while military communism was still in effect, deals in part with aspects still essentially unchanged. It was written for the British Labour Mission of 1920 and is included in their report.

The memorandum dated just a few months before his death in 1921 deals with the revolution in much more general terms. It was not completed, and should not be regarded as his full thought on the question that prompted it,— *What to do?* It was written in response to repeated appeals by his family and friends for his view of what should be done by anarchists in Russia.

THE RUSSIAN REVOLUTION AND THE SOVIET GOVERNMENT

LETTER TO THE WORKERS OF WESTERN EUROPE *

Dmitrov, Russia,
April 28, 1919.

I HAVE been asked if I did not have a message for the workers of the western world. Certainly there is plenty to say and learn of the actual events in Russia. As the message would have to be long to cover all, I will indicate only the principal points.

First, the workers of the civilized world and their friends in other classes ought to prevail on their governments to abandon entirely the idea of armed intervention in Russia, whether openly or secretly. Russia is undergoing now a revolution of the same extent and importance as England underwent in 1639 to '48, and France in 1789 to '94. Every nation should refuse to play the shameful role played by England, Prussia, Austria and Russia during the French Revolution.

Further, it must be borne in mind that the Russian Revolution—which is trying to build a society in which all productive work, technical ability and scientific knowledge will be entirely communal—is not a mere accident in the struggle of contending parties. It was prepared by almost a century of socialist and communist propaganda, since the days of Robert Owen, Saint Simon and Fourier. And although the effort to introduce the new social system by means of a party dictatorship is apparently condemned to failure,

---

* Published first in English in the *Labour Leader* of July 22, 1920, later in the *Temps Nouveaux*, from which this is translated.

it must be recognized that already the revolution has introduced into our daily lives new conceptions of the rights of
labor, its rightful place in society and the duties of each
citizen,—and that they will endure.

Not only the workers, but all the progressive forces in
the civilized world should put an end to the support given
until now to the enemies of the revolution. Not that there
is nothing to oppose in the methods of the Bolshevik government. Far from it! But all foreign armed intervention
necessarily strengthens the dictatorial tendencies of the government, and paralyzes the efforts of those Russians who are
ready to aid Russia, independently of the government, in the
restoration of its life.

The evils inherent in a party dictatorship have been accentuated by the conditions of war in which this party maintains its power. This state of war has been the pretext for
strengthening dictatorial methods which centralize the control of every detail of life in the hands of the government,
with the effect of stopping an immense part of the ordinary
activities of the country. The evils natural to state communism have been increased ten-fold under the pretext that
all our misery is due to foreign intervention.

I should also point out that if Allied military intervention
continues, it will certainly develop in Russia a bitter feeling
toward the western nations, a feeling which will be used some
day in future conflicts. That bitterness is always developing.

In short, it is high time that the nations of Europe enter
into direct relations with the Russian nation. And from this
point of view, you—the working class and the progressive
elements of all nations—should have your word to say.

A word more on the general question. The re-establish-
ment of relations between the European and American nations and Russia does not mean the supremacy of the Russian
nation over the nationalities that composed the Czarist empire. Imperialist Russia is dead and will not be revived. The
future of these different provinces lies in a great federation.
The natural territories of the various parts of this federation

are quite distinct, as those of us familiar with Russian history and ethnography well know. All efforts to reunite under a central control the naturally separate parts of the Russian Empire are predestined to failure. It is therefore fitting that the western nations should recognize the right of independence of each part of the old Russian Empire.

My opinion is that this development will continue. I see the time coming when each part of this federation will be itself a federation of rural communes and free cities. And I believe also that certain parts of western Europe will soon follow the same course.

As to our present economic and political situation, the Russian revolution, being a continuation of the great revolutions of England and France, is trying to reach the point where the French revolution stopped before it succeeded in creating what they called "equality in fact," that is, economic equality.

Unhappily, this effort has been made in Russia under a strongly centralized party dictatorship. This effort was made in the same way as the extremely centralized and Jacobin endeavor of Baboeuf. I owe it to you to say frankly that, according to my view, this effort to build a communist republic on the basis of a strongly centralized state communism under the iron law of party dictatorship is bound to end in failure. We are learning to know in Russia how *not* to introduce communism, even with a people tired of the old régime and opposing no active resistance to the experiments of the new rulers.

The idea of soviets, that is to say, of councils of workers and peasants, conceived first at the time of the revolutionary attempt in 1905, and immediately realized by the revolution of February, 1917, as soon as Czarism was overthrown,—the idea of such councils controlling the economic and political life of the country is a great idea. All the more so, since it necessarily follows that these councils should be composed of all who take a real part in the production of national wealth by their own efforts.

But as long as the country is governed by a party dic-

tatorship, the workers' and peasants' councils evidently lose
their entire significance. They are reduced to the passive
role formerly played by the "States General," when they were
convoked by the king and had to combat an all-powerful
royal council.

A council of workers ceases to be free and of any use when
liberty of the press no longer exists, and we have been in
that condition for two years,—under a pretext that we are
in a state of war. But more still. The workers' and peasants'
councils lose their significance when the elections are not preceded by a free electoral campaign, and when the elections
are conducted under pressure by a party dictatorship. Naturally, the usual excuse is that a dictatorship is inevitable in
order to combat the old régime. But such a state of affairs is
evidently a step backwards, since the revolution is committed
to the construction of a new society on a new economic base.
It means the death-knell of the new system.

The methods of overthrowing an already enfeebled government are well known to ancient and modern history. But
when it is necessary to create new forms of life, especially new
forms of production and exchange, without having examples
to imitate; when everything must be constructed anew; when
a government which undertakes to furnish every citizen with
a lamp and even the match to light it, and then cannot do
it even with a limitless number of officials,—that government
becomes a nuisance. It develops a bureaucracy so formidable
that the French bureaucracy, which requires the help of forty
officials to sell a tree broken down by a storm on the national
highway, is a mere bagatelle in comparison. That is what
we are learning in Russia. And that is what you workers of
the west should avoid by every means, since you have at
heart the success of a real social reconstruction. Send your
delegates here to see how a social revolution is working in
real life.

The immense constructive work demanded by a social revolution cannot be accomplished by a central government, even
if it had to guide it something more substantial than a few

socialist and anarchist hand-books. It has need of knowledge, of brains and of the voluntary collaboration of a host of local and specialized forces which alone can attack the diversity of economic problems in their local aspects. To reject this collaboration and to turn everything over to the genius of party dictators is to destroy the independent centers of our life, the trade unions and the local cooperative organizations, by changing them into bureaucratic organs of the party, as is the case at this time. That is the way *not* to accomplish the revolution, to make its realization impossible. And that is why I consider it my duty to put you on guard against borrowing any such methods. . . .

The late war has brought about new conditions of life for the whole civilized world. Socialism will certainly make considerable progress, and new forms of more independent life will be created based on local autonomy and free initiative. They will be created either peacefully, or by revolutionary means.

But the success of this reconstruction will depend in great part on the possibility of direct cooperation between the different peoples. To achieve that, it is necessary that the working classes of all nations should be directly united and that the idea of a great international of all the workers of the world should be taken up again, but not in the form of a union directed by a single political party, as in the case of the Second and Third Internationals. Such unions have of course plenty of reason to exist, but outside of them, and uniting all, there should be a union of all the workers' organizations of the world, federated to deliver world production from its present subjection to capitalism.

WHAT TO DO?

The revolution we have gone through is the sum total, not of the efforts of separate individuals, *but a natural phenomenon, independent of the human will*, a natural phenomenon similar to a typhoon such as rises suddenly on the coasts of Eastern Asia.

Thousands of causes, in which the work of separate individuals and even of parties has been only a grain of sand, one of the minute local whirlwinds, have contributed to form the great natural phenomenon, the great catastrophe which shall either renew, or destroy; or perhaps both destroy and renew.

All of us prepared this great inevitable change. But it was also prepared by all the previous revolutions of 1793, 1848-1871; by all the writings of the Jacobins, socialists; by all the achievements of science, industry, art and so on. In a word, millions of natural causes have contributed just in the same way as millions of movements of particles of air or water cause the sudden storm which sinks hundreds of ships or destroys thousands of houses—as the trembling of the earth in an earthquake is caused by thousands of small tremors and by the preparatory movements of separate particles.

In general, people do not see events concretely, solidly. They think more in words than in clearly-imagined pictures, and they have absolutely no idea what a revolution is,—of those many millions of causes which have gone to give it its present form,—and they are therefore inclined to exaggerate the importance in the progress of the revolution of their personality and of that attitude which they, their friends and co-thinkers will take up in this enormous upheaval. And of course they are absolutely incapable of understanding how powerless is any individual, whatever his intelligence and experience, in this whirlpool of hundreds of thousands of forces which have been put into motion by the upheaval.

They do not understand that once such a great natural phenomenon has begun, such as an earthquake, or, rather, such as a typhoon, separate individuals are powerless to exercise any kind of influence on the course of events. A party perhaps can do something,—far less than is usually thought,—and on the surface of the oncoming waves, its influence may, perhaps, be very slightly noticeable. But separate small aggregations not forming a fairly large mass are undoubtedly powerless—their powers are certainly *nil*. . . .

It is in this position that I, an anarchist, find myself. But even parties of far greater numbers in Russia at the present moment are in a very similar position.

I will even go farther; the governing party itself is in the some position. It no longer governs, it is being carried along by the current which it helped to create but which is now already a thousand times stronger than the party itself. . . .

What is then to be done?

We are experiencing a revolution which has advanced not at all along those ways which we had prepared for it, but which we had no time to prepare sufficiently. What is to be done now?

To prevent the revolution? Absurd!

Too late. The revolution will advance in its own way, in the direction of the least resistance, without paying the least attention to our efforts.

At the present moment the Russian revolution is in the following position. It is perpetrating horrors. It is ruining the whole country. In its mad fury it is annihilating human lives. That is why it is a revolution and not a peaceful progress, because it is destroying without regarding what it destroys and whither it goes.

And we are powerless for the present to direct it into another channel, until such time as it will have played itself out. It must wear itself out.

And then? *Then—inevitably will come a reaction.* Such is the law of history, and it is easy to understand why this cannot be otherwise. People imagine that we can change the form of development of a revolution. That is a childish illusion. A revolution is such a force that its growth cannot be changed. *And a reaction is absolutely inevitable,* just as a hollow in the water is inevitable after every wave, as weakness is inevitable in a human being after a period of feverish activity.

Therefore the only thing we can do is to use our energy to lessen the fury and force of the oncoming reaction.

But of what can our efforts consist?

To modify the passions—on one as on the other side? Who is likely to listen to us? Even if there exist such diplomats as can do anything in this role, the time for their *début* has not yet come; neither the one nor the other side is as yet disposed to listen to them. I see one thing; we must gather together people *who will be capable of undertaking constructive work in each and every party after the revolution has worn itself out.* (Italics Kropotkin's.)

NOTE FOR "AN APPEAL TO THE YOUNG"

This plea to young men and women of the upper classes to join the workers' revolutionary cause is one of the best known and most widely read of Kropotkin's "editorials." It appeared first in *Le Révolté* in 1880 and was soon published in pamphlet form, being later included in the book *Paroles d'un Révolté*.

It is directed specifically to professional young men and women,—lawyers, doctors, teachers, scientists,—urging them to put their talents and technical training at the service of the workers and to forego lives of personal gain. Kropotkin pictures the compensations in larger lives of comradeship and joy and in the growth of creative powers of expression.

It is well calculated to fire the idealism of youth, though like all such appeals it is weak on the practical side of just what to do and how to do it. Its impulse must have been drawn largely from Kropotkin's own experience in Russia, and in the "to the people" movement of the students and professional men and women who championed the revolutionary cause.

AN APPEAL TO THE YOUNG

IT IS to the young that I wish to address myself. Let the old—I mean of course the old in heart and mind—lay this down without tiring their eyes in reading what will tell them nothing.

I assume that you are about eighteen or twenty years of age, that you have finished your apprenticeship or your studies, that you are just entering on life. I take it for granted that you have a mind free from the superstition which your teachers have sought to force upon you; that you do not fear the devil, and that you do not go to hear parsons and ministers rant. More, that you are not one of the fops, sad products of a society in decay, who display their well-cut trousers and their monkey faces in the park, and who even at their early age have only an insatiable longing for pleasure at any price . . . I assume on the contrary that you have a warm heart and for this reason I talk to you.

A first question, I know, occurs to you. You have often asked yourself—"What am I going to be?" In fact when a man is young he understands that after having studied a trade or a science for several years—at the cost of society, mark—he has not done this in order that he should make use of his acquirements as instruments of plunder for his own gain, and he must be depraved indeed and utterly cankered by vice, who has not dreamed that one day he would apply his intelligence, his abilities, his knowledge to help on the enfranchisement of those who today grovel in misery and in ignorance.

You are one of those who has had such a vision, are you not? Very well, let us see what you must do to make your dream a reality.

I do not know in what rank you were born. Perhaps, favored by fortune, you have turned your attention to the study of science; you are to be a doctor, a lawyer, a man of letters, or a scientific man. A wide field opens up before you. You enter upon life with extensive knowledge, with a trained intelligence. Or on the other hand, you are perhaps only an artisan whose knowledge of science is limited by the little you learned at school. But you have had the advantage of learning at first hand what a life of exhausting toil is the lot of the worker of our time.

TO THE "INTELLECTUALS"

To Doctors

I stop at the first supposition, to return afterwards to the second; I assume then that you have received a scientific education. Let us suppose you intend to be a doctor.

Tomorrow a man attired in rough clothes will come to fetch you to see a sick woman. He will lead you into one of those alleys where the neighbors opposite can almost shake hands over the heads of the passers-by. You ascend into a foul atmosphere by the flickering light of a little ill-trimmed lamp. You climb two, three, four, five flights of filthy stairs, and in a dark, cold room you find the sick woman lying on a pallet covered with dirty rags. Pale, livid children, shivering under their scanty garments, gaze with their big eyes wide open. The husband has worked all his life twelve or thirteen hours a day at no matter what. Now he has been out of work for three months. To be out of employment is not rare in his trade; it happens every year, periodically. But formerly when he was out of work his wife went out as a charwoman—perhaps to wash your shirts; now she has been bedridden for two months, and misery glares upon the family in all its squalid hideousness.

What will you prescribe for the sick woman, doctor? You have seen at a glance that the cause of her illness is a general anaemia, want of good food, lack of fresh air. Say a good beefsteak every day? A little exercise in the country? A dry and well-ventilated bedroom? What irony! If she could have afforded it this would have been done long since without waiting for your advice.

If you have a good heart, a frank address, an honest face, the family will tell you many things. They will tell you that the woman on the other side of the partition, who coughs a cough which tears your heart, is a poor ironer; that a flight of stairs lower down all the children have the fever; that the washwoman who occupies the ground floor will not live to see the spring; and that in the house next door things are worse.

What will you say to all these sick people? Recommend them generous diet, change of air, less exhausting toil. . . . You only wish you could, but you daren't and you go out heartbroken with a curse on your lips.

The next day, as you still brood over the fate of the dwellers in this dog house, your partner tells you that yesterday a footman came to fetch him, this time in a carriage. It was for the owner of a fine house, for a lady worn out with sleepless nights, who devotes all her life to dressing, visits, balls and squabbles with a stupid husband. Your friend has prescribed for her a less preposterous habit of life, a less heating diet, walks in the fresh air, an even temperament, and, in order to make up in some measure for the want of useful work, a little gymnastic exercise in her bedroom.

The one is dying because she has never had enough food nor enough rest in her whole life. The other pines because she has never known what work is since she was born.

If you are one of those characterless natures who adapt themselves to anything, who at the sight of the most revolting spectacles console themselves with a gentle sigh, then you will gradually become used to these contrasts, and the nature of the beast favoring your endeavors, your sole idea will be to maintain yourself in the ranks of pleasure-seekers, so that you may never find yourself among the wretched. But if you are a *Man*, if every sentiment is translated in your case into an action of the will, if in you the beast has not crushed the intelligent being, then you will return home one day saying to yourself: "No, it is unjust: this must not go on any longer. It is not enough to cure diseases; we must prevent them. A little good living and intellectual development would score off our lists half the patients and half the diseases. Throw physic to the dogs! Air, good diet, less crushing toil—that is how we must begin. Without this, the whole profession of a doctor is nothing but trickery and humbug."

That very day you will understand socialism. You will wish to know it thoroughly, and if altruism is not a word devoid of significance for you, if you apply to the study of the social question the rigid induction of the natural philosopher, you will end by finding yourself in our ranks, and you will work, as we work, to bring about the social revolution.

To Scientists

But perhaps you will say, "Mere practical business may go to the devil! As an astronomer, a physiologist, a chemist, I will devote myself to science. Such work as that always bears fruit, if only for future generations."

Let us first try to understand what you seek in devoting yourself to science. Is it only the pleasure—doubtless immense—which we derive from the study of nature and the exercise of our mental faculties? In that case I ask you in what respect does the philosopher, who pursues science in order that he may pass life pleasantly to himself, differ from that drunkard there, who only seeks the immediate gratification that gin affords him? The philosopher has, past all question, chosen his enjoyment more wisely, since it affords him a pleasure far deeper and more lasting than that of the toper. But that is all! Both one and the other have the same selfish end in view, personal gratification.

But no, you have no wish to lead this selfish life. By working at science you mean to work for humanity, and this is the idea which will guide you in your investigations. A charming illusion! Which of us has not hugged it for a moment when giving himself up for the first time to science?

But then, if you are really thinking about humanity, if it is the good of mankind at which you aim, a formidable question arises before you; for, however little you may have of critical spirit, you must at once note that in our society of today science is only an appendage to luxury, rendering life pleasanter for the few, but remaining absolutely inaccessible to the bulk of mankind.

More than a century has passed since science laid down sound propositions as to the origin of the universe, but how many have mastered them or possess the really scientific spirit of criticism? A few thousands at the outside, who are lost in the midst of hundreds of millions still steeped in prejudices and superstitions worthy of savages, who are consequently ever ready to serve as puppets for religious impostors.

Or, to go a step further, let us glance at what science has done to establish rational foundations for physical and moral health. Science tells us how we ought to live in order to preserve the health of our own bodies, how to maintain in good condition the crowded masses of our population. But does not all the vast amount of work done in these two directions remain a dead letter in our books? We know it does. And why? Because science today exists only for a handful of privileged persons, because social inequality, which divides society into two classes—the wage-slaves and the grabbers of capital—renders all its teachings as to the conditions of a rational existence only the bitterest irony to nine-tenths of mankind.

At the present moment we no longer need to accumulate scientific truths and discoveries. The most important thing is to spread the truths already acquired, to practice them in daily life, to make of them a common inheritance. We have to order things in such wise that all humanity may be capable of assimilating and applying them, so that science ceasing to be a luxury becomes the basis of everyday life. Justice requires this.

Furthermore, the very interests of science require it. Science only makes real progress when its truths find environments ready prepared for their reception. The theory of the mechanical origin of heat remained for eighty years buried in academic records until such knowledge of physics had spread widely enough to create a public capable of accepting it. Three generations had to go before the ideas of Erasmus Darwin on the variation of species could be favorably received from his grandson and admitted by academic philosophers, and even then not without pressure from public opinion. The philosopher like the poet or artist is always the product of the society in which he moves and teaches.

But if you are imbued with these ideas, you will understand that it is important above all to bring about a radical change in this state of affairs which today condemns the philosopher to be crammed with scientific truths, and almost the whole of the rest of human beings to remain what they were five or ten centuries ago,—that is to say, in the state of slaves and machines, incapable of mastering established truths. And the day when you are imbued with wide, deep, humane, and profoundly scientific truth, that day will you lose your taste for pure science. You will set to work to find out the means to effect this transformation, and if you bring to your investigations the impartiality which has guided you in your scientific researches you will of necessity adopt the cause of socialism; you will make an end of sophisms and you will come among us. Weary of working to procure pleasures for this small group, which already has a large share of them, you will place your information and devotion at the service of the oppressed.

And be sure that the feeling of duty accomplished and of a real accord established between your sentiments and your actions, you will then find powers in yourself of whose existence you never even dreamed. When, too, one day—it is not far distant in any case, saving the presence of our professors—when one day, I say, the change for which you are working shall have been brought about, then, deriving new forces from collective scientific work, and from the powerful help of armies of laborers who will come to place their energies at its service, science will take a new bound forward, in comparison with which the slow progress of today will appear the simple exercise of tyros. Then you will enjoy science; that pleasure will be a pleasure for all.

To Lawyers

If you have finished reading law and are about to be called to the bar, perhaps you, too, have some illusions as to your future activity—I assume that you are one of the nobler spirits, that you know what altruism means. Perhaps you think, "To devote my life to an unceasing and vigorous struggle against all injustice; to apply my whole faculties to bringing about the triumph of law, the public expression of supreme justice—can any career be nobler!" You begin the real work of life confident in yourself and the profession you have chosen.

Very well; let us turn to any page of the law reports and see what actual life will tell you.

Here we have a rich landowner. He demands the eviction of a farmer tenant who has not paid his rent. From a legal point of view the case is beyond dispute. Since the poor farmer can't pay, out he must go. But if we look into the facts we shall learn something like this. The landlord has squandered his rents persistently in rollicking pleasure; the tenant has worked hard all day and every day. The landlord has done nothing to improve his estate. Nevertheless its value has trebled in fifty years owing to the rise in price of land due to the construction of a railway, to the making of new highroads, to the draining of a marsh, to the enclosure and cultivation of waste lands. But the tenant who has contributed largely towards this increase has ruined himself. He fell into the hands of usurers, and head over ears in debt, he can no longer pay the landlord. The law, always on the side of property, is quite clear; the landlord is in the right. But you, whose feeling of justice has not yet been stifled by legal fictions, what will you do? Will you contend that the farmer ought to be turned out upon the highroad—for that is what the law ordains—or will you urge that the landlord should pay back to the farmer the whole of the increase of value in his property which is due to the farmer's labor—this is what equity decrees? Which side will you take? For the law and against justice, or for justice and against the law?

Or when workmen have gone out on strike against a master, without notice, which side will you take then? The side of the law, that is to say the part of the master, who, taking advantage of a period of crisis, has made outrageous profits, or against the law but on the side of the workers who received during the whole time only miserable wages, and saw their wives and children fade away before their eyes? Will you stand up for that piece of chicanery which consists in affirming "freedom of contract"? Or will you uphold equity, according to which a contract entered into between a man who has dined well and a man who sells his labor for a bare subsistence, between the strong and the weak, is not a contract at all?

Take another case. Here in London a man was loitering near a butcher's shop. He stole a beefsteak and ran off with it. Arrested and questioned, it turns out that he is an artisan out of work, and that he and his family have had nothing to eat for four days. The butcher is asked to let the man off but he is all for the triumph of justice! He prosecutes and the man is sentenced to six months' imprisonment. Does not your conscience revolt against society when you hear similar judgments pronounced every day?

Or again, will you call for the enforcement of the law against this man, who badly brought up and ill-used from his childhood, has arrived at man's estate without having heard one sympathetic word, and completes his career by murdering his neighbor in order to rob him? Will you demand his execution, or, worse still, that he should be imprisoned for twenty years, when you know very well that he is rather a madman than a criminal, and, in any case, that his crime is the fault of our entire society?

Will you claim that these weavers should be thrown into prison who in a moment of desperation have set fire to a mill; that this man who shot at a crowned murderer should be imprisoned for life; that these insurgents should be shot down who plant the flag of the future on the barricades? No, a thousand times no!

If you *reason* instead of repeat what is taught you; if you analyze the law and strip off those cloudy fictions with which it has been draped in order to conceal its real origin, which is the right of the stronger, and its substance, which has ever been the consecration of all the tyrannies handed down to mankind through its long and bloody history; when you have comprehended this your contempt for the law will be profound indeed. You will understand that to remain the servant of the written law is to place yourself every day in opposition to the law of conscience, and to make a bargain on the wrong side, and since this struggle cannot go on for ever, you will either silence your conscience and become a scoundrel, or you will break with tradition, and you will work with us for the utter destruction of all this injustice, economic, social and political. But then you will be a *socialist, you will be a revolutionist!*

To Engineers

And you, young engineer, who dream of bettering the lot of the workers by applying the inventions of science to industry, what a sad disenchantment, what deceptions await you. You devote the youthful energy of your intellect to working out the plan of some railway which, winding round by the edges of precipices, and piercing the heart of huge mountains, will unite two countries separated by nature. But when once the work is on foot you see whole regiments of workers decimated by privations and sickness in this gloomy tunnel, you see others returning home taking with them only a little money and the seeds of consumption, you will see each yard of the line marked off by human corpses, the result of grovelling greed, and finally, when the line is at last opened, you see it used as the highway for the artillery of an invading army.

You have devoted your youth to make a discovery destined to simplify production, and after many efforts, many sleepless nights, you have at last this valuable invention. You put it into practice and the result surpasses your expectations. Ten, twenty thousand beings are thrown out of work; those who remain, mostly children, are reduced to the condition of mere machines! Three, four, or maybe ten capitalists will make a fortune and drink champagne by the bottleful. Was that your dream?

Finally, you study recent industrial advances, and you see that the seamstress has gained nothing, absolutely nothing, by the invention of the sewing machine; that the laborer in the St. Gothard tunnel dies of ankylostomiasis, notwithstanding diamond drills; that the mason and the day laborer are out of work just as before. If you discuss social problems with the same independence of spirit which has guided you in your mechanical investigations, you necessarily come to the conclusion that under the domination of private property and wage-slavery, every new invention, far from increasing the well-being of the worker, only makes his slavery heavier, his labor more degrading, the periods of slack work more frequent, the crisis sharper, and that the man who already has every conceivable pleasure for himself is the only one who profits by it.

What will you do when you have once come to this conclusion? Either you will begin by silencing your conscience by sophisms; then one fine day you will bid farewell to the honest dreams of your youth and you will try to obtain, for yourself, what commands pleasure and enjoyment—you will then go over to the camp of the exploiters. Or, if you have a tender heart, you will say to yourself:—"No, this is not the time for inventions. Let us work first to transform the domain of production. When private property is put to an end, then each new advance in industry will be made for the benefit of all mankind, and this mass of workers, mere machines as they are to-day, will then become thinking beings who apply to industry their intelligence, strengthened by study and skilled in manual labor, and thus mechanical progress will take a bound forward which will carry out in fifty years what now-a-days we cannot even dream of."

To Teachers

And what shall I say to the schoolmaster—not to the man who looks upon his profession as a wearisome business, but to him who, when surrounded by a joyous band of youngsters, feels exhilarated by their cheery looks and in the midst of their happy laughter; to him who tries to plant in their little heads those ideas of humanity which he cherished himself when he was young.

Often I see that you are sad, and I know what it is that makes you knit your brows. This very day, your favorite pupil, who is not very well up in Latin, it is true, but who has none the less an excellent heart, recited the story of William Tell with so much vigor! His eyes sparkled; he seemed to wish to stab all tyrants there and then; he gave with such fire the passionate lines of Schiller:—

> Before the slave when he breaks his chain,
> Before the free man tremble not.

But when he returned home, his mother, his father, his uncle, sharply rebuked him for want of respect to the minister or the rural policeman. They held forth to him by the hour on "prudence, respect for authority, submission to his betters," till he put Schiller aside in order to read *Self-Help*.

And then only yesterday you were told that your best pupils have all turned out badly. One does nothing but dream of becoming an officer; another in league with his master robs the workers of their slender wages; and you, who had such hopes of these young people, you now brood over the sad contrast between your ideal and life as it is.

You still brood over it. Then I foresee that in two years at the outside, after having suffered disappointment after disappointment, you will lay your favorite authors on the shelf, and you will end by saying that Tell was no doubt a very honest fellow, but after all a trifle cracked; that poetry is a first-rate thing for the fireside, especially when a man has been teaching the rule-of-three all day long, but still poets are always in the clouds and their views have nothing to do with the life of today, nor with the next visit of the inspector of schools. . . .

Or, on the other hand, the dreams of your youth will become the firm convictions of your mature age. You will wish to have wide, human education for all, in school and out of school. And seeing that this is impossible in existing conditions, you will attack the very foundations of bourgeois society. Then discharged as you will be by the board of education, you will leave your school and come among us and be of us. You will tell men of riper years but of smaller attainments than yourself how enticing knowledge is, what mankind ought to be, nay, what we could be. You will come and work with socialists for the complete transformation of the existing system, will strive side by side with us to attain true equality, true fraternity, never-ending liberty for the world.

To Artists

Lastly, you, young artist, sculptor, painter, poet, musician, do you not observe that the sacred fire which inspired your predecessors is wanting in the men of today; that art is commonplace and mediocrity reigns supreme?

Could it be otherwise? The delight at having rediscovered the ancient world, of having bathed afresh in the springs of nature which created the masterpieces of the Renaissance no longer exists for the art of our time. The revolutionary ideal has left it cold until now, and failing an ideal, our art fancies that it has found one in realism when it painfully photographs in colors the dewdrop on the leaf of a plant, imitates the muscles in the leg of a cow, or describes minutely in prose and in verse the suffocating filth of a sewer, the boudoir of a whore of high degree.

"But if this is so, what is to be done?" you say. If, I reply, the sacred fire that you say you possess is nothing better than a smouldering wick, then you will go on doing as you have done, and your art will speedily degenerate into the trade of decorator of tradesmen's shops, of a purveyor of libretti to third-rate operettas and tales for Christmas books—most of you are already running down that grade with a fine head of steam on. . . .

But, if your heart really beats in unison with that of humanity, if like a true poet you have an ear for Life, then, gazing out upon this sea of sorrow whose tide sweeps up around you, face to face with these people dying of hunger, in the presence of these corpses piled up in these mines, and these mutilated bodies lying in heaps on the barricades, in full view of this desperate battle which is being fought, amid the cries of pain from the conquered and the orgies of the victors, of heroism in conflict with cowardice, of noble determination face to face with contemptible cunning—you cannot remain neutral. You will come and take the side of the oppressed because you know that the beautiful, the sublime, the spirit of life itself are on the side of those who fight for light, for humanity, for justice!

WHAT YOU CAN DO

You stop me at last! "What the devil!" you say. "But if abstract science is a luxury and practice of medicine mere chicane; if law spells injustice, and mechanical invention is but a means of robbery; if the school, at variance with the wisdom of the 'practical man,' is sure to be overcome, and art without the revolutionary idea can only degenerate, what remains for me to do?"

A vast and most enthralling task, a work in which your actions will be in complete harmony with your conscience, an undertaking capable of rousing the noblest and most vigorous natures.

What work? I will now tell you.

Two courses are open to you. You can either tamper for ever with your conscience and finish one day by saying "Humanity can go to the devil as long as I am enjoying every pleasure to the full and so long as the people are foolish enough to let me do so." Or else you will join the ranks of the socialists and work with them for the complete transformation of society. Such is the necessary result of the analysis we have made. Such is the logical conclusion at which every intelligent being must arrive provided he judge impartially the things he sees around him, and disregard the sophisms suggested to him by his middle-class education and the interested views of his friends.

Having once reached this conclusion, the question which arises is "what is to be done?" The answer is easy. Quit the environment in which you are placed and in which it is customary to speak of the workers as a lot of brutes; go among the people, and the question will solve itself.

You will find that everywhere in England as in Germany, in Italy as in the United States, wherever there are privileged classes and oppressed, a tremendous movement is on foot among the working-classes, the aim of which is to destroy once and for ever the slavery imposed by capitalists, and to lay the foundations of a new society based on the principles of justice and equality. It no longer suffices for the people to voice their misery in those songs whose melody breaks one's heart, and which the serfs of the eighteenth century sang. He works today fully conscious of what he has done, in spite of every obstacle to his enfranchisement. His thoughts are continually occupied in considering what to do so that life instead of being a mere curse to three-fourths of the human race may be a blessing to all. He attacks the most difficult problems of sociology, and strives to solve them with his

sound common sense, his observation, and his sad experience.
To come to a common understanding with his fellows in
misfortune, he tries to form groups and to organize. He
forms societies, sustained with difficulty by slender contributions. He tries to make terms with his fellows beyond the
frontier. And he does more than all the loud-mouthed philanthropists to hasten the advent of the day when wars between
nations will become impossible. To know what his brothers
are doing, to improve his acquaintance with them, to elaborate and propagate his ideas, he sustains, at the cost of what
efforts, his working-class press. What a ceaseless struggle!
What labor, constantly requiring to be recommenced. Sometimes to fill the gaps made by desertion—the result of lassi-
tude, of corruption, of persecutions; sometimes to reorganize
the ranks decimated by fusillades and grape shot, sometimes
to resume studies suddenly cut short by wholesale massacres.

The papers are conducted by men who have had to snatch
from society scraps of knowledge by depriving themselves of
food and sleep. The agitation is supported with the pennies
of the workers saved from the strict necessaries of life. And
all this is done, shadowed by the continual apprehension of
seeing their families plunged into destitution as soon as the
master perceives that his worker, his slave, is a socialist.

These are the things you will see if you go among the
people. And in this ceaseless struggle how often has the
worker, sinking under the weight of difficulties, exclaimed
in vain: "Where then are those young men who have been
educated at our expense, whom we have clothed and fed while
they studied? For whom, with backs bowed down under
heavy loads, and with empty stomachs, we have built these
houses, these academies, these museums? For whom we, with
pallid faces, have printed those fine books we cannot so much
as read? Where are they, those professors who claim to possess the science of humanity, and yet in whose eyes mankind
is not worth a rare species of caterpillar? Where are those
men who preach of liberty and who never rise to defend
ours, daily trodden under foot? These writers, these poets,

these painters, all this band of hypocrites, in short, who speak of the people with tears in their eyes, and who nevertheless never come among us to help us in our work?"

Some complacently enjoy their condition of cowardly indifference, others, the majority, despise the "rabble" and are ever ready to pounce down on it if it dare to attack their privileges.

From time to time, it is true, a young man appears on the scene who dreams of drums and barricades, and who is in search of sensational scenes and situations, but who deserts the cause of the people as soon as he perceives that the road to the barricades is long, that the laurels he counts on winning on the way are mixed with thorns. Generally these men are ambitious adventurers, who after failing in their first attempts, seek to obtain the votes of the people, but who later on will be the first to denounce it, if it dare to try and put into practice the principles they themselves advocated, and who perhaps will even point the cannon at the proletariat if it dare move before they, the leaders, have given the word of command.

Add to this stupid insults, haughty contempt, and cowardly calumny on the part of a great number, and you have all the help that the middle-class youth give the people in their powerful social evolution.

And then you ask, "what shall we do?" when there is everything to be done! When a whole army of young people would find plenty to employ the entire vigor of their youthful energy, the full force of their intelligence and their talents to help the people in the vast enterprise they have undertaken!

What shall we do? Listen.

You lovers of pure science, if you are imbued with the principles of socialism, if you have understood the real meaning of the revolution which is even now knocking at the door, do you not see that all science has to be recast in order to place it in harmony with the new principles? That it is your business to accomplish in this field a revolution far

greater than that which was accomplished in every branch
of science during the eighteenth century? Do you not understand that history—which today is an old woman's tale about
great kings, great statesmen and great parliaments—that history itself has to be written from the point of view of the
people in the long evolution of mankind? That social economy—which today is merely the sanctification of capitalist
robbery—has to be worked out afresh in its fundamental principles as well as in its innumerable applications? That anthropology, sociology, ethics, must be completely recast, and
that the natural sciences themselves, regarded from another
point of view, must undergo a profound modification, alike
in regard to the conception of natural phenomena and with
respect to the method of exposition?

Very well, then, set to work! Place your abilities at the
command of the good cause. Especially help us with your
clear logic to combat prejudice and to lay by your synthesis
the foundation of a better organization. Yet more, teach
us to apply in our daily arguments the fearlessness of true
scientific investigation, and show us as your predecessors did,
how man dare sacrifice even life itself for the triumph of the
truth.

You, doctors who have learnt socialism by a bitter experience, never weary of telling us today, tomorrow, in and out
of season, that humanity itself hurries onward to decay if man
remain in the present conditions of existence and work; that
all your medicaments must be powerless against disease while
the majority of mankind vegetate in conditions absolutely
contrary to those which science tells us are healthful. Convince the people that it is the causes of disease which must be
uprooted, and show us all what is necessary to remove them.

Come with your scalpel and dissect for us with unerring
hand this society of ours fast hastening to putrefaction. Tell
us what a rational existence should and might be. Insist, as
true surgeons, that a gangrenous limb must be amputated
when it may poison the whole body.

You who have worked at the application of science to

industry, come and tell us frankly what has been the outcome of your discoveries. Convince those who dare not march boldly towards the future what new inventions the knowledge we have already acquired carries in its womb, what industry could do under better conditions, what man might easily produce if he produced always with a view to enhance his own productions.

You poets, painters, sculptors, musicians, if you understand your true mission and the very interests of art itself, come with us. Place your pen, your pencil, your chisel, your ideas at the service of the revolution. Figure forth to us, in your eloquent style, or your impressive pictures, the heroic struggles of the people against their oppressors, fire the hearts of our youth with that glorious revolutionary enthusiasm which inflamed the souls of our ancestors. Tell women what a noble career is that of a husband who devotes his life to the great cause of social emancipation! Show the people how hideous is their actual life, and place your hands on the causes of its ugliness. Tell us what a rational life would be, if it did not encounter at every step the follies and the ignominies of our present social order.

Lastly, all of you who possess knowledge, talent, capacity, industry, if you have a spark of sympathy in your nature, come you, and your companions, come and place your services at the disposal of those who most need them. And remember, if you do come, that you come not as masters, but as comrades in the struggle; that you come not to govern but to gain strength for yourselves in a new life which sweeps upwards to the conquest of the future: that you come less to teach than to grasp the aspiration of the many; to divine them, to give them shape, and then to work, without rest and without haste, with all the fire of youth and all the judgment of age, to realize them in actual life. Then and then only, will you lead a complete, a noble, a rational existence. Then you will see that your every effort on this path bears with it fruit in abundance, and this sublime harmony once established between your actions and the dictates of your conscience will give you powers you never dreamt lay dormant in yourselves, the never-ceasing struggle for truth, justice, and equality among the people, whose gratitude you will earn—what nobler career can the youth of all nations desire than this?

It has taken me long to show you of the well-to-do classes that in view of the dilemma which life presents to you, you will be forced, if courageous and sincere, to come and work side by side with the socialists, and champion in their ranks, the cause of the social revolution.

And yet how simple this truth is after all! But when one is speaking to those who have suffered from the effects of bourgeois surroundings, how many sophisms must be combated, how many prejudices overcome, how many interested objections put aside!

TO WORKING CLASS YOUTHS

It is easy to be brief today in addressing you, the youth of the people. The very pressure of events impels you to become socialists, however little you may have the courage to reason and to act.

To rise from the ranks of the working people, and not devote oneself to bringing about the triumph of socialism, is to misconceive the real interests at stake, to give up the cause, and the true historic mission.

Do you remember the time, when still a mere lad, you went down one winter's day to play in your dark court? The cold nipped your shoulders through your thin clothes, and the mud worked into your worn-out shoes. Even then when you saw chubby children richly clad pass in the distance, looking at you with an air of contempt, you knew right well that these imps were not the equals of yourself and your comrades, either in intelligence, common sense or energy. But later when you were forced to shut yourself up in a filthy factory from seven o'clock in the morning, to remain hours on end close to a whirling machine, and, a machine yourself, you were forced to follow day after day for whole years in succession its movements with relentless throbbing—during all this time they, the others, were going quietly to be taught at fine schools, at academies, at the universities. And now these same children, less intelligent, but better taught than you, have become your masters, are enjoying all the pleasures of life and all the advantages of civilization. And you? What sort of lot awaits you?

You return to little, dark, damp lodgings where five or six human beings pig together within a few square feet. Where your mother, sick of life, aged by care rather than years, offers you dry bread and potatoes as your only food, washed down by a blackish fluid called in irony "tea." And to distract your thoughts you have ever the same never-ending question, "How shall I be able to pay the baker tomorrow, and the landlord the day after?"

What! must you drag on the same weary existence as your father and mother for thirty and forty years? Must you toil your life long to procure for others all the pleasures of well-being, of knowledge, of art, and keep for yourself only the eternal anxiety as to whether you can get a bit of bread? Will you forever give up all that makes life so beautiful to devote yourself to providing every luxury for a handful of idlers? Will you wear yourself out with toil and have in return only trouble, if not misery, when hard times—the fearful hard times—come upon you? Is this what you long for in life?

Perhaps you will give up. Seeing no way whatever out of your condition, maybe you say to yourself, "Whole generations have undergone the same lot, and I, who can alter nothing in the matter, I must submit also. Let us work on then and endeavor to live as well as we can!"

Very well. In that case life itself will take pains to enlighten you. One day a crisis comes, one of those crises which are no longer mere passing phenomena, as they were formerly, but a crisis which destroys a whole industry, which plunges thousands of workers into misery, which crushes whole families. You struggle against the calamity like the rest. But

you will soon see how your wife, your child, your friend, little
by little succumb to privations, fade away under your very
eyes. For sheer want of food, for lack of care and medical
assistance, they end their days on the pauper's stretcher, whilst
the life of the rich flows on joyously midst the sunny streets
of the great city, careless of those who starve and perish.
You will then understand how utterly revolting is this society.
You will then reflect upon the causes of this crisis, and your
examinations will scrutinize to the depths that abomination
which puts millions of human beings at the mercy of the
brutal greed of a handful of useless triflers. Then you will
understand that socialists are right when they say that our
present society can be, that it must be, reorganized from top
to bottom.

To pass from general crises to your particular case. One
day when your master tries by a new reduction of wages to
squeeze out of you a few more dollars in order to increase
his fortune still further you will protest. But he will haught-
ily answer, "Go and eat grass, if you will not work at
the price I offer." Then you will understand that your master
not only tries to shear you like a sheep, but that he looks
upon you as an inferior kind of animal altogether; that not
content with holding you in his relentless grip by means of
the wage system, he is further anxious to make you a slave
in every respect. Then you will, perhaps, bow down before
him, you will give up the feeling of human dignity, and you
will end by suffering every possible humiliation. Or the blood
will rush to your head, you shudder at the hideous slope on
which you are slipping down, you will retort, and, turned
out workless on the street, you will understand how right
socialists are when they say, "Revolt! rise against this economic slavery!" Then you will come and take your place in
the ranks of the socialists, and you will work with them for
the complete destruction of all slavery—economic, social and
political.

Every one of you then, honest young people, men and
women, peasants, laborers, artisans, and soldiers, you will

understand what are your rights and you will come along with us. You will come in order to work with your brethren in the preparation of that revolution which is sweeping away every vestige of slavery, tearing the fetters asunder, breaking with the old worn-out traditions and opening to all mankind a new and wider scope of joyous existence, and which shall at length establish true liberty, real equality, ungrudging fraternity throughout human society. Work with all, work for all—the full enjoyment of the fruits of their labor, the complete development of all their faculties, a rational, human and happy life!

Don't let anyone tell us that we—but a small band—are too weak to attain unto the magnificent end at which we aim. Count and see how many there are who suffer this injustice. We peasants who work for others, and who mumble the straw while our master eats the wheat, we by ourselves are millions of men. We workers who weave silks and velvet in order that we may be clothed in rags, we, too, are a great multitude; and when the clang of the factories permits us a moment's repose, we overflow the streets and squares like the sea in a spring tide. We soldiers who are driven along to the word of command, or by blows, we who receive the bullets for which our officers get crosses and pensions, we, too, poor fools who have hitherto known no better than to shoot our brothers, why we have only to make a right about face towards these plumed and decorated personages who are so good as to command us, to see a ghastly pallor overspread their faces.

Ay, all of us together, we who suffer and are insulted daily, we are a multitude whom no man can number, we are the ocean that can embrace and swallow up all else. When we have but the will to do it, that very moment will justice be done: that very instant the tyrants of the earth shall bite the dust.

Note on Article from "The Encyclopedia Britannica"

This scholarly article written in 1905 for the eleventh edition of *The Encyclopedia Britannica* is included because it is the best brief statement in English of the precursors of anarchist thought. Its objective treatment detaches it at once from propaganda, and its appearance in so authoritative a publication was intended to present a statement of the anarchist position to those not connected with the labor or revolutionary movement. It is useful for those who want a compact view of communist-anarchism by the man best qualified to state it,—and the kind of thing to show an unfamiliar inquirer who wants to know, what it is all about.

It of course has no place in Kropotkin's own teaching. Its merit and usefulness as a dispassionate statement is the sole reason for reprinting it.

ANARCHISM

ANARCHISM (from the Gr. ἀυ-, and ἀρχη, contrary to authority), is the name given to a principle or theory of life and conduct under which society is conceived without government—harmony in such a society being obtained, not by submission to law, or by obedience to any authority, but by free agreements concluded between the various groups, territorial and professional, freely constituted for the sake of production and consumption, as also for the satisfaction of the infinite variety of needs and aspirations of a civilized being.

In a society developed on these lines, the voluntary associations which already now begin to cover all the fields of human activity would take a still greater extension so as to substitute themselves for the State in all its functions. They would represent an interwoven network, composed of an infinite variety of groups and federations of all sizes and degrees, local, regional, national and international—temporary or more or less permanent—for all possible puposes: production, consumption and exchange, communications, sanitary arrangements, education, mutual protection, defense of the territory, and so on; and, on the other side, for the satisfaction of an ever-increasing number of scientific, artistic, literary and sociable needs.

Moreover, such a society would represent nothing immutable. On the contrary—as is seen in organic life at large—harmony would (it is contended) result from an ever-changing adjustment and readjustment of equilibrium between the multitudes of forces and influences, and this adjustment would be the easier to obtain as none of the forces would enjoy a special protection from the State.

If, it is contended, society were organized on these principles, man would not be limited in the free exercise of his powers in productive work by a capitalist monopoly, maintained by the State; nor would he be limited in the exercise of his will by a fear of punishment, or by obedience towards individuals or metaphysical entities, which both lead to depression of initiative and servility of mind. He would be guided in his actions by his own understanding, which necessarily would bear the impression of a free action and reaction between his own self and the ethical conceptions of his surroundings. Man would thus be enabled to obtain the full development of all his faculties, intellectual, artistic and moral, without being hampered by overwork for the monopolists, or by the servility and inertia of mind of the great number. He would thus be able to reach full *individualization*, which is not possible either under the present system of *individualism*, or under any system of State socialism in the so-called *Volkstaat* (popular State).

The anarchist writers consider, moreover, that their conception is not a Utopia, constructed on the *a priori* method, after a few desiderata have been taken as postulates. It is derived, they maintain, from an *analysis of tendencies* that are at work already, even though state socialism may find a temporary favor with the reformers. The progress of modern technics, which wonderfully simplifies the production of all the necessaries of life; the growing spirit of independence, and the rapid spread of free initiative and free understanding in all branches of activity—including those which formerly were considered as the proper attribution of church and State—are steadily reinforcing the no-government tendency.

As to their economical conceptions, the anarchists, in common with all socialists, of whom they constitute the left wing, maintain that the now prevailing system of private ownership in land, and our capitalist production for the sake of profits, represent a monopoly which runs against both the principles of justice and the dictates of utility. They are the main obstacle which prevents the successes of modern technics from being brought into the service of all, so as to produce general well-being. The anarchists consider the wage-system and capitalist production altogether as an obstacle to progress. But they point out also that the State was, and continues to be, the chief instrument for permitting the few to monopolize the land, and the capitalists to appropriate for themselves a quite disproportionate share of the yearly accumulated surplus of production. Consequently, while combating the present monopolization of land, and capitalism altogether, the anarchists combat with the same energy the State as the main support of that system. Not this or that special form, but the State altogether, whether it be a monarchy or even a republic governed by means of the *referendum*.

The State organization, having always been, both in ancient and modern history (Macedonian empire, Roman empire, modern European states grown up on the ruins of the autonomous cities), the instrument for establishing monopolies in favor of the ruling minorities, cannot be made to work for the destruction of these monopolies. The anarchists consider, therefore, that to hand over to the State all the main sources of economic life—the land, the mines, the railways, banking, insurance, and so on—as also the management of all the main branches of industry, in addition to all the functions already accumulated in its hands (education, State-supported religions, defense of the territory, etc.), would mean to create a new instrument of tyranny. State capitalism would only increase the powers of bureaucracy and capitalism. True progress lies in the direction of decentralization, both *territorial* and *functional,* in the development of the spirit of local and personal initiative, and of free federation from the simple to the compound, *in lieu* of the present hierarchy from the center to the periphery.

In common with most socialists, the anarchists recognize that, like all evolution in nature, the slow evolution of society is followed from time to time by periods of accelerated evolution which are called revolutions; and they think that the era of revolutions is not yet closed. Periods of rapid changes will follow the periods of slow evolution, and these periods must be taken advantage of—not for increasing and widening the powers of the State, but for reducing them, through the organization in every township or commune of the local groups of producers and consumers, as also the regional, and eventually the international, federations of these groups.

In virtue of the above principles the anarchists refuse to be party to the present-State organization and to support it by infusing fresh blood into it. They do not seek to constitute, and invite the workingmen not to constitute, political parties in the parliaments. Accordingly, since the foundation of the International Working Men's Association in 1864-1866, they have endeavored to promote their ideas directly amongst the labor organizations and to induce those unions to a direct struggle against capital, without placing their faith in parliamentary legislation.

THE HISTORICAL DEVELOPMENT OF ANARCHISM

The conception of society just sketched, and the tendency which is its dynamic expression, have always existed in mankind, in opposition to the governing hierarchic conception and tendency—now the one and now the other taking the upper hand at different periods of history. To the former tendency we owe the evolution, by the masses themselves, of those institutions—the clan, the village community, the guild, the free medieval city—by means of which the masses resisted the encroachments of the conquerors and the power-seeking minorities. The same tendency asserted itself with great energy in the great religious movements of medieval times, especially in the early movements of the reform and its forerunners. At the same time it evidently found its expression in the writings of some thinkers, since the times of Lao-tze, although, owing to its non-scholastic and popular origin, it obviously found less sympathy among the scholars than the opposed tendency.

As has been pointed out by Prof. Adler in his *Geschichte des Sozialismus und Kommunismus,* Aristippus (b. c. 430 B.C), one of the founders of the Cyrenaic school, already taught that the wise must not give up their liberty to the State, and in reply to a question by Socrates he said that he did not desire to belong either to the governing or the governed class. Such an attitude, however, seems to have been dictated merely by an Epicurean attitude towards the life of the masses.

The best exponent of anarchist philosophy in ancient Greece was Zeno (342-267 or 270 B.C.), from Crete, the founder of the Stoic philosophy, who distinctly opposed his conception of a free community without government to the state-Utopia of Plato. He repudiated the omnipotence of the State, its intervention and regimentation, and proclaimed the sovereignty of the moral law of the individual—remarking already that, while the necessary instinct of self-preservation leads man to egotism, nature has supplied a corrective to it by providing man with another instinct—that of sociability. When men are reasonable enough to follow their natural instincts, they will unite across the frontiers and constitute the Cosmos. They will have no need of law-courts or police, will have no temples and no public worship, and use no money—free gifts taking the place of the exchanges. Unfortunately, the writings of Zeno have not reached us and are only known through fragmentary quotations. However, the fact that his very wording is similar to the wording now in use, shows how deeply is laid the tendency of human nature of which he was the mouth-piece.

In medieval times we find the same views on the State expressed by the illustrious bishop of Alba, Marco Girolamo Vida, in his first dialogue *De dignitate reipublicae* (Ferd. Cavalli, in *Men. dell' Istituto Vento,* xiii.; Dr. E. Nys, *Researches in the History of Economics*). But it is especially in several early Christian movements, beginning with the ninth century in Armenia, and in the preachings of the early Hussites, particularly Chojecki, and the early Anabaptists, especially

Hans Denk (cf. Keller, *Ein Apostel der Wiedertäufer*), that one finds the same ideas forcibly expressed—special stress being laid of course on their moral aspects.

Rabelais and Fénelon, in their Utopias, have also expressed similar ideas, and they were also current in the eighteenth century amongst the French Encyclopaedists, as may be concluded from separate expressions occasionally met with in the writings of Rousseau, from Diderot's *Preface* to the *Voyage* of Bougainville, and so on. However, in all probability such ideas could not be developed then, owing to the rigorous censorship of the Roman Catholic Church.

These ideas found their expression later during the great French Revolution. While the Jacobins did all in their power to centralize everything in the hands of the government, it appears now, from recently published documents, that the masses of the people, in their municipalities and "sections," accomplished a considerable constructive work. They appropriated for themselves the election of the judges, the organization of supplies and equipment for the army, as also for the large cities, work for the unemployed, the management of charities, and so on. They even tried to establish a direct correspondence between the 36,000 communes of France through the intermediary of a special board, outside the National Assembly (cf. Sigismund Lacroix, *Actes de la commune de Paris*).

It was Godwin, in his *Enquiry concerning Political Justice* (2 vols., 1793), who was the first to formulate the political and economical conceptions of anarchism, even though he did not give that name to the ideas developed in his remarkable work. Laws, he wrote, are not a product of the wisdom of our ancestors: they are the product of their passions, their timidity, their jealousies and their ambition. The remedy they offer is worse than the evils they pretend to cure. If and only if all laws and courts were abolished, and the decisions in the arising contests were left to reasonable men chosen for that purpose, real justice would gradually be evolved. As to the State, Godwin frankly claimed its abolition. A society, he wrote, can perfectly well exist without any government: only the communities should be small and perfectly autonomous. Speaking of property, he stated that the rights of every one "to every substance capable of contributing to the benefit of a human being" must be regulated by justice alone: the substance must go "to him who most wants it." His conclusion was communism. Godwin, however, had not the courage to maintain his opinions. He entirely rewrote later on his chapter on property and mitigated his communist views in the second edition of *Political Justice* (8vo, 1796).

Proudhon was the first to use, in 1840 (*Qu'est-ce que la propriété?* first memoir), the name of anarchy with application to the no-government state of society. The name of "anarchists" had been freely applied during the French Revolution by the Girondists to those revolutionaries who did not consider that the task of the Revolution was accomplished with the overthrow of Louis XVI, and insisted upon a series of economical measures being taken (the abolition of feudal rights without redemption, the return to the village communities of the communal lands enclosed since 1669, the limitation of landed property to 120 acres, progressive income-tax, the national organization of exchanges on a just value basis, which already received a beginning of practical realization, and so on).

Now Proudhon advocated a society without government, and used the word anarchy to describe it. Proudhon repudiated, as is known, all schemes of communism, according to which mankind would be driven into communistic monasteries or barracks, as also all the schemes of state or state-aided socialism which were advocated by Louis Blanc and the collectivists. When he proclaimed in his first memoir on property that "Property is theft," he meant only property in its present, Roman-law, sense of "right of use and abuse;" in property-rights, on the other hand, understood in the limited sense of *possession,* he saw the best protection against the encroachments of the State. At the same time he did not want violently to dispossess the present owners of land, dwelling-houses, mines, factories and so on. He preferred to attain the same end by rendering capital incapable of earning interest; and this he proposed to obtain by means of a national bank, based on the mutual confidence of all those who are engaged in production, who would agree to exchange among themselves their produces at cost-value, by means of labor checks representing the hours of labor required to produce every given commodity. Under such a system, which Proudhon described as "Mutuellisme," all the exchanges of services would be strictly equivalent. Besides, such a bank would be enabled to lend money without interest, levying only something like 1 per cent, or even less, for covering the cost of administration. Every one being thus enabled to borrow the money that would be required to buy a house, nobody would agree to pay any more a yearly rent for the use of it. A general "social liquidation" would thus be rendered easy, without expropriation. The same applied to mines, railways, factories and so on.

In a society of this type the State would be useless. The chief relations between citizens would be based on free agreement and regulated by mere account keeping. The contests might be settled by arbitration. A penetrating criticism of the State and all possible forms of government and a deep insight into all economic problems, were well-known characteristics of Proudhon's work.

It is worth noticing that French mutualism had its precursor in England, in William Thompson, who began by mutualism before he became a communist, and in his followers John Gray (*A Lecture on Human Happiness*, 1825; *The Social System*, 1831) and J. F. Bray (*Labour's Wrongs and Labour's Remedy*, 1839). It had also its precursor in America. Josiah Warren, who was born in 1798 (cf W. Bailie, *Josiah Warren, the First American Anarchist*, Boston, 1900), and belonged to Owen's "New Harmony," considered that the failure of this enterprise was chiefly due to the suppression of individuality and the lack of initiative and responsibility. These defects, he taught, were inherent to every scheme based upon authority and the community of goods. He advocated, therefore, complete individual liberty. In 1827 he opened in Cincinnati a little country store which was the first "Equity Store," and which the people called "Time Store," because it was based on labor being exchanged hour for hour in all sorts of produce. "Cost—the limit of price," and consequently "no interest," was the motto of his store, and later on of his "Equity Village," near New York, which was still in existence in 1865. Mr. Keith's "House of Equity" at Boston, founded in 1855, is also worthy of notice.

While the economic, and especially the mutual-banking, ideas of Proudhon found supporters and even a practical application in the United States, his political conception of anarchy found but little echo in France, where the christian socialism of Lamennais and the Fourierists, and the state socialism of Louis Blanc and the followers of Saint-Simon, were dominating. These ideas found, however, some temporary support among the left-wing Hegelians in Germany, Moses Hess in 1843, and Karl Grün in 1845, who advocated anarchism. Besides, the authoritarian communism of Wilhelm Weitling having given origin to opposition amongst the Swiss workingmen, Wilhelm Marr gave expression to it in the forties.

On the other side, individualist anarchism found, also in Germany, its fullest expression in Max Stirner (Kaspar Schmidt), whose remarkable works (*Der Einzige und sein Eigenthum* and articles contributed to the *Rheinische Zeitung*) remained quite overlooked until they were brought into prominence by John Henry Mackay.

Prof. V. Basch, in a very able introduction to his interesting book, *L'Individualisme anarchiste: Max Stirner* (1904), has shown how the development of the German philosophy from Kant to Hegel, and "the absolute" of Schelling and the *Geist* of Hegel, necessarily provoked, when the anti-Hegelian revolt began, the preaching of the same "absolute" in the camp of the rebels. This was done by Stirner, who advocated, not only a complete revolt against the State and against the servitude which authoritarian communism would impose upon men, but also the full liberation of the individual from all social and moral bonds—the rehabilitation of the "I," the supremacy of the individual, complete "a-moralism," and the "association of the egotists." The final conclusion of that sort of individual anarchism has been indicated by Prof. Basch. It maintains that the aim of all superior civilization is, not to permit *all* members of the community to develop in a normal way, but to permit certain better endowed individuals "fully to develop," even at the cost of the happiness and the very existence of the mass of mankind. It is thus a return towards the most common individualism, advocated by all the would-be superior minorities, to which indeed man owes in his history precisely the State and the rest, which these individualists combat. Their individualism goes so far as to end in a negation of their own starting-point,—to say nothing of the impossibility for the individual to attain a really full development in the conditions of oppression of the masses by the "beautiful aristocracies." His development would remain uni-lateral. This is why this direction of thought, notwithstanding its undoubtedly correct and useful advocacy of the full development of each individuality, finds a hearing only in limited artistic and literary circles.

ANARCHISM IN THE INTERNATIONAL WORKING MEN'S ASSOCIATION

A general depression in the propaganda of all fractions of socialism followed, as is known, after the defeat of the uprising of the Paris workingmen in June 1848 and the fall of the Republic. All the socialist press was gagged during the reaction period, which lasted fully twenty years. Nevertheless, even anarchist thought began to make some progress, namely in the writings of Bellegarrique (*Cœurderoy*), and especially Joseph Déjacque (*Les Lazaréennes, L'Humanisphère,* an anarchist-communist Utopia, lately discovered and reprinted). The socialist movement revived only after 1864, when some French workingmen, all "mutualists," meeting in London during the Universal Exhibition with English followers of Robert Owen, founded the International Working Men's Association. This association developed very rapidly and adopted a policy of direct economic struggle against capitalism, without interfering in the political parliamentary agitation, and this policy was followed until 1871. However, after the Franco-German War, when the International Association was prohibited in France after the uprising of the Commune, the German workingmen, who had received manhood suffrage for elections to the newly constituted imperial parliament, insisted upon modifying the tactics of the International, and began to build up a social-democratic political party. This soon led to a division in the Working Men's Association, and the Latin federations, Spanish, Italian, Belgian and Jurassic (France could not be represented), constituted among themselves a federal union which broke entirely with the Marxist general council of the International. Within these federations developed now what may be described as *modern anarchism*. After the names of "federalists" and "anti-authoritarians" had been used for some time by these federations the name of "anarchists," which their adversaries insisted upon applying to them, prevailed, and finally it was revindicated.

Bakunin soon became the leading spirit among these Latin federations for the development of the principles of anarchism, which he did in a number of writings, pamphlets and letters, He demanded the complete abolition of the State, which—he wrote—is a product of religion, belongs to a lower state of civilization, represents the negation of liberty, and spoils even that which it undertakes to do for the sake of general wellbeing. The State was an historically necessary evil, but its complete extinction will be, sooner or later, equally necessary. Repudiating all legislation, even when issuing from universal suffrage, Bakunin claimed for each nation, each region and each commune, full autonomy, so long as it is not a menace to its neighbors, and full independence for the individual, adding that one becomes really free only when, and in proportion as, all others are free. Free federations of the communes would constitute free nations.

As to his economic conceptions, Bakunin described himself, in common with his federalist comrades of the International, a "collectivist anarchist"—not in the sense of Vidal and Pecqueur in the forties, or of their modern social-democratic followers, but to express a state of things in which all necessaries for production are owned in common by the labor groups and the free communes, while the ways of retribution of labor, communist or otherwise, would be settled by each group for itself. Social revolution, the near approach of which was foretold at that time by all socialists, would be the means of bringing into life the new conditions.

The Jurassic, the Spanish, and the Italian federations and sections of the International Working Men's Association, as also the French, the German and the American anarchist groups, were for the next years the chief centers of anarchist thought and propaganda. They refrained from any participation in parliamentary politics, and always kept in close contact with the labor organizations. However, in the second half of the eighties and the early nineties of the nineteenth century, when the influence of the anarchists began to be felt in strikes, in the first of May demonstrations, where they promoted the idea of a general strike for an eight hours' day, and in the anti-militarist propaganda in the army, violent prosecutions were directed against them, especially in the Latin countries (including physical torture in the Barcelona Castle) and the United States (the execution of five Chicago anarchists in 1887). Against these prosecutions the anarchists retaliated by acts of violence which in their turn were followed by more executions from above, and new acts of revenge from below. This created in the general public the impression that violence is the substance of anarchism, a view repudiated by its supporters, who hold that in reality violence is resorted to by all parties in proportion as their open action is obstructed by repression, and exceptional laws render them outlaws.

Anarchism continued to develop, partly in the direction of Proudhonian "Mutuellisme," but chiefly as communist-anarchism, to which a third direction, christian-anarchism, was added by Leo Tolstoy, and a fourth, which might be described as literary-anarchism, began amongst some prominent modern writers.

The ideas of Proudhon, especially as regards mutual banking, corresponding with those of Josiah Warren, found a considerable following in the United States, creating quite a school, of which the main writers are Stephen Pearl Andrews, William Greene, Lysander Spooner (who began to write in 1850, and whose unfinished work, *Natural Law*, was full of promise), and several others, whose names will be found in Dr. Nettlau's *Bibliographie de l'anarchie*.

A prominent position among the individualist anarchists in America has been occupied by Benjamin R. Tucker, whose journal *Liberty* was started in 1881 and whose conceptions are a combination of those of Proudhon with those of Herbert Spencer. Starting from the statement that anarchists are egotists, strictly speaking, and that every group of individuals, be it a secret league of a few persons, or the Congress of the United States, has the right to oppress all mankind, provided it has the power to do so, that equal liberty for all and absolute equality ought to be the law, and "mind every one your own business" is the unique moral law of anarchism, Tucker goes on to prove that a general and thorough application of these principles would be beneficial and would offer no danger, because the powers of every individual would be limited by the exercise of the equal rights of all others. He further indicated (following H. Spencer) the difference which exists between the encroachment on somebody's rights and resistance to such an encroachment; between domination and defense: the former being equally condemnable, whether it be encroachment of a criminal upon an individual, or the encroachment of one upon all others, or of all others upon one; while resistance to encroachment is defensible and necessary. For their self-defense, both the citizen and the group have the right to any violence, including capital punishment. Violence is also justified for enforcing the duty of keeping an agreement. Tucker thus follows Spencer, and, like him, opens (in the present writer's opinion) the way for reconstituting under the heading of "defense" all the functions of the State. His criticism of the present State is very searching, and his defense of the rights of the individual very powerful. As regards his economic views B. R. Tucker follows Proudhon.

The individualist anarchism of the American Proudhonians finds, however, but little sympathy amongst the working masses. Those who profess it—they are chiefly "intellectuals"—soon realize that the *individualization* they so highly praise is not attainable by individual efforts, and either abandon the ranks of the anarchists, and are driven into the liberal individualism of the classical economists, or they retire into a sort of Epicurean a-moralism, or super-man-theory, similar to that of Stirner and Nietzsche. The great bulk of the anarchist workingmen prefer the anarchist-communist ideas which have gradually evolved out of the anarchist collectivism of the International Working Men's Association. To this direction belong—to name only the better known exponents of anarchism—Élisée Reclus, Jean Grave, Sebastien Fauré, Emile Pouget in France; Enrico Malatesta and Covelli in Italy; R. Mella, A. Lorenzo, and the mostly unknown authors of many excellent manifestos in Spain; John Most amongst the Germans; Spies, Parsons and their followers in the United States, and so on; while Domela Nieuwenhuis occupies an intermediate position in Holland. The chief anarchist papers which have been published since 1880 also belong to that direction; while a number of anarchists of this direction have joined the so-called syndicalist movement—the French name for the non-political labor movement, devoted to direct struggle with capitalism, which has lately become so prominent in Europe.

As one of the anarchist-communist direction, the present writer for many years endeavored to develop the following ideas: to show the intimate, logical connection which exists between the modern philosophy of natural sciences and anarchism; to put anarchism on a scientific basis by the study of the tendencies that are apparent now in society and may indicate its further evolution; and to work out the basis of anarchist ethics. As regards the substance of anarchism itself, it was Kropotkin's aim to prove that communism—at least partial—has more chances of being established than collectivism, especially in communes taking the lead, and that free, or anarchist-communism is the only form of communism that has any chance of being accepted in civilized societies; communism and anarchy are therefore two terms of evolution which complete each other, the one rendering the other possible and acceptable. He has tried, moreover, to indicate how, during a revolutionary period, a large city—if its inhabitants have accepted the idea—could organize itself on the lines of free communism; the city guaranteeing to every inhabitant dwelling, food and clothing to an extent corresponding to the comfort now available to the middle classes only, in exchange for a half-day's, or a five-hours' work; and how all those things which would be considered as luxuries might be obtained by every one if he joins for the other half of the day all sorts of free associations pursuing all possible aims— educational, literary, scientific, artistic, sports and so on. In order to prove the first of these assertions he has analyzed the possibilities of agriculture and industrial work, both being combined with brain work. And in order to elucidate the main factors of human evolution, he has analyzed the part played in history by the popular constructive agencies of mutual aid and the historical role of the State.

Without naming himself an anarchist, Leo Tolstoy, like his predecessors in the popular religious movements of the fifteenth and sixteenth centuries, Chojecki, Denk and many others, took the anarchist position as regards the State and property rights, deducing his conclusions from the general spirit of the teachings of the Christ and from the necessary dictates of reason. With all the might of his talent he made (especially in *The Kingdom of God in Yourselves*) a powerful criticism of the church, the State and law altogether, and especially of the present property laws. He describes the State as the domination of the wicked ones, supported by brutal force. Robbers, he says, are far less dangerous than a well-organized government. He makes a searching criticism of the prejudices which are current now concerning the benefits conferred upon men by the church, the State and the existing distribution of property, and from the teachings of the Christ he deduces the rule of non-resistance and the absolute condemnation of all wars. His religious arguments are, however, so well combined with arguments borrowed from a dispassionate observation of the present evils, that the anarchist portions of his works appeal to the religious and the non-religious reader alike.

It would be impossible to represent here, in a short sketch, the penetration, on the one hand, of anarchist ideas into modern literature, and the influence, on the other hand, which the libertarian ideas of the best comtemporary writers have exercised upon the development of anarchism. One ought to consult the ten big volumes of the *Supplement littéraire* to the paper *La Révolte* and later the *Temps Nouveaux,* which contain reproductions from the works of hundreds of modern authors expressing anarchist ideas, in order to realize how closely anarchism is connected with all the intellectual movement of our own times. J. S. Mill's *Liberty,* Spencer's *Individual versus The State,* Marc Guyau's *Morality without Obligation or Sanction,* and Fouillée's *La morale, l'art et la religion,* the works of Multatuli (E. Douwes Dekker), Richard Wagner's *Art and Revolution,* the works of Nietzsche, Emerson, W. Lloyd Garrison, Thoreau, Alexander Herzen, Edward Carpenter and so on; and in the domain of fiction, the dramas of Ibsen, the poetry of Walt Whitman, Tolstoy's *War and*

Peace, Zola's *Paris* and *Le Travail*, the latest works of Merezh-kovsky, and an infinity of works of less known authors,—are full of ideas which show how closely anarchism is inter-woven with the work that is going on in modern thought in the same direction of enfranchisement of man from the bonds of the State as well as from those of capitalism.

PARTIAL BIBLIOGRAPHY OF KROPOTKIN'S REVOLUTIONARY, HISTORICAL AND SOCIOLOGICAL WRITINGS

BOOKS IN ENGLISH

The Conquest of Bread. 299 pages, Chapman and Hall, London, 1906 (out of print); Putnam's, New York, 1907 (out of print); Vanguard Press, New York, 1926.

Ethics: Origin and Development. 350 pages, L. McVeagh, New York, 1924.

Fields, Factories and Workshops. 475 pages, Houghton Mifflin and Company, Boston, 1899 (original edition, 315 pages); Putnam's, New York, 1913 (revised edition 477 pages); T. Nelson and Sons, London, 1919 (same).

The Great French Revolution. 610 pages, Heinemann, London (out of print); Putnam's, New York, 1909 (out of print); Vanguard Press, New York, 1927.

Ideals and Realities in Russian Literature. 341 pages, Alfred A. Knopf, New York, 1915. (Original edition as *Russian Literature*, New York, 1905.) This work has some material related to Kropotkin's social thought.

In Russian and French Prisons. 387 pages, Ward and Downey, London, 1887. (Long out of print.)

Modern Science and Anarchism. Booklet, 112 pages, Freedom Press, London, 1912; Social Science Club, Philadelphia, 1903, 94 pages. Reprinted in part in this volume.

Memoirs of a Revolutionist. 519 pages, Houghton Mifflin and Company, Boston, 1899.

Mutual Aid. 348 pages, Heinemann, London, 1902; (revised edition, 1904); Alfred A. Knopf, New York, 1921, 240 pages.

The Terror in Russia. 75 pages, Issued by the (British) Parliamentary Russian Committee, published by Methuen and Company, London, 1909. (Report on the Czarist terror against political opponents; out of print.)

Anarchism: Its Philosophy and Ideal. Freedom Press, London. (Revision of a speech; reprinted in this volume.)

Anarchist Communism: Its Basis and Principles. 35 pages, Freedom Press, 1891. Also published by the Fellowship Press, London, 1899. (Reprinted in this volume.)

Anarchist Morality. 36 pages, Freedom Press, London, 1909; American edition, Mother Earth Publishing Company, 1916. (Reprinted in this volume.)

An Appeal to the Young. 16 pages, Freedom Press, London; Kerr and Company, Chicago, 1899. Written for *Le Révolté* (Paris) June-August, 1880; translated by H. M. Hyndman for *Justice,* London, 1884. (Reprinted in this volume.)

The Commune of Paris. 16 pages, Freedom Press, London, 1909; Liberty Library, Iowa, 1896.

Expropriation. 39 pages, Freedom Press, London, 1909. (Reprinted from *The Conquest of Bread.*)

Law and Authority. 23 pages, Freedom Press, London, 1886. (Reprinted in this volume.)

The Place of Anarchism in Socialist Evolution. 16 pages, H. Seymour, London, 1887. (Revision of a speech.)

Revolutionary Government. 16 pages, Freedom Press, 1892. (Reprinted in this volume.)

Revolutionary Studies. 31 pages, *The Commonweal,* London, 1892. Translated from *La Révolté,* "Etude sur la Revolution," but not published as a pamphlet in French or in any other language.

The State: Its Historic Role. 42 pages, Freedom Press, London, 1903; a better translation is reprinted in *Man or the State,* a collection of essays compiled by Waldo R. Browne, published by B. W. Huebsch, New York, 1921.

The Wage System.   15 pages, Freedom Press, London, 1920. (First published in 1889. Reprinted from *The Conquest of Bread.*)

War.   H. Seymour, London, 1888.

War and Capitalism.   20 pages, Freedom Press, London, 1914. (Reprinted from *Modern Science and Anarchism.*)

IN OTHER LANGUAGES

Paroles d'un Révolté.   343 pages, a collection of articles from *Le Révolté,* 1879-1882, selected by Élisée Reclus, Paris, 1885.   The chapters translated and published in English pamphlets (listed above) are: Appeal to the Young, The Commune of Paris, War, Revolutionary Government, Law and Authority, and Expropriation.   The last appears also as a chapter in *The Conquest of Bread.* A new translation of The Spirit of Revolt appears in this volume. The chapters not translated are: Decomposition of the State, The Necessity of the Revolution, The Next Revolution, Political Rights, The Coming Order, Theory and Practice, The Revolutionary Minorities, Representative Government, The Agrarian Question, and All Socialists.

Les Prisons.   (Revision of a speech; translated and printed in this volume.)   This also appears, with some changes, in *Russian and French Prisons.*

L'Organization de la Vindicte appelée Justice.   (Organized Vengeance called Justice.)   16 pages, *Temps Nouveaux,* Paris, 1901.

La Science Moderne et L'Anarchie.   402 pages, P. V. Stock et Cie., Paris, 1913.   This contains: *La Science Moderne et l'Anarchie,* 136 pages; *Communisme et Anarchie,* 32 pages; *L'État: son rôle historique,* 63 pages; *L'État Moderne,* 102 pages; and *Herbert Spencer: sa Philosophie,* 25 pages.   Most of these essays appeared previously in separate form and were translated in almost all civilized languages, particularly, *L'État: son rôle historique.*

Un Siècle d'Attente: 1789-1889.   32 pages, *La Révolté,* 1893.

Syndikalismus und Anarchismus.   11 pages, Der Syndikalist,

Berlin, 1908. This was taken from *Les Temps Nouveaux* and did not appear in pamphlet form in French or English.

Les Temps Nouveaux. 63 pages, *La Révolté*, Paris, 1894.

NOTES ON KROPOTKIN'S BOOKS AS AN AID TO FURTHER READING

The Conquest of Bread.

This is Kropotkin's most thorough study of the tendencies toward free cooperation as the best means to abolish capitalism, class control, the wage system and above all, the State. It deals only with the economic and political factors,—chiefly the reorganization of production and distribution. Present evils are analyzed in the light of historic examples of voluntary cooperation as the driving force toward larger freedom. The workability of anarchist-communism is predicated on that experience.

Most of the book is an argument,—exceedingly simple and clear,—for the conquest of economic power by the workers without resort to the State to do it. He argues the case with the state socialists of course,—and adds his views for intensified agriculture and decentralized industry.

Ethics.

This book, assembled from Kropotkin's notes, and published posthumously, is an elaboration and development of articles which appeared in the London magazine *Nineteenth Century* between 1904 and 1906.

After tracing ethical principles in nature and among the primitives, Kropotkin gives a history of ethical theories and teachings beginning with those of the ancient Greeks, followed by those of medieval Christianity, the Renaissance and the nineteenth century. He discusses the evolution of the conceptions of justice, the ethics of socialism, altruism and egoism, etc., and concludes with showing the necessity of envisaging ethics from the sociological point of view.

Kropotkin denies the connection of morality with religion and metaphysics, and tries to establish its purely scientific basis. His ethical theory could be expressed in one word,—solidarity,—for he considers solidarity and equality necessary conditions for the establishment of social justice. Hence his formula: "Without equality no justice and without justice no morality."

Fields, Factories, and Workshops.

This book, published in 1912, is a revision of magazine articles written between 1888 and 1890. It discusses "the advantages which civilized societies would derive from a combination of industrial pursuits with intensive agriculture, and of brain work with manual work."

Tracing the gradual spread of manufacture from its original centers in England and France, Kropotkin comes to the conclusion that each nation will in its turn become a manufacturing nation, and that each region, therefore, will have to become its own producer and its own consumer of manufactured goods. From a study of the results of intensive agriculture he concludes, also, that an "economy of space and labor," representing a combination of machinery and manual labor would enable almost every nation to grow on its own soil the food and most of the raw material required for its own use. Moreover, the abolition of the distinction between city and village, by the increased use of applied science in agriculture and by the easy transmission of electric power to places at great distances from its source, will make possible a "synthesis of human activities."

For an all-round technical and "integral" education Kropotkin would substitute for the division of society into brain workers and manual workers a combination of both kinds of activities. The results would be a greater economy of human effort, a better balance of individual life, and the happiness that can be found in the full exercise and development of the different and dormant capacities of the human being.

Thus country and city, factory and laboratory, workshop and studio would no longer divide human beings into various classes; instead these activities would be simultaneous aspects of the future integrated life of the individual.

The Great French Revolution.

This history of the French Revolution was undertaken because Kropotkin felt that previous historians had wholly neglected the two essential factors that made that revolution so significant,—the intellectuals who prepared it and the masses who gave it its force. Besides being an excellent piece of historical writing, it has the merit of carrying throughout an interpretation which is unique. It has nothing to do with anarchist propaganda; the word anarchism is not mentioned in it. It is faithful historical interpretation,—the only work of its sort which Kropotkin did,—and one which is regarded by many as his crowning achievement.

Mutual Aid.

This scientific study is the most generally known of Kropotkin's work, for it dealt with a controversial issue of lively interest to the whole "intelligent minority." It is an answer to the school of "the survival of the fittest," and was directly inspired by revolt against Huxley's interpretation of Darwinism. In it Kropotkin sets forth the principle of mutual cooperation within species as the chief force for survival, protection and progress. One chapter is devoted to its influence in animal societies, the rest to an historical study of its growth and power from primitive tribes to the present. While it is free of propaganda, anarchist philosophy obviously is based upon such an interpretation of social life. He sums up his thesis by saying: "For individual progress, as for each other conquest over nature, mutual aid and close intercourse are, as they have always been, much more advantageous than mutual struggle."

Modern Science and Anarchism.

The essential parts of this work are reprinted in this volume. The later revised French edition expanded it. In that book were published also three other studies,—*The State, its*

Historic Role, The Modern State, and *Communism and Anarchism.* Only the first has been translated and published in English.

The State is an historical study of the origin and function of the State, confined chiefly to Europe in the middle ages, when the modern State arose and destroyed the free communes. Kropotkin looks upon the free cities, not only of medieval Europe, but of Greece as well, as the natural inspirers of the art, thought and well-being that made them significant. He sees the State as the destroyer of creative power, and of free initiative, He says, "Throughout the whole history of our civilization, two opposed tendencies have been in conflict: the Roman tradition and the popular tradition; the imperialist tradition and the federalist tradition; the authoritarian and the libertarian."

The study is of course an argument for free federation in all its forms as against the State and its subjects.

In *The Modern State,* he continues the study through the nineteenth century, with particular relation to the growth of monopolies under State protection, especially in England and Germany. The part played by war in impoverishing the masses and making the rich richer is also set forth. The State, he says, cannot help free the masses, not in its modern constitutional form any more than in its monarchical. Therefore any attempt to strengthen it, to extend its power or functions, merely increases the enslavement of the masses.

In *Communism and Anarchism,* his familiar principles are set forth in new form, with additional material on why isolated communist communities fail, on whether the family is the necessary basis of sex relationships, and on the question of individual freedom under communism.

A CATALOG OF SELECTED
DOVER BOOKS
IN ALL FIELDS OF INTEREST

A CATALOG OF SELECTED DOVER
BOOKS IN ALL FIELDS OF INTEREST

CONCERNING THE SPIRITUAL IN ART, Wassily Kandinsky. Pioneering work by father of abstract art. Thoughts on color theory, nature of art. Analysis of earlier masters. 12 illustrations. 80pp. of text. 5⅜ x 8½. 23411-8

ANIMALS: 1,419 Copyright-Free Illustrations of Mammals, Birds, Fish, Insects, etc., Jim Harter (ed.). Clear wood engravings present, in extremely lifelike poses, over 1,000 species of animals. One of the most extensive pictorial sourcebooks of its kind. Captions. Index. 284pp. 9 x 12. 23766-4

CELTIC ART: The Methods of Construction, George Bain. Simple geometric techniques for making Celtic interlacements, spirals, Kells-type initials, animals, humans, etc. Over 500 illustrations. 160pp. 9 x 12. (Available in U.S. only.) 22923-8

AN ATLAS OF ANATOMY FOR ARTISTS, Fritz Schider. Most thorough reference work on art anatomy in the world. Hundreds of illustrations, including selections from works by Vesalius, Leonardo, Goya, Ingres, Michelangelo, others. 593 illustrations. 192pp. 7⅛ x 10¼. 20241-0

CELTIC HAND STROKE-BY-STROKE (Irish Half-Uncial from "The Book of Kells"): An Arthur Baker Calligraphy Manual, Arthur Baker. Complete guide to creating each letter of the alphabet in distinctive Celtic manner. Covers hand position, strokes, pens, inks, paper, more. Illustrated. 48pp. 8¼ x 11. 24336-2

EASY ORIGAMI, John Montroll. Charming collection of 32 projects (hat, cup, pelican, piano, swan, many more) specially designed for the novice origami hobbyist. Clearly illustrated easy-to-follow instructions insure that even beginning papercrafters will achieve successful results. 48pp. 8¼ x 11. 27298-2

THE COMPLETE BOOK OF BIRDHOUSE CONSTRUCTION FOR WOODWORKERS, Scott D. Campbell. Detailed instructions, illustrations, tables. Also data on bird habitat and instinct patterns. Bibliography. 3 tables. 63 illustrations in 15 figures. 48pp. 5¼ x 8½. 24407-5

BLOOMINGDALE'S ILLUSTRATED 1886 CATALOG: Fashions, Dry Goods and Housewares, Bloomingdale Brothers. Famed merchants' extremely rare catalog depicting about 1,700 products: clothing, housewares, firearms, dry goods, jewelry, more. Invaluable for dating, identifying vintage items. Also, copyright-free graphics for artists, designers. Co-published with Henry Ford Museum & Greenfield Village. 160pp. 8¼ x 11. 25780-0

HISTORIC COSTUME IN PICTURES, Braun & Schneider. Over 1,450 costumed figures in clearly detailed engravings–from dawn of civilization to end of 19th century. Captions. Many folk costumes. 256pp. 8⅜ x 11¾. 23150-X

STICKLEY CRAFTSMAN FURNITURE CATALOGS, Gustav Stickley and L. & J. G. Stickley. Beautiful, functional furniture in two authentic catalogs from 1910. 594 illustrations, including 277 photos, show settles, rockers, armchairs, reclining chairs, bookcases, desks, tables. 183pp. 6½ x 9¼.   23838-5

AMERICAN LOCOMOTIVES IN HISTORIC PHOTOGRAPHS: 1858 to 1949, Ron Ziel (ed.). A rare collection of 126 meticulously detailed official photographs, called "builder portraits," of American locomotives that majestically chronicle the rise of steam locomotive power in America. Introduction. Detailed captions. xi+ 129pp. 9 x 12.   27393-8

AMERICA'S LIGHTHOUSES: An Illustrated History, Francis Ross Holland, Jr. Delightfully written, profusely illustrated fact-filled survey of over 200 American light-houses since 1716. History, anecdotes, technological advances, more. 240pp. 8 x 10¾.
                                                                      25576-X

TOWARDS A NEW ARCHITECTURE, Le Corbusier. Pioneering manifesto by founder of "International School." Technical and aesthetic theories, views of industry, eco-nomics, relation of form to function, "mass-production split" and much more. Profusely illustrated. 320pp. 6⅛ x 9¼. (Available in U.S. only.)   25023-7

HOW THE OTHER HALF LIVES, Jacob Riis. Famous journalistic record, expos-ing poverty and degradation of New York slums around 1900, by major social reformer. 100 striking and influential photographs. 233pp. 10 x 7⅞.   22012-5

FRUIT KEY AND TWIG KEY TO TREES AND SHRUBS, William M. Harlow. One of the handiest and most widely used identification aids. Fruit key covers 120 deciduous and evergreen species; twig key 160 deciduous species. Easily used. Over 300 photographs. 126pp. 5⅜ x 8½.   20511-8

COMMON BIRD SONGS, Dr. Donald J. Borror. Songs of 60 most common U.S. birds: robins, sparrows, cardinals, bluejays, finches, more—arranged in order of increasing complexity. Up to 9 variations of songs of each species.
                                                 Cassette and manual 99911-4

ORCHIDS AS HOUSE PLANTS, Rebecca Tyson Northen. Grow cattleyas and many other kinds of orchids—in a window, in a case, or under artificial light. 63 illus-trations. 148pp. 5⅜ x 8½.   23261-1

MONSTER MAZES, Dave Phillips. Masterful mazes at four levels of difficulty. Avoid deadly perils and evil creatures to find magical treasures. Solutions for all 32 exciting illustrated puzzles. 48pp. 8¼ x 11.   26005-4

MOZART'S DON GIOVANNI (DOVER OPERA LIBRETTO SERIES), Wolfgang Amadeus Mozart. Introduced and translated by Ellen H. Bleiler. Standard Italian libretto, with complete English translation. Convenient and thoroughly portable—an ideal companion for reading along with a recording or the performance itself. Introduction. List of characters. Plot summary. 121pp. 5¼ x 8½.   24944-1

TECHNICAL MANUAL AND DICTIONARY OF CLASSICAL BALLET, Gail Grant. Defines, explains, comments on steps, movements, poses and concepts. 15-page pictorial section. Basic book for student, viewer. 127pp. 5⅜ x 8½.   21843-0

THE CLARINET AND CLARINET PLAYING, David Pino. Lively, comprehensive work features suggestions about technique, musicianship, and musical interpretation, as well as guidelines for teaching, making your own reeds, and preparing for public performance. Includes an intriguing look at clarinet history. "A godsend," *The Clarinet*, Journal of the International Clarinet Society. Appendixes. 7 illus. 320pp. 5⅜ x 8½. 40270-3

HOLLYWOOD GLAMOR PORTRAITS, John Kobal (ed.). 145 photos from 1926-49. Harlow, Gable, Bogart, Bacall; 94 stars in all. Full background on photographers, technical aspects. 160pp. 8⅜ x 11¼. 23352-9

THE ANNOTATED CASEY AT THE BAT: A Collection of Ballads about the Mighty Casey/Third, Revised Edition, Martin Gardner (ed.). Amusing sequels and parodies of one of America's best-loved poems: Casey's Revenge, Why Casey Whiffed, Casey's Sister at the Bat, others. 256pp. 5⅜ x 8½. 28598-7

THE RAVEN AND OTHER FAVORITE POEMS, Edgar Allan Poe. Over 40 of the author's most memorable poems: "The Bells," "Ulalume," "Israfel," "To Helen," "The Conqueror Worm," "Eldorado," "Annabel Lee," many more. Alphabetic lists of titles and first lines. 64pp. 5³⁄₁₆ x 8¼. 26685-0

PERSONAL MEMOIRS OF U. S. GRANT, Ulysses Simpson Grant. Intelligent, deeply moving firsthand account of Civil War campaigns, considered by many the finest military memoirs ever written. Includes letters, historic photographs, maps and more. 528pp. 6⅛ x 9¼. 28587-1

ANCIENT EGYPTIAN MATERIALS AND INDUSTRIES, A. Lucas and J. Harris. Fascinating, comprehensive, thoroughly documented text describes this ancient civilization's vast resources and the processes that incorporated them in daily life, including the use of animal products, building materials, cosmetics, perfumes and incense, fibers, glazed ware, glass and its manufacture, materials used in the mummification process, and much more. 544pp. 6⅛ x 9¼. (Available in U.S. only.) 40446-3

RUSSIAN STORIES/RUSSKIE RASSKAZY: A Dual-Language Book, edited by Gleb Struve. Twelve tales by such masters as Chekhov, Tolstoy, Dostoevsky, Pushkin, others. Excellent word-for-word English translations on facing pages, plus teaching and study aids, Russian/English vocabulary, biographical/critical introductions, more. 416pp. 5⅜ x 8½. 26244-8

PHILADELPHIA THEN AND NOW: 60 Sites Photographed in the Past and Present, Kenneth Finkel and Susan Oyama. Rare photographs of City Hall, Logan Square, Independence Hall, Betsy Ross House, other landmarks juxtaposed with contemporary views. Captures changing face of historic city. Introduction. Captions. 128pp. 8¼ x 11. 25790-8

AIA ARCHITECTURAL GUIDE TO NASSAU AND SUFFOLK COUNTIES, LONG ISLAND, The American Institute of Architects, Long Island Chapter, and the Society for the Preservation of Long Island Antiquities. Comprehensive, well-researched and generously illustrated volume brings to life over three centuries of Long Island's great architectural heritage. More than 240 photographs with authoritative, extensively detailed captions. 176pp. 8¼ x 11. 26946-9

NORTH AMERICAN INDIAN LIFE: Customs and Traditions of 23 Tribes, Elsie Clews Parsons (ed.). 27 fictionalized essays by noted anthropologists examine religion, customs, government, additional facets of life among the Winnebago, Crow, Zuni, Eskimo, other tribes. 480pp. 6⅛ x 9¼. 27377-6

CATALOG OF DOVER BOOKS

FRANK LLOYD WRIGHT'S DANA HOUSE, Donald Hoffmann. Pictorial essay of residential masterpiece with over 160 interior and exterior photos, plans, elevations, sketches and studies. 128pp. 9¼ x 10¾.   29120-0

THE MALE AND FEMALE FIGURE IN MOTION: 60 Classic Photographic Sequences, Eadweard Muybridge. 60 true-action photographs of men and women walking, running, climbing, bending, turning, etc., reproduced from rare 19th-century masterpiece. vi + 121pp. 9 x 12.   24745-7

1001 QUESTIONS ANSWERED ABOUT THE SEASHORE, N. J. Berrill and Jacquelyn Berrill. Queries answered about dolphins, sea snails, sponges, starfish, fishes, shore birds, many others. Covers appearance, breeding, growth, feeding, much more. 305pp. 5¼ x 8¼.   23366-9

ATTRACTING BIRDS TO YOUR YARD, William J. Weber. Easy-to-follow guide offers advice on how to attract the greatest diversity of birds: birdhouses, feeders, water and waterers, much more. 96pp. 5³⁄₁₆ x 8¼.   28927-3

MEDICINAL AND OTHER USES OF NORTH AMERICAN PLANTS: A Historical Survey with Special Reference to the Eastern Indian Tribes, Charlotte Erichsen-Brown. Chronological historical citations document 500 years of usage of plants, trees, shrubs native to eastern Canada, northeastern U.S. Also complete identifying information. 343 illustrations. 544pp. 6½ x 9¼.   25951-X

STORYBOOK MAZES, Dave Phillips. 23 stories and mazes on two-page spreads: Wizard of Oz, Treasure Island, Robin Hood, etc. Solutions. 64pp. 8¼ x 11.   23628-5

AMERICAN NEGRO SONGS: 230 Folk Songs and Spirituals, Religious and Secular, John W. Work. This authoritative study traces the African influences of songs sung and played by black Americans at work, in church, and as entertainment. The author discusses the lyric significance of such songs as "Swing Low, Sweet Chariot," "John Henry," and others and offers the words and music for 230 songs. Bibliography. Index of Song Titles. 272pp. 6½ x 9¼.   40271-1

MOVIE-STAR PORTRAITS OF THE FORTIES, John Kobal (ed.). 163 glamor, studio photos of 106 stars of the 1940s: Rita Hayworth, Ava Gardner, Marlon Brando, Clark Gable, many more. 176pp. 8⅜ x 11¼.   23546-7

BENCHLEY LOST AND FOUND, Robert Benchley. Finest humor from early 30s, about pet peeves, child psychologists, post office and others. Mostly unavailable elsewhere. 73 illustrations by Peter Arno and others. 183pp. 5⅜ x 8½.   22410-4

YEKL and THE IMPORTED BRIDEGROOM AND OTHER STORIES OF YIDDISH NEW YORK, Abraham Cahan. Film Hester Street based on *Yekl* (1896). Novel, other stories among first about Jewish immigrants on N.Y.'s East Side. 240pp. 5⅜ x 8½.   22427-9

SELECTED POEMS, Walt Whitman. Generous sampling from *Leaves of Grass*. Twenty-four poems include "I Hear America Singing," "Song of the Open Road," "I Sing the Body Electric," "When Lilacs Last in the Dooryard Bloom'd," "O Captain! My Captain!"—all reprinted from an authoritative edition. Lists of titles and first lines. 128pp. 5³⁄₁₆ x 8¼.   26878-0

THE BEST TALES OF HOFFMANN, E. T. A. Hoffmann. 10 of Hoffmann's most important stories: "Nutcracker and the King of Mice," "The Golden Flowerpot," etc. 458pp. 5⅜ x 8½. 21793-0

FROM FETISH TO GOD IN ANCIENT EGYPT, E. A. Wallis Budge. Rich detailed survey of Egyptian conception of "God" and gods, magic, cult of animals, Osiris, more. Also, superb English translations of hymns and legends. 240 illustrations. 545pp. 5⅜ x 8½. 25803-3

FRENCH STORIES/CONTES FRANÇAIS: A Dual-Language Book, Wallace Fowlie. Ten stories by French masters, Voltaire to Camus: "Micromegas" by Voltaire; "The Atheist's Mass" by Balzac; "Minuet" by de Maupassant; "The Guest" by Camus, six more. Excellent English translations on facing pages. Also French-English vocabulary list, exercises, more. 352pp. 5⅜ x 8½. 26443-2

CHICAGO AT THE TURN OF THE CENTURY IN PHOTOGRAPHS: 122 Historic Views from the Collections of the Chicago Historical Society, Larry A. Viskochil. Rare large-format prints offer detailed views of City Hall, State Street, the Loop, Hull House, Union Station, many other landmarks, circa 1904-1913. Introduction. Captions. Maps. 144pp. 9⅜ x 12¼. 24656-6

OLD BROOKLYN IN EARLY PHOTOGRAPHS, 1865-1929, William Lee Younger. Luna Park, Gravesend race track, construction of Grand Army Plaza, moving of Hotel Brighton, etc. 157 previously unpublished photographs. 165pp. 8⅞ x 11¾. 23587-4

THE MYTHS OF THE NORTH AMERICAN INDIANS, Lewis Spence. Rich anthology of the myths and legends of the Algonquins, Iroquois, Pawnees and Sioux, prefaced by an extensive historical and ethnological commentary. 36 illustrations. 480pp. 5⅜ x 8½. 25967-6

AN ENCYCLOPEDIA OF BATTLES: Accounts of Over 1,560 Battles from 1479 B.C. to the Present, David Eggenberger. Essential details of every major battle in recorded history from the first battle of Megiddo in 1479 B.C. to Grenada in 1984. List of Battle Maps. New Appendix covering the years 1967-1984. Index. 99 illustrations. 544pp. 6½ x 9¼. 24913-1

SAILING ALONE AROUND THE WORLD, Captain Joshua Slocum. First man to sail around the world, alone, in small boat. One of great feats of seamanship told in delightful manner. 67 illustrations. 294pp. 5⅜ x 8½. 20326-3

ANARCHISM AND OTHER ESSAYS, Emma Goldman. Powerful, penetrating, prophetic essays on direct action, role of minorities, prison reform, puritan hypocrisy, violence, etc. 271pp. 5⅜ x 8½. 22484-8

MYTHS OF THE HINDUS AND BUDDHISTS, Ananda K. Coomaraswamy and Sister Nivedita. Great stories of the epics; deeds of Krishna, Shiva, taken from puranas, Vedas, folk tales; etc. 32 illustrations. 400pp. 5⅜ x 8½. 21759-0

THE TRAUMA OF BIRTH, Otto Rank. Rank's controversial thesis that anxiety neurosis is caused by profound psychological trauma which occurs at birth. 256pp. 5⅜ x 8½. 27974-X

A THEOLOGICO-POLITICAL TREATISE, Benedict Spinoza. Also contains unfinished Political Treatise. Great classic on religious liberty, theory of government on common consent. R. Elwes translation. Total of 421pp. 5⅜ x 8½. 20249-6

MY BONDAGE AND MY FREEDOM, Frederick Douglass. Born a slave, Douglass became outspoken force in antislavery movement. The best of Douglass' autobiographies. Graphic description of slave life. 464pp. 5⅜ x 8½. 22457-0

FOLLOWING THE EQUATOR: A Journey Around the World, Mark Twain. Fascinating humorous account of 1897 voyage to Hawaii, Australia, India, New Zealand, etc. Ironic, bemused reports on peoples, customs, climate, flora and fauna, politics, much more. 197 illustrations. 720pp. 5⅜ x 8½. 26113-1

THE PEOPLE CALLED SHAKERS, Edward D. Andrews. Definitive study of Shakers: origins, beliefs, practices, dances, social organization, furniture and crafts, etc. 33 illustrations. 351pp. 5⅜ x 8½. 21081-2

THE MYTHS OF GREECE AND ROME, H. A. Guerber. A classic of mythology, generously illustrated, long prized for its simple, graphic, accurate retelling of the principal myths of Greece and Rome, and for its commentary on their origins and significance. With 64 illustrations by Michelangelo, Raphael, Titian, Rubens, Canova, Bernini and others. 480pp. 5⅜ x 8½. 27584-1

PSYCHOLOGY OF MUSIC, Carl E. Seashore. Classic work discusses music as a medium from psychological viewpoint. Clear treatment of physical acoustics, auditory apparatus, sound perception, development of musical skills, nature of musical feeling, host of other topics. 88 figures. 408pp. 5⅜ x 8½. 21851-1

THE PHILOSOPHY OF HISTORY, Georg W. Hegel. Great classic of Western thought develops concept that history is not chance but rational process, the evolution of freedom. 457pp. 5⅜ x 8½. 20112-0

THE BOOK OF TEA, Kakuzo Okakura. Minor classic of the Orient: entertaining, charming explanation, interpretation of traditional Japanese culture in terms of tea ceremony. 94pp. 5⅜ x 8½. 20070-1

LIFE IN ANCIENT EGYPT, Adolf Erman. Fullest, most thorough, detailed older account with much not in more recent books, domestic life, religion, magic, medicine, commerce, much more. Many illustrations reproduce tomb paintings, carvings, hieroglyphs, etc. 597pp. 5⅜ x 8½. 22632-8

SUNDIALS, Their Theory and Construction, Albert Waugh. Far and away the best, most thorough coverage of ideas, mathematics concerned, types, construction, adjusting anywhere. Simple, nontechnical treatment allows even children to build several of these dials. Over 100 illustrations. 230pp. 5⅜ x 8½. 22947-5

THEORETICAL HYDRODYNAMICS, L. M. Milne-Thomson. Classic exposition of the mathematical theory of fluid motion, applicable to both hydrodynamics and aerodynamics. Over 600 exercises. 768pp. 6⅛ x 9¼. 68970-0

SONGS OF EXPERIENCE: Facsimile Reproduction with 26 Plates in Full Color, William Blake. 26 full-color plates from a rare 1826 edition. Includes "The Tyger," "London," "Holy Thursday," and other poems. Printed text of poems. 48pp. 5¼ x 7. 24636-1

OLD-TIME VIGNETTES IN FULL COLOR, Carol Belanger Grafton (ed.). Over 390 charming, often sentimental illustrations, selected from archives of Victorian graphics—pretty women posing, children playing, food, flowers, kittens and puppies, smiling cherubs, birds and butterflies, much more. All copyright-free. 48pp. 9¼ x 12¼. 27269-9

PERSPECTIVE FOR ARTISTS, Rex Vicat Cole. Depth, perspective of sky and sea, shadows, much more, not usually covered. 391 diagrams, 81 reproductions of drawings and paintings. 279pp. 5⅜ x 8½. 22487-2

DRAWING THE LIVING FIGURE, Joseph Sheppard. Innovative approach to artistic anatomy focuses on specifics of surface anatomy, rather than muscles and bones. Over 170 drawings of live models in front, back and side views, and in widely varying poses. Accompanying diagrams. 177 illustrations. Introduction. Index. 144pp. 8⅜ x11¼. 26723-7

GOTHIC AND OLD ENGLISH ALPHABETS: 100 Complete Fonts, Dan X. Solo. Add power, elegance to posters, signs, other graphics with 100 stunning copyright-free alphabets: Blackstone, Dolbey, Germania, 97 more–including many lower-case, numerals, punctuation marks. 104pp. 8⅛ x 11. 24695-7

HOW TO DO BEADWORK, Mary White. Fundamental book on craft from simple projects to five-bead chains and woven works. 106 illustrations. 142pp. 5⅜ x 8. 20697-1

THE BOOK OF WOOD CARVING, Charles Marshall Sayers. Finest book for beginners discusses fundamentals and offers 34 designs. "Absolutely first rate . . . well thought out and well executed."–E. J. Tangerman. 118pp. 7¾ x 10⅝. 23654-4

ILLUSTRATED CATALOG OF CIVIL WAR MILITARY GOODS: Union Army Weapons, Insignia, Uniform Accessories, and Other Equipment, Schuyler, Hartley, and Graham. Rare, profusely illustrated 1846 catalog includes Union Army uniform and dress regulations, arms and ammunition, coats, insignia, flags, swords, rifles, etc. 226 illustrations. 160pp. 9 x 12. 24939-5

WOMEN'S FASHIONS OF THE EARLY 1900s: An Unabridged Republication of "New York Fashions, 1909," National Cloak & Suit Co. Rare catalog of mail-order fashions documents women's and children's clothing styles shortly after the turn of the century. Captions offer full descriptions, prices. Invaluable resource for fashion, costume historians. Approximately 725 illustrations. 128pp. 8⅜ x 11¼. 27276-1

THE 1912 AND 1915 GUSTAV STICKLEY FURNITURE CATALOGS, Gustav Stickley. With over 200 detailed illustrations and descriptions, these two catalogs are essential reading and reference materials and identification guides for Stickley furniture. Captions cite materials, dimensions and prices. 112pp. 6½ x 9¼. 26676-1

EARLY AMERICAN LOCOMOTIVES, John H. White, Jr. Finest locomotive engravings from early 19th century: historical (1804–74), main-line (after 1870), special, foreign, etc. 147 plates. 142pp. 11⅜ x 8¼. 22772-3

THE TALL SHIPS OF TODAY IN PHOTOGRAPHS, Frank O. Braynard. Lavishly illustrated tribute to nearly 100 majestic contemporary sailing vessels: Amerigo Vespucci, Clearwater, Constitution, Eagle, Mayflower, Sea Cloud, Victory, many more. Authoritative captions provide statistics, background on each ship. 190 black-and-white photographs and illustrations. Introduction. 128pp. 8⅞ x 11¾. 27163-3

LITTLE BOOK OF EARLY AMERICAN CRAFTS AND TRADES, Peter Stockham (ed.). 1807 children's book explains crafts and trades: baker, hatter, cooper, potter, and many others. 23 copperplate illustrations. 140pp. 4⅝ x 6.   23336-7

VICTORIAN FASHIONS AND COSTUMES FROM HARPER'S BAZAR, 1867–1898, Stella Blum (ed.). Day costumes, evening wear, sports clothes, shoes, hats, other accessories in over 1,000 detailed engravings. 320pp. 9⅜ x 12¼. 22990-4

GUSTAV STICKLEY, THE CRAFTSMAN, Mary Ann Smith. Superb study surveys broad scope of Stickley's achievement, especially in architecture. Design philosophy, rise and fall of the Craftsman empire, descriptions and floor plans for many Craftsman houses, more. 86 black-and-white halftones. 31 line illustrations. Introduction 208pp. 6½ x 9¼.   27210-9

THE LONG ISLAND RAIL ROAD IN EARLY PHOTOGRAPHS, Ron Ziel. Over 220 rare photos, informative text document origin (1844) and development of rail service on Long Island. Vintage views of early trains, locomotives, stations, passengers, crews, much more. Captions. 8⅞ x 11¾.   26301-0

VOYAGE OF THE LIBERDADE, Joshua Slocum. Great 19th-century mariner's thrilling, first-hand account of the wreck of his ship off South America, the 35-foot boat he built from the wreckage, and its remarkable voyage home. 128pp. 5⅜ x 8½.
40022-0

TEN BOOKS ON ARCHITECTURE, Vitruvius. The most important book ever written on architecture. Early Roman aesthetics, technology, classical orders, site selection, all other aspects. Morgan translation. 331pp. 5⅜ x 8½.   20645-9

THE HUMAN FIGURE IN MOTION, Eadweard Muybridge. More than 4,500 stopped-action photos, in action series, showing undraped men, women, children jumping, lying down, throwing, sitting, wrestling, carrying, etc. 390pp. 7⅞ x 10⅝.
20204-6 Clothbd.

TREES OF THE EASTERN AND CENTRAL UNITED STATES AND CANADA, William M. Harlow. Best one-volume guide to 140 trees. Full descriptions, woodlore, range, etc. Over 600 illustrations. Handy size. 288pp. 4½ x 6⅜.   20395-6

SONGS OF WESTERN BIRDS, Dr. Donald J. Borror. Complete song and call repertoire of 60 western species, including flycatchers, juncoes, cactus wrens, many more–includes fully illustrated booklet.   Cassette and manual 99913-0

GROWING AND USING HERBS AND SPICES, Milo Miloradovich. Versatile handbook provides all the information needed for cultivation and use of all the herbs and spices available in North America. 4 illustrations. Index. Glossary. 236pp. 5⅜ x 8½.
25058-X

BIG BOOK OF MAZES AND LABYRINTHS, Walter Shepherd. 50 mazes and labyrinths in all–classical, solid, ripple, and more–in one great volume. Perfect inexpensive puzzler for clever youngsters. Full solutions. 112pp. 8⅛ x 11.   22951-3

PIANO TUNING, J. Cree Fischer. Clearest, best book for beginner, amateur. Simple repairs, raising dropped notes, tuning by easy method of flattened fifths. No previous skills needed. 4 illustrations. 201pp. 5⅜ x 8½. 23267-0

HINTS TO SINGERS, Lillian Nordica. Selecting the right teacher, developing confidence, overcoming stage fright, and many other important skills receive thoughtful discussion in this indispensible guide, written by a world-famous diva of four decades' experience. 96pp. 5⅜ x 8½. 40094-8

THE COMPLETE NONSENSE OF EDWARD LEAR, Edward Lear. All nonsense limericks, zany alphabets, Owl and Pussycat, songs, nonsense botany, etc., illustrated by Lear. Total of 320pp. 5⅜ x 8½. (Available in U.S. only.) 20167-8

VICTORIAN PARLOUR POETRY: An Annotated Anthology, Michael R. Turner. 117 gems by Longfellow, Tennyson, Browning, many lesser-known poets. "The Village Blacksmith," "Curfew Must Not Ring Tonight," "Only a Baby Small," dozens more, often difficult to find elsewhere. Index of poets, titles, first lines. xxiii + 325pp. 5⅜ x 8¼. 27044-0

DUBLINERS, James Joyce. Fifteen stories offer vivid, tightly focused observations of the lives of Dublin's poorer classes. At least one, "The Dead," is considered a masterpiece. Reprinted complete and unabridged from standard edition. 160pp. 5³⁄₁₆ x 8¼. 26870-5

GREAT WEIRD TALES: 14 Stories by Lovecraft, Blackwood, Machen and Others, S. T. Joshi (ed.). 14 spellbinding tales, including "The Sin Eater," by Fiona McLeod, "The Eye Above the Mantel," by Frank Belknap Long, as well as renowned works by R. H. Barlow, Lord Dunsany, Arthur Machen, W. C. Morrow and eight other masters of the genre. 256pp. 5⅜ x 8½. (Available in U.S. only.) 40436-6

THE BOOK OF THE SACRED MAGIC OF ABRAMELIN THE MAGE, translated by S. MacGregor Mathers. Medieval manuscript of ceremonial magic. Basic document in Aleister Crowley, Golden Dawn groups. 268pp. 5⅜ x 8½. 23211-5

NEW RUSSIAN-ENGLISH AND ENGLISH-RUSSIAN DICTIONARY, M. A. O'Brien. This is a remarkably handy Russian dictionary, containing a surprising amount of information, including over 70,000 entries. 366pp. 4½ x 6⅛. 20208-9

HISTORIC HOMES OF THE AMERICAN PRESIDENTS, Second, Revised Edition, Irvin Haas. A traveler's guide to American Presidential homes, most open to the public, depicting and describing homes occupied by every American President from George Washington to George Bush. With visiting hours, admission charges, travel routes. 175 photographs. Index. 160pp. 8¼ x 11. 26751-2

NEW YORK IN THE FORTIES, Andreas Feininger. 162 brilliant photographs by the well-known photographer, formerly with *Life* magazine. Commuters, shoppers, Times Square at night, much else from city at its peak. Captions by John von Hartz. 181pp. 9¼ x 10¾. 23585-8

INDIAN SIGN LANGUAGE, William Tomkins. Over 525 signs developed by Sioux and other tribes. Written instructions and diagrams. Also 290 pictographs. 111pp. 6⅛ x 9¼. 22029-X

ANATOMY: A Complete Guide for Artists, Joseph Sheppard. A master of figure drawing shows artists how to render human anatomy convincingly. Over 460 illustrations. 224pp. 8⅜ x 11¼. 27279-6

MEDIEVAL CALLIGRAPHY: Its History and Technique, Marc Drogin. Spirited history, comprehensive instruction manual covers 13 styles (ca. 4th century through 15th). Excellent photographs; directions for duplicating medieval techniques with modern tools. 224pp. 8⅜ x 11¼. 26142-5

DRIED FLOWERS: How to Prepare Them, Sarah Whitlock and Martha Rankin. Complete instructions on how to use silica gel, meal and borax, perlite aggregate, sand and borax, glycerine and water to create attractive permanent flower arrangements. 12 illustrations. 32pp. 5⅜ x 8½. 21802-3

EASY-TO-MAKE BIRD FEEDERS FOR WOODWORKERS, Scott D. Campbell. Detailed, simple-to-use guide for designing, constructing, caring for and using feeders. Text, illustrations for 12 classic and contemporary designs. 96pp. 5⅜ x 8½. 25847-5

SCOTTISH WONDER TALES FROM MYTH AND LEGEND, Donald A. Mackenzie. 16 lively tales tell of giants rumbling down mountainsides, of a magic wand that turns stone pillars into warriors, of gods and goddesses, evil hags, powerful forces and more. 240pp. 5⅜ x 8½. 29677-6

THE HISTORY OF UNDERCLOTHES, C. Willett Cunnington and Phyllis Cunnington. Fascinating, well-documented survey covering six centuries of English undergarments, enhanced with over 100 illustrations: 12th-century laced-up bodice, footed long drawers (1795), 19th-century bustles, 19th-century corsets for men, Victorian "bust improvers," much more. 272pp. 5⅝ x 8¼. 27124-2

ARTS AND CRAFTS FURNITURE: The Complete Brooks Catalog of 1912, Brooks Manufacturing Co. Photos and detailed descriptions of more than 150 now very collectible furniture designs from the Arts and Crafts movement depict davenports, settees, buffets, desks, tables, chairs, bedsteads, dressers and more, all built of solid, quarter-sawed oak. Invaluable for students and enthusiasts of antiques, Americana and the decorative arts. 80pp. 6½ x 9¼. 27471-3

WILBUR AND ORVILLE: A Biography of the Wright Brothers, Fred Howard. Definitive, crisply written study tells the full story of the brothers' lives and work. A vividly written biography, unparalleled in scope and color, that also captures the spirit of an extraordinary era. 560pp. 6⅛ x 9¼. 40297-5

THE ARTS OF THE SAILOR: Knotting, Splicing and Ropework, Hervey Garrett Smith. Indispensable shipboard reference covers tools, basic knots and useful hitches; handsewing and canvas work, more. Over 100 illustrations. Delightful reading for sea lovers. 256pp. 5⅜ x 8½. 26440-8

FRANK LLOYD WRIGHT'S FALLINGWATER: The House and Its History, Second, Revised Edition, Donald Hoffmann. A total revision–both in text and illustrations–of the standard document on Fallingwater, the boldest, most personal architectural statement of Wright's mature years, updated with valuable new material from the recently opened Frank Lloyd Wright Archives. "Fascinating"–*The New York Times*. 116 illustrations. 128pp. 9¼ x 10¾. 27430-6

PHOTOGRAPHIC SKETCHBOOK OF THE CIVIL WAR, Alexander Gardner. 100 photos taken on field during the Civil War. Famous shots of Manassas Harper's Ferry, Lincoln, Richmond, slave pens, etc. 244pp. 10⅝ x 8¼. 22731-6

FIVE ACRES AND INDEPENDENCE, Maurice G. Kains. Great back-to-the-land classic explains basics of self-sufficient farming. The one book to get. 95 illustrations. 397pp. 5⅜ x 8½. 20974-1

SONGS OF EASTERN BIRDS, Dr. Donald J. Borror. Songs and calls of 60 species most common to eastern U.S.: warblers, woodpeckers, flycatchers, thrushes, larks, many more in high-quality recording. Cassette and manual 99912-2

A MODERN HERBAL, Margaret Grieve. Much the fullest, most exact, most useful compilation of herbal material. Gigantic alphabetical encyclopedia, from aconite to zedoary, gives botanical information, medical properties, folklore, economic uses, much else. Indispensable to serious reader. 161 illustrations. 888pp. 6½ x 9¼. 2-vol. set. (Available in U.S. only.) Vol. I: 22798-7
Vol. II: 22799-5

HIDDEN TREASURE MAZE BOOK, Dave Phillips. Solve 34 challenging mazes accompanied by heroic tales of adventure. Evil dragons, people-eating plants, blood-thirsty giants, many more dangerous adversaries lurk at every twist and turn. 34 mazes, stories, solutions. 48pp. 8¼ x 11. 24566-7

LETTERS OF W. A. MOZART, Wolfgang A. Mozart. Remarkable letters show bawdy wit, humor, imagination, musical insights, contemporary musical world; includes some letters from Leopold Mozart. 276pp. 5⅜ x 8½. 22859-2

BASIC PRINCIPLES OF CLASSICAL BALLET, Agrippina Vaganova. Great Russian theoretician, teacher explains methods for teaching classical ballet. 118 illustrations. 175pp. 5⅜ x 8½. 22036-2

THE JUMPING FROG, Mark Twain. Revenge edition. The original story of The Celebrated Jumping Frog of Calaveras County, a hapless French translation, and Twain's hilarious "retranslation" from the French. 12 illustrations. 66pp. 5⅜ x 8½. 22686-7

BEST REMEMBERED POEMS, Martin Gardner (ed.). The 126 poems in this superb collection of 19th- and 20th-century British and American verse range from Shelley's "To a Skylark" to the impassioned "Renascence" of Edna St. Vincent Millay and to Edward Lear's whimsical "The Owl and the Pussycat." 224pp. 5⅜ x 8½. 27165-X

COMPLETE SONNETS, William Shakespeare. Over 150 exquisite poems deal with love, friendship, the tyranny of time, beauty's evanescence, death and other themes in language of remarkable power, precision and beauty. Glossary of archaic terms. 80pp. 5³⁄₁₆ x 8¼. 26686-9

THE BATTLES THAT CHANGED HISTORY, Fletcher Pratt. Eminent historian profiles 16 crucial conflicts, ancient to modern, that changed the course of civilization. 352pp. 5⅜ x 8½. 41129-X

THE WIT AND HUMOR OF OSCAR WILDE, Alvin Redman (ed.). More than 1,000 ripostes, paradoxes, wisecracks: Work is the curse of the drinking classes; I can resist everything except temptation; etc. 258pp. 5⅜ x 8½. 20602-5

SHAKESPEARE LEXICON AND QUOTATION DICTIONARY, Alexander Schmidt. Full definitions, locations, shades of meaning in every word in plays and poems. More than 50,000 exact quotations. 1,485pp. 6½ x 9¼. 2-vol. set.
Vol. 1: 22726-X
Vol. 2: 22727-8

SELECTED POEMS, Emily Dickinson. Over 100 best-known, best-loved poems by one of America's foremost poets, reprinted from authoritative early editions. No comparable edition at this price. Index of first lines. 64pp. 5³⁄₁₆ x 8¼. 26466-1

THE INSIDIOUS DR. FU-MANCHU, Sax Rohmer. The first of the popular mystery series introduces a pair of English detectives to their archnemesis, the diabolical Dr. Fu-Manchu. Flavorful atmosphere, fast-paced action, and colorful characters enliven this classic of the genre. 208pp. 5³⁄₁₆ x 8¼. 29898-1

THE MALLEUS MALEFICARUM OF KRAMER AND SPRENGER, translated by Montague Summers. Full text of most important witchhunter's "bible," used by both Catholics and Protestants. 278pp. 6⅝ x 10. 22802-9

SPANISH STORIES/CUENTOS ESPAÑOLES: A Dual-Language Book, Angel Flores (ed.). Unique format offers 13 great stories in Spanish by Cervantes, Borges, others. Faithful English translations on facing pages. 352pp. 5⅜ x 8½. 25399-6

GARDEN CITY, LONG ISLAND, IN EARLY PHOTOGRAPHS, 1869–1919, Mildred H. Smith. Handsome treasury of 118 vintage pictures, accompanied by carefully researched captions, document the Garden City Hotel fire (1899), the Vanderbilt Cup Race (1908), the first airmail flight departing from the Nassau Boulevard Aerodrome (1911), and much more. 96pp. 8⅞ x 11¾. 40669-5

OLD QUEENS, N.Y., IN EARLY PHOTOGRAPHS, Vincent F. Seyfried and William Asadorian. Over 160 rare photographs of Maspeth, Jamaica, Jackson Heights, and other areas. Vintage views of DeWitt Clinton mansion, 1939 World's Fair and more. Captions. 192pp. 8⅞ x 11. 26358-4

CAPTURED BY THE INDIANS: 15 Firsthand Accounts, 1750-1870, Frederick Drimmer. Astounding true historical accounts of grisly torture, bloody conflicts, relentless pursuits, miraculous escapes and more, by people who lived to tell the tale. 384pp. 5⅜ x 8½. 24901-8

THE WORLD'S GREAT SPEECHES (Fourth Enlarged Edition), Lewis Copeland, Lawrence W. Lamm, and Stephen J. McKenna. Nearly 300 speeches provide public speakers with a wealth of updated quotes and inspiration–from Pericles' funeral oration and William Jennings Bryan's "Cross of Gold Speech" to Malcolm X's powerful words on the Black Revolution and Earl of Spenser's tribute to his sister, Diana, Princess of Wales. 944pp. 5⅜ x 8⅜. 40903-1

THE BOOK OF THE SWORD, Sir Richard F. Burton. Great Victorian scholar/adventurer's eloquent, erudite history of the "queen of weapons"–from prehistory to early Roman Empire. Evolution and development of early swords, variations (sabre, broadsword, cutlass, scimitar, etc.), much more. 336pp. 6⅛ x 9¼.
25434-8

AUTOBIOGRAPHY: The Story of My Experiments with Truth, Mohandas K. Gandhi. Boyhood, legal studies, purification, the growth of the Satyagraha (nonviolent protest) movement. Critical, inspiring work of the man responsible for the freedom of India. 480pp. 5⅜ x 8½. (Available in U.S. only.) 24593-4

CELTIC MYTHS AND LEGENDS, T. W. Rolleston. Masterful retelling of Irish and Welsh stories and tales. Cuchulain, King Arthur, Deirdre, the Grail, many more. First paperback edition. 58 full-page illustrations. 512pp. 5⅜ x 8½. 26507-2

THE PRINCIPLES OF PSYCHOLOGY, William James. Famous long course complete, unabridged. Stream of thought, time perception, memory, experimental methods; great work decades ahead of its time. 94 figures. 1,391pp. 5⅜ x 8½. 2-vol. set.
Vol. I: 20381-6   Vol. II: 20382-4

THE WORLD AS WILL AND REPRESENTATION, Arthur Schopenhauer. Definitive English translation of Schopenhauer's life work, correcting more than 1,000 errors, omissions in earlier translations. Translated by E. F. J. Payne. Total of 1,269pp. 5⅜ x 8½. 2-vol. set.   Vol. 1: 21761-2   Vol. 2: 21762-0

MAGIC AND MYSTERY IN TIBET, Madame Alexandra David-Neel. Experiences among lamas, magicians, sages, sorcerers, Bonpa wizards. A true psychic discovery. 32 illustrations. 321pp. 5⅜ x 8½. (Available in U.S. only.) 22682-4

THE EGYPTIAN BOOK OF THE DEAD, E. A. Wallis Budge. Complete reproduction of Ani's papyrus, finest ever found. Full hieroglyphic text, interlinear transliteration, word-for-word translation, smooth translation. 533pp. 6½ x 9¼. 21866-X

MATHEMATICS FOR THE NONMATHEMATICIAN, Morris Kline. Detailed, college-level treatment of mathematics in cultural and historical context, with numerous exercises. Recommended Reading Lists. Tables. Numerous figures. 641pp. 5⅜ x 8½. 24823-2

PROBABILISTIC METHODS IN THE THEORY OF STRUCTURES, Isaac Elishakoff. Well-written introduction covers the elements of the theory of probability from two or more random variables, the reliability of such multivariable structures, the theory of random function, Monte Carlo methods of treating problems incapable of exact solution, and more. Examples. 502pp. 5⅜ x 8½. 40691-1

THE RIME OF THE ANCIENT MARINER, Gustave Doré, S. T. Coleridge. Doré's finest work; 34 plates capture moods, subtleties of poem. Flawless full-size reproductions printed on facing pages with authoritative text of poem. "Beautiful. Simply beautiful."–*Publisher's Weekly.* 77pp. 9¼ x 12. 22305-1

NORTH AMERICAN INDIAN DESIGNS FOR ARTISTS AND CRAFTSPEOPLE, Eva Wilson. Over 360 authentic copyright-free designs adapted from Navajo blankets, Hopi pottery, Sioux buffalo hides, more. Geometrics, symbolic figures, plant and animal motifs, etc. 128pp. 8⅜ x 11. (Not for sale in the United Kingdom.) 25341-4

SCULPTURE: Principles and Practice, Louis Slobodkin. Step-by-step approach to clay, plaster, metals, stone; classical and modern. 253 drawings, photos. 255pp. 8⅛ x 11. 22960-2

THE INFLUENCE OF SEA POWER UPON HISTORY, 1660–1783, A. T. Mahan. Influential classic of naval history and tactics still used as text in war colleges. First paperback edition. 4 maps. 24 battle plans. 640pp. 5⅜ x 8½. 25509-3

CATALOG OF DOVER BOOKS

THE STORY OF THE TITANIC AS TOLD BY ITS SURVIVORS, Jack Winocour (ed.). What it was really like. Panic, despair, shocking inefficiency, and a little heroism. More thrilling than any fictional account. 26 illustrations. 320pp. 5⅜ x 8½.
20610-6

FAIRY AND FOLK TALES OF THE IRISH PEASANTRY, William Butler Yeats (ed.). Treasury of 64 tales from the twilight world of Celtic myth and legend: "The Soul Cages," "The Kildare Pooka," "King O'Toole and his Goose," many more. Introduction and Notes by W. B. Yeats. 352pp. 5⅜ x 8½.
26941-8

BUDDHIST MAHAYANA TEXTS, E. B. Cowell and others (eds.). Superb, accurate translations of basic documents in Mahayana Buddhism, highly important in history of religions. The Buddha-karita of Asvaghosha, Larger Sukhavativyuha, more. 448pp. 5⅜ x 8½.
25552-2

ONE TWO THREE . . . INFINITY: Facts and Speculations of Science, George Gamow. Great physicist's fascinating, readable overview of contemporary science: number theory, relativity, fourth dimension, entropy, genes, atomic structure, much more. 128 illustrations. Index. 352pp. 5⅜ x 8½.
25664-2

EXPERIMENTATION AND MEASUREMENT, W. J. Youden. Introductory manual explains laws of measurement in simple terms and offers tips for achieving accuracy and minimizing errors. Mathematics of measurement, use of instruments, experimenting with machines. 1994 edition. Foreword. Preface. Introduction. Epilogue. Selected Readings. Glossary. Index. Tables and figures. 128pp. 5⅜ x 8½.
40451-X

DALÍ ON MODERN ART: The Cuckolds of Antiquated Modern Art, Salvador Dalí. Influential painter skewers modern art and its practitioners. Outrageous evaluations of Picasso, Cézanne, Turner, more. 15 renderings of paintings discussed. 44 calligraphic decorations by Dalí. 96pp. 5⅜ x 8½. (Available in U.S. only.)
29220-7

ANTIQUE PLAYING CARDS: A Pictorial History, Henry René D'Allemagne. Over 900 elaborate, decorative images from rare playing cards (14th–20th centuries): Bacchus, death, dancing dogs, hunting scenes, royal coats of arms, players cheating, much more. 96pp. 9¼ x 12¼.
29265-7

MAKING FURNITURE MASTERPIECES: 30 Projects with Measured Drawings, Franklin H. Gottshall. Step-by-step instructions, illustrations for constructing handsome, useful pieces, among them a Sheraton desk, Chippendale chair, Spanish desk, Queen Anne table and a William and Mary dressing mirror. 224pp. 8⅛ x 11¼.
29338-6

THE FOSSIL BOOK: A Record of Prehistoric Life, Patricia V. Rich et al. Profusely illustrated definitive guide covers everything from single-celled organisms and dinosaurs to birds and mammals and the interplay between climate and man. Over 1,500 illustrations. 760pp. 7½ x 10⅛.
29371-8

Paperbound unless otherwise indicated. Available at your book dealer, online at **www.doverpublications.com**, or by writing to Dept. GI, Dover Publications, Inc., 31 East 2nd Street, Mineola, NY 11501. For current price information or for free catalogues (please indicate field of interest), write to Dover Publications or log on to **www.doverpublications.com** and see every Dover book in print. Dover publishes more than 500 books each year on science, elementary and advanced mathematics, biology, music, art, literary history, social sciences, and other areas.